HOW TO WIN

THE ONE IMPORTANT THING TO KNOW ABOUT GAMBLING is that there is no guaranteed way to win all the time. But there is a guaranteed way to lose constantly, and that is when you don't understand the basic rules of playing and betting. It is appalling how many people, even big-money gamblers, lose consistently and don't know why. There are only two types of gamblers—those who really know the game and suckers. Mike Goodman, a veteran professional gambler, gives you an amazing, easy-to-understand insight on how to gamble and win.

HORSE RACING

. . . watch those second favorites; let the suckers play the favorites, they're usually overplayed!

DICE

. . . you're a sucker if you don't take advantage of the odds, but the real pay-off comes when you know how to bet!

SLOTS

. . . there's only one way to beat those "one-arm bandits," but, unfortunately, it's against the law!

ROULETTE

. . . it's tough to beat the house percentage, but there are ways to lose less, keep you in the game, and then, who knows?

BLACKJACK "21"

. . . here's a game you can win at consistently if you learn the tricks and how to put "lady luck" on your side!

POKER

. . . you get real help here; tips that'll open your eyes, make you play a better game and win!

BY **MIKE GOODMAN**
PROFESSIONAL GAMBLER AND
CASINO EXECUTIVE

HOW TO Win

**DICE
ROULETTE
POKER
BLACKJACK (21)
HORSE RACING
BETTING SYSTEMS
MONEY MANAGEMENT
INTERNATIONAL GAMBLING**

An Original Holloway House Edition

HOLLOWAY HOUSE PUBLISHING CO.
LOS ANGELES, CALIFORNIA

To all the losers
who gave me the inspiration
to write this book

PUBLISHED BY

Holloway House Publishing Company
8060 Melrose Avenue
Los Angeles, California 90046

International Standard Book Number 0-87067-617-2

Printed in the United States of America

ABOUT THE AUTHOR

MIKE GOODMAN is a professional gambler, rated as one of the two or three top men in the gambling industry. He is married, has three children, two in college, and owns a beautiful home in Las Vegas. He is an executive in one of the largest gambling casinos in the world in Las Vegas.

Mike is friendly, easy-to-like, and fascinating to talk to, especially when relating his many experiences in and out of Las Vegas. He was born in Rochester, New York, and started to gamble at the age of eight while selling papers after school. When other boys were playing with toy automobiles and boats, Mike was playing with dice and cards. When only sixteen, he ran a crap table and started dealing 21.

He learned his A-B-C's of big-time gambling from three of the smartest men in the profession. Two are now deceased. One owned a plush gambling club and taught him the inside of club operation and the pitfalls. The other two taught him the methods cheaters use to beat a club and how to protect himself from such hazards. Mike proved to be an apt student. Wherever big money was at stake, whenever real trouble was brewing, the call went out for Mike Goodman. He also proved to be one of the most competent teachers in the country.

Before taking his marriage vows and settling down, Mike was constantly on the move. As gambler and house man he worked in the biggest clubs on the East Coast--New York, Saratoga, New Jersey, Washington, Hot Springs and Florida. He also worked many small hit-and-run clubs as well as the largest cash money banking games ever known.

TABLE OF CONTENTS

1

COMING OUT

One of the 18,000,000 people who pass through Nevada each year is comedian, singer, raconteur George Burns. Next to telling a joke that gets boffs, George would rather win at 21. As who wouldn't, you say? Well, not like George.

For years George has looked at a deck of cards as if it were his sworn enemy. The cards have teased him, disappointed him, tricked him, gave him a smile or two and discouraged him. But he has never stopped trying to woo them.

On this particular hot day in July, as a pit boss of the Dunes, I stood surrounded by about 9 tables of 21 all going on at the same time. At one table George had passed through two moods—happiness and resignation—and was deep in a third—irrascibility.

All these were inspired of course by cards that were dealing him losses.

Bosses or no bosses, I couldn't stand it anymore and I took George by the arm, brought him out to the swimming pool area and explained the facts of life to him.

"George. From this moment on I never want to see you draw to a 12 or over—a breaking hand—when the dealer has a 6, 5, 4, 3 or 2 showing. On the other hand when he has a 7, 8, 9, picture card or ace showing, I want you to draw cards and come as close to 21 as possible regardless of the consequences."

"That is your first lesson: "I will give you others. But if you adhere to that rule, you won't suffer near as much. Right?"

George promised he'd follow my advice.

Just 24 hours later, George, looking as if he had 3 hit shows under his belt, told me he had two winning sessions of 21. He was doing better already and he had learned only the first simple steps on the road to profit-making on the 21 table.

On, he'd have losing days, but I promised him when I got through with him, I'd make him a winner instead of a loser.

In fact this book was written for losers, out of compassion for lambs led daily to slaughter by hungry wolves.

You don't have to be a loser. You too can be a wolf.

Oh, I know there have been many magazine pieces by amateurs for amateurs relating some system with a pot of gold at the end of it (that's what they said was in the pot) but not only in every case was the system not workable but usually it was unintelligible.

Here's a typical paragraph from an article titled "A Prof Beats The Gamblers" in Atlantic.

"Just then a one percent advantage arose. I decided to go to the $2 to $20 scale and bet $4. I won, and the advantage coincidentally advanced to 2 percent. I let my $8 ride and won again. I left $20 on the table with the remark that it was time to take a small profit. I continued with $20 bets as the deck remained favorable.

At the end of the deck, I had recouped my $100 loss and had a few dollars profit besides."

(I realize this is out of context but you must believe me that not only was the 21 system unworkable, but the explanation a challenge to Einstein for understanding.)

The date and author's name escape me but about ten years ago Esquire magazine had a get-rich-scheme for the crap tables. Believe me any casino owners who read it did not shake with fear. It made good reading but we'd swim the ocean to get any such players.

I've worked in gambling houses for 30 years and have never seen a winning system. People have read Scarne's books, McDougal's articles and literature of all kinds from other experts and have never seen any suggestions from them that would make a losing player a winning player.

I can just see you, the reader, saying to himself, "Wise Guy. He says nobody else can make a winning gambler but he can."

Yes, brother, I can. I haven't been part of gambling operations for 30 years without learning plenty. I've been behind the scene watching the magic from close up and brother I know how the rabbit comes out of the hat.

Gambling, legal and illegal, is the biggest industry in America. It gets bigger every year. If you're the average sucker gambler you're stupid and I'm going to do my best to wisen you up.

I cannot promise to make everyone who follows my instructions happy but I will promise to give him a fair share of winnings. I tell you why I won't promise happiness. One night a loveable Jewish garment manufacturer who comes to Las Vegas once every year decided to plan some games in the casino.

"I lost 100 dollars," he moaned. He asked what the biggest odds were that he could get for his money, as he only had three dollars left.

He was told, 25,000 for 3 at Keno. In order to win you

have to pick 10 numbers, all of which must appear out of the 80 selections.

He bet his three dollars and wouldn't you know it his ten numbers were picked giving him a total win of $25,000.

He wasn't jubilant. "Would you believe it? I hit such big odds and I only have $3 to bet!"

On the other hand I see players who are always cheerful no matter what happens.

One old dowager is suffering from asthma. She's very rich and all day long she sips whiskey, plays 21 and says "I'll take another hundred." She's happy with her lot and it makes little difference if she wins or loses.

I think it was Gallup who took a poll some years ago to find out how many people gamble. Well the amazing results showed 93% of all people gamble in some fashion. It's amazing because most people know so little about gambling games.

Another time I noticed a woman sticking on 8 and 9 (two card total) in 21 which is silly because for nothing she could draw one or more cards to get closer to 21. I looked at the dealer's hand and told her he had 20. That didn't move her. A friend told her to stick after two cards and that damn well is what she is going to do.

You know it's amazing but a woman who has a very nice allowance will go to three markets to price watermelon in order to save 12 cents. But in a gambling casino she'll blow $30 on the dice table because she doesn't know that betting on the "Field" is not one of the best bets she can make. In a few minutes study with a lowly night school acquaintanceship with mathematics she could learn a lot more about the game. But she has been told that when you gamble you have little chance to win so she does little about it. She's resigned to her losses.

Every day as I maintain my job as pit boss people ask me countless questions: "Why do you use red dice?" "Can I bet nickels on the roulette table?" "What do the colored checks mean on the roulette layout?" "How do you play 'Big Six'?" Hundreds of other questions. But maybe twice have I been asked by players, "What is the best way to play for my money?" I, or any other pit boss would be delighted to tell them and explain what they were doing wrong.

I know powerful lobbies of every kind have tried since Washington threw a dollar across the Delaware to squelch gambling especially on a big business basis but they have failed. It is bigger than ever. In fact the individual's need to gamble is constantly so pitted against the law's requirements that you see much ironies as legal race-tracks teaching people how to bet on races in the same city but outside the race track, if they bet they are arrested.

I'll tell you how violently I feel about every living person knowing how to gamble. One time one of my three children came home to say he lost money playing poker. I taught all three of them the fine points of every gambling game. I believe every teen-ager should be taught how to gamble. They are going to gamble sooner or later and when they do they'll be better off in many ways if they win.

So you ask me, "How do I learn how to gamble and win?" Easy. Just finish reading this book. If you go to any other printed material it might be dangerous. I just finished reading a book on dice which was so outdated a three (ace and deuce) was considered a stand-off bet. Nobody won. And to further laugh, that book stated, "If you bet on a seven to show in one roll you get three to one for your money. The proper odds are 5 to 1.

I can without many words or too much effort convince you that I can make you a winning gambler. And I can easily convince you that Lady Luck was little influence over a period of time. It's like a baby, walk one step at a time.

Joe Sloan is a crack gin player. His wife, Sally, a beauty, is nevertheless a lousy player. Occasionally Sally wins in an evening. But in those years they've been playing at a penny a point, Sally owes her husband $131,000 on paper. That is true of every gambling game that requires any skill at all or *proper and skillful money management*—a good player will make money and a poor player will lose. Luck will only enter into the game at sporadic intervals. *She will have no influence* over the long run.

Show me a skillful, professional dice, 21 player or even horse player and I'll show you a man that the bosses fear. That is not as true at Roulette because chance has more accent. Learn the game well, learn money management and learn the psychology of the House and you'll win and I'll tell you how to win, or at the very least I'll improve your style so much you'll be on near even terms with the house, an enviable spot to be.

I'll tell you what a difference a knowledge of a game can make. One of our wealthiest gamblers, who comes to Las Vegas about once a month dropped $25,000 on the dice table during a weekend. He's a nervous impatient player who bets every come-out and bets on everything. He constantly bets on the Field, eleven, seven, the Hard Ways, all the bets where the House gets as much as 16 percent. Yet if he were to bet only on the "Pass" line and "Come" and back up his 4, 5, 6, 8, 9, and 10 numbers the House would be getting an average of 1.4 *percent*. I figured with all the money he was just handing to the house over and over again of the $25,000 he lost $21,000 could have been saved. Only the $4,000 was legitimate loss. It was as if he took the $21,000 and handed it to the House before play.

I must tell you that bosses worry as much when everybody's losing (well almost!) as when everyone's winning. It doesn't take much brains to know that if everyone lost at a casino there wouldn't be any players and all the casinos would have to close, and I would have to go to work for a living. There's nothing that will soup up a casino's play more than a couple of hot tables.

Even club owners hearing of dice passing in another casino, will quickly hop by cab to take advantage of it. Games do run in cycles and when the tables are passing is when the professionals try to take advantage of it. More about that anon.

As a gambling house employer, I must tell you that gamblers are like my children. Dear Abby. I listen to their troubles, aympathize or advise them. They are my charges and I have a warm feeling for them. You maybe won't believe it but I very often feel sad when a friend loses. I would much rather he'd win.

2

WINNING AT 21

Now to make good my promise—that I'd show you how to become a winning gambler. Let's start with the game of 21 also called "Blackjack."

The game can be described in two sentences yet many players play it all their lives and never learn to play it correctly. In fact an attractive girl who I've seen gambling with high stakes at the 21 table for years only recently asked me what "splitting" was and how and why you do it, I can only tell you that without knowing how to split cards through the years she placed herself at a terrible disadvantage enough edge to put her in the loss column.

The object of 21 is to draw cards which when added

together make 21 or as close to 21 as you can without going over. If your hand is closer to 21 than the dealer's, you win, if there is a tie, you break even.

Yet with this simple concept, a smart player could have his steady share of winnings. But on the other hand thousands of players lose millions every year because they don't know what they are doing.

Of course there are no sure things. Wait, I take that back. One night Jerry Lewis (and Polly Bergen too) began dealing behind the blackjack table. They saw to it that everyone at the table won to the dismay of the House. When cards didn't add up to win, Jerry or Polly would see to it that they were switched.

It was Christmas for all the players. But Christmas comes but once a year and on the other days you must know how to play.

As a pit boss I see amazing things. One gentleman sat down at the table, ordered a drink, opened his tie and best $100 on his cards. He did this about a half-dozen times and lost each time. Then he turned to me and said, "Say, how do you play this game?"

But the most amazing thing about people at the 21 table is that so many can't count. They actually can't add. I constantly see people hit 20 and 21 even. It's enough to send the cold shakes down your back to see a sure winner convert to a loser because he can't add 5, 7 and 9. People shaky about their simple addition should bone up before sitting down at the 21 table.

Occasionally a dealer will recognize a poor player's difficulty with addition and help but usually the game is moving too fast for him to be able to help. It isn't unusual at all to have a player ask something like, "Say, how much is eight and nine?" It certainly doesn't speak well for American education.

As I mentioned before one of the marks of a good player is one who knows how and when to split. It means that when his first two cards are alike he is permitted, if he wishes to, to turn them up, bet the same amount on the second hand as he had on the first and draw to each as if

18

they were separate hands.

Never split 4's, 5's, 9's or 10's (10, J, Q, K). The reason is obvious. Two 4's add to eight, which is a good start for a hand, two 5's add to ten, even better, etc. You usually split 2's, 3's, 6's and 7's. You split 8's when the dealer's show card is a seven to a deuce. For example, if you are dealt a pair of eight's and the dealer has a 7 showing, split. It is to your advantage.

The ace because it can be used as either one or eleven is the most complicated part of 21. It sounds simple but the ace confuses almost every beginner.

It creates amazing situations. I have seen a player with an ace, a 4 and a 6 (called a *soft* 21) draw, instead of stopping, and draw a picture card (making a hard 21) or a 5 or a 6 making a bad hand.

I often see players stop on an ace and a 5 or an ace and a 4 when drawing another card is free and couldn't possibly put them over.

The trouble with most 21 players isthat they guess their way from hand to hand never quite being certain of what to do. I want to relieve the pain of indecision and anxiety. And that's what I'm going to do.

There comes a time when a professional, like myself, can't stand watching the many ways the players have found to butcher perfectly good hands. And I see new boners made all the time.

When I take enough of an interest to kindly query people about a particularly dumb move I am astounded by their reply.

"Why," I asked a steady customer, "did you stop on a soft 16?"

He looked at me as if I were crazy. "I have a friend who lives in Las Vegas so of course he knows all about gambling. He says to never hit on a 16."

Living in Vegas is no certainty of gambling knowledge. And a 16 is not the same as a *soft* 16. But I failed to convince the customer.

I've seen 21 players toss a coin to make a decision. That's certain death. A player can't be undecided, he must know.

The psychology of most players is discouraging. They tell me, "I brought $50 along to lose. Then I'll stop." They seldom say, "I have $50 and with it I'm going to win." They're beaten before they start with this attitude.

A player will say, "I think I'll play roulette, the other tables are crowded." He should plan what game he's going to play and stick to the plan—not let crowds make his decision for him.

Or a player will tell me, "Let's see, I have five 5-dollar chips so I'll play for five dollars a hand." He should know long before he plays what unit of money he's going to use and not let what he has in his hand dictate to him. That's what the change booths or cashier's window are for.

Another kind of player looks at his watch and says, "I have a half-hour to play 21 then I have to meet my wife." That's the worst way to play—to be pressed for time. He's the kind of player who wins five ten-dollar hands and then because he has to run bets $50 on the next hand and loses it. It makes no sense at all.

It's important in 21 for the dealers to have respect for the player. It creates the right atmosphere.

In order to gain respect, the player must know what he's doing. There can be no guessing. If he stumbles and guesses, he's referred to as "a live one" especially if he's betting big money. He's thought of as a chump.

When finished with this chapter, play some practice games with friends. You'll soon know when you are ready to play for the money.

And when you have learned your lesson well, don't be influenced to change your game by the actions of big money players. They often play as stupidly as any dollar player.

A customer said to me, "I found a perfect way to play 21. You never hit a breaking hand (never draw to a 12 or over) no matter what the dealer has up. If you don't hit you can never go over. I saw this man win $40,000 at a hotel playing this way."

The man she mentioned is a consistent loser in Las

Vegas—he has lost over $1,000,000. And like most players he likes to talk about his great winnings but he never mentions his losings. It's the old story of the gambler who lost $1,000 Monday night, again Tuesday and again Wednesday but on Thursday he won $500. Late that night he celebrated spending $500 for the party and you never saw a happier fellow. He never mentioned his losings. In fact he didn't at all want to be reminded of them. We send cabs for players like that.

A sure way to draw a crowd to the table will be for a gambler to sit with a big pile of chips and cash in front of him, betting heavily in each hand. For some odd reason, probably snobbery, he gains the respect of his audience. He might be a bad player and a loser but they watch him in awe and often ape his style of play. And strangely enough a player sitting with loads of cash and checks in front of him is always thought to be a winner when actually he might be a heavy loser.

Many gamblers are actors. They consider the seat at the table their stage. They buy large amounts of chips even if they don't use them. They enjoy the spotlight. They do everything but bow when they win a hand and I think they'd do that if someone applauded. These are the gamblers to be wary of—they must prove themselves just as anyone else must. They have to show that they are fine players before their play is imitated.

The most obstinate and stubborn people in the world are people who gamble. They usually don't want to be told what to do no matter how wrong they are and no matter how wrong they know they are.

I have walked through the casino, stopped at a 21 dealer's table, picked up his cards and showed it to a player. The player, a young woman, had a 16, the dealer had a 20. "Draw," I told her. She refused even though she had to lose this way.

When the dealer collected I asked her why she didn't draw. "I thought it was a trick," she said.

Another time I looked at the dealer's cards and told a player he had a 19. She had 16. She wouldn't draw and explained, "I was told never to draw on 16." How silly can you be?

At still another table I asked a player who was betting big money why he stuck on a soft 15 (an ace and 4) when he could get another card free.

His answer was, "It's my money and I can do what I want with it." It's a logical answer but obstinate people like that end in the poorhouse.

There's always something suspicious about people who lose money carelessly and react without much emotion to losses. Once I was fascinated with such a player and his great aplomb. Several days later I discovered he was a bank teller who had been arrested for absconding with bank cash.

You wouldn't believe some of the inane things that happen at a 21 table. Two women walked over to a table one evening and it was clear by their conversation that one had never been inside a casino before but the other knew how to play. So the woman who knew how to play stood in back of the other one while she played, and told her what to do. The novice in the third or fourth deal drew a 16 and asked what she should do.

"You stand on 16," advised the woman. (That means stop drawing.)

The woman immediately stood up.

It's funny but a pit boss doesn't dare laugh. It's serious business to players.

One man who comes to Las Vegas quite frequently, tips hotel personnel generously just to save him a chair so he can be sure to play immediately after dinner.

He's unusual in that veteran 21 players would rather skip two or three meals than risk the chance of losing their seat. In fact the old joke—which has a lot of truth in it—goes that one man asked another in Las Vegas what Hotel he was stopping. "None," replied the gambler. "I'm only staying three days."

It is really not unusual for a gambler to sit at a 21 table (tme out for bathroom) for 24 hours.

For some reason 21 is a popular women's game. Probably because you can sit down, bet leisurely and it looks so simply to play (but isn't). Yet one day a husband was betting $500 a hand at 21. His beautiful Southern wife would take a few dollars, go to the roulette wheel, lose and come back. She was pestering her husband to leave because, "Honey, I don't understand nothing about any game." The husband looked at the roulette croupier and winked. From then on the roulette wheel "paid" the pretty little Southern girl something so she'd be kept out of her husband's hair.

3

TIPS FOR YOU

Many players have a pat answer when you criticize their style of play and to them it excuses everything. They say, "I have been playing this way for years." They don't tell you they've been losing for years too, sometimes I'm firm with them and answer, "You've been playing for money, not peanuts and you've been losing. Why don't you try to find out what's wrong? This game of 21 isn't like a slot machine where you pull a lever and pray for a jackpot. In 21 skill and knowledge count. You say the game is hard to beat. True. But it can be beaten."

I explain to them that they couldn't win even if the cards were breaking for them. I admit the casino has a percentage breaking for them, but it isn't as strong as the public thinks. I repeat over and over again: *The Club never beats a player. He beats himself,* by the way he plays.

Never forget you are being asked to play your opponent's game. You have a double whammy to start with right away. You have to be better than your opponent at his own game. Years ago when I was in my teens, we would play softball. If it started to rain the fellows would run to the shelter where the girls were playing jacks. I used to play too while waiting for the rain to stop. Years later I taught my daughter to play and trying to beat her after a while I became very good at it. It happens that in one of the clubs I worked at there was a know-it-all. He was good at everything he did. One day we had a heated discussion over gambling and he challenged me to my best game. He said he didn't care what it was. Well, you know what happened. We put the hundred dollar bet in escrow and next day I brought in the jacks and said triumphantly, "This is my best game." I won by default.

He stayed away from me after that. You can see that there's a moral here. Don't play anybody at their own game unless you are very good at it.

As I said there are all kinds who make up the percentage of the casino. A woman who I know to be a fine 21 player was watching the games instead of playing and I asked her why. "They're all playing with $25 chips and I play with silver dollars. I'd feel embarrassed." I assured her that the dollar player is the backbone of our play. That is so true as there are millions more of small players than big players, and if we had to just wait for big players we would have to close most of the big clubs. "We are especially careful to hold onto our dollar bettors and you go and play and there will be no reason for embarrassment." She played. And, incidentally, she won.

Most dealers are courteous and are trained to be polite to all players. If a dealer makes a mistake, the player should correct him. If you make a mistake, you usually have to suffer. Play thoughtfully. Don't talk unnecessarily while you are playing. Don't be the life of the table. Especially don't worry about another player's hand. You have enough trouble playing your own. That isn't your responsibility.

One of the worst habits of players is their need to be funny at a table. And frankly I have never heard an amateur comic who was funny. "I'm new here," says one. "I'm from New Brunswick, New Jersey." She laughs but no one else does. Another says, "Hit me" and she slaps herself loudly and roars. Other players smile sickly. We pay top money for comics in our show rooms and there's no need for free comics in the casinos.

I know it sounds silly to say money is very valuable. But in gambling it is more than money. It is a commodity.

While you still have one dollar left you can still play and you never know when fortunes will turn. Every dollar is valuable even if you have a thousand. That dollar might save you. Be serious and extremely careful about wasting money.

We have an axiom in the casinos which goes: "Don't 'chase' your money." It is excellent advice. What it means is this: Many players are progression players. If they lose a dollar, they bet two dollars and if they lose two, they bet four and so forth. This is an over-simplification but they do bet more each time. What they are doing is chasing the original dollar they lost. It makes no sense to be betting $256 to win a dollar. Chasing money is doubly dangerous because the house always has a limit and there will come a time when you will not be allowed to bet enough to get your dollar back. Then not only will you lose your dollar but lots more. The time to increase your bets (intelligently) is when you are winning so that you can take advantage of the break in the cards.

A player should know his game so well that he has a prepared plan of action that he is sure of, already prepared before he plays, that will cover every emergency. But a "losing progression" should not be part of his plan. Also, Caution: too many people make out complicated rules for themselves which they've copied from some book or a friend. After a few minutes of play, in the excitement of the game, their face flushes and they can't possibly remember everything they planned to do. Flustered, with the game running over them they go back to just playing and lose fast.

You know it's amazing that people will spend big money for years in the learning of bridge and when they play consider it a misfortune if they lose $5. But they'll lose $50 at 21 in a casino and not spend one hour learning the niceties of the game before they play. How do you figure it?

I think the lavishness of Las Vegas makes their small bankroll (average is $50 to $300) seem infinitesimal by comparison and so they lose it carelessly feeling they shouldn't care. On the other hand, they believe they are unimportant and feel uneasy to be taking up all that space on the small amount of money they have. And how wrong they are! They should play carefully, take their time and watch every dollar.

One time in the casino I was annoyed by the treatment of Mr. R. gave his wife. He bet a lot of money and she nursed her $5 bets. They both played 21 next to each other. One evening I took her aside and taught her a few fine points about the game. That's all I told her. I didn't want to load her down with advice.

Well, with some good run of cards, she won the next three times out, while Mr. R. was losing plenty. It wasn't long before he had figured out his wife's play and was doing the same. He doesn't kid her anymore.

Recently a bright young fellow stopped at the 21 table. He bet $50 on each hand and won four in a row for a cool $200 profit in 5 minutes. He grinned at me and said, "I've got enough." What could I do but nod. He winked at his girl friend as he showed her the $200 and he left. Having been around casinos all my life, I can tell you the only sure thing about cards is that they run in good cycles and in bad cycles and you never know when each will hit you. *Never* but *never* quit a winning cycle—let it quit you. Ride it all the way. Press it—bet more and more, even if you have to stay all week, take full advantage of it. It might not happen again for a long time. But don't stop until a few losses turn up and you are sure the hot streak is over. You must take advantage of hot cards. You'll need to for the many times you must lose. If you lose $50 at five different losing sessions and then hit a winning cycle for $500, you're in good shape. But you can't just win $50 in the win cycle. You must squeeze it dry.

There's an axiom for stock market players that applies to 21 players or for that matter any casino games. "Don't try to sell at the very peak and buy at the very bottom. If you do, sooner or later you'll court trouble."

Anyway that bright young fellow, as I knew he would, came back to play about an hour later—but this time the cards weren't the same. He had his chance and didn't take advantage of it. He kept losing and losing but didn't stop. I never understood this. Why will a player stop when he's winning and keep playing when he's losing. And you see it all the time.

I thought I might say a word to this fellow whom I knew. I hit him hard with the truth, "You play a good game of 21. What you need is a course in money management. You play like a pit boss I know. He gets scared when he wins a little, but shows all the wrong kind of courage when he's losing. He owns a boat named "Deep In Hock" and it always is." I convinced the boy he was handling his money wrong. And he felt better because a professional like a pit boss was doing the same as he was.

Talking about gambling house personnel, you'd be surprised how little some of the boys know about gambling. Especially in the so-called specialization of the men. They are like medical specialists. A 21 dealer often knows nothing about craps. Likewise a crap dealer often doesn't even know how to play 21. In some cases the hotel employees often don't know anything about any game. But they should. People ask them questions and expect sensible answers. Every hotel in a city where there is legal gambling should have symposiums for the men so they understand the games thoroughly. Certainly they should be well-coached on how to talk to customers.

I overheard a woman ask a bell captain, who is a fine

crap shooter, what the "Field" meant in dice. "I'm sorry, Lady," he said, "I don't work in the casino." It reminds me of the lecture in which the lecturer told a funny story and everyone laughed except one man. His neighbor asked him why he didn't laugh, "Simple," he answered, "I'm not a member of your club."

Though it's foolish I have an idea why the bell captain answered the way he did. The most superstitious people in the world are people who gamble. That bell captain probably didn't want to be blamed for any losses that happened to the woman. You'd be surprised the blame that's put on the hotel because of superstition. One man said accusingly to the cashier, "You gave me Room 27 and I played number 27 on the roulette wheel all weekend and I lost several hundred dollars."

Another time two brothers from Stockholm won a lot of money playing a waitress' badge number for a week. They bought her a beautiful jacket.

You'd be surprised to what extremes the superstitious will go. One woman will not play at a 21 table if there are an odd number of people there. A man will only shoot crap if there are no women at the table. One man will gamble only between the hours of 2 and 4 A.M. A couple will only play cards when it is raining. And so it goes. I have always felt superstition was an excuse for a lack of game skill. A gambler who is sure of his talent cares nothing about the superstitions.

From our objective elevation of the pit we see players with x-ray eyes. Usually we know more about the players' styles than the players themselves. They are often bewildered when we analyze their style of play and make recommendations.

For instance there are many players we call "desperados." They play with short bankrolls, are fine players, and bet high with winnings. They beat your brains out and take advantage of every card break. Bosses often sweat when they sit down at a game. They come to Las Vegas a few times a year and lose a little but when they win, they win big.

29

There are some unpleasant players who don't have a name to describe them and thank goodness there are just a few of them. Usually they are betting more than everyone else at the table and they're telling everyone else how to play their hand. When he is winning he's unbearable. He lords it over everyone. He knows everything about the game. No one can tell him anything and he has the money to prove it. And if anyone makes a mistake in hitting that has an influence on his hand, he goes out of his mind. When he makes a mistake he blames the dealer. Or he blames the casino or the hotel or his wife—anyone but where the blame lies. My advice to you is if you ever find yourself in a game with this character, just leave the table.

It's amazing how many timid souls there are at the 21 table. I've stopped by a woman with a 14 or 15 and said, "Hit it." She sighed and said, "I don't have the nerve. What if I go over?" I told her, "If you can sit at a 21 table and play for pretty high stakes you surely have the nerve to play correctly and take the necessary chances." But I couldn't convince her—she was one of the timid souls.

And most pitied players—and there are a lot of them—are the moaners, the "red board" players who constantly do something wrong or silly and then commiserate with themselves out loud.

4

21, A SURE GAME

Players never cease to fascinate me. Once a dealer told a player. "You only have eleven. You must draw." The man got very belligerent. He was playing badly but he resented being told so. He screamed, "Mind your own business." Another woman hit on an ace, 3 and 6 (20). She drew a 6 and now had 16. She stopped. After the play was over and she had lost, the dealer told her she had hit a 20. She was furious. "I know how to count—I went to school. You just deal the cards, that's what you get paid for." You can be sure from then on the dealer had no helpful advice for her.

Players can be boorish and ungrateful. I saw a man with 13 draw an ace and turn his cards over thinking he had lost.

The dealer told him he was not over. The man reddened and shouted, "I know how to play. Don't tell me what to do."

The most colorful players are the "praying players." They look heavensward, roll their eyes and intone. "Please hit me with a six or seven." They give the impression that all the Lord had to do is to see that they get a winning 21 hand. Often they'll pray for a card, the dealer will hit, they'll keep their eyes closed and nudge the person next to them, asking, "Is it a 6? Tell me. Is it a 6?"

Other players have their own language. A player says to the dealer, "Hit me with a baby, please." Since she's a beautiful young girl, he's taken back. Seeing his hesitation, she says impatiently, "A small card, please.".

One of the types of people I find hard to understand, is the ever-jovial player. He draws 23 and howls with laughter. He loses all his money, and he hits the dealer on the back and goes off into the night, laughing heartily. Of course, he laughs at other people's misfortune too and that often doesn't sit well.

Then there are the "believers". No matter what you tell them—they believe. Don't you be like that. I saw a "believer" get 21. The dealer went over with 22 and said kiddingly, "I beat you." The man pushed over his money and started to leave. The dealer had to call him back.

Then there's the "in-a-hurry" player. He comes running off the plane on Friday at 7 P.M. (expecting to stay for the weekend) runs to the tables before he checks in, bets heavily, loses his money in an hour or so and grabs the 11 P.M. plane back. He's out of money, never saw his room or even unpacked his bags.

There's the nuisance player, who is almost in a daze, slow and deliberate. Everyone waits while he "thinks." He aggravates everyone. He never seems to be aware that anyone is waiting for him to make up his alleged mind.

An odd type and there are a lot of them, are the men who call all women "knishes", and will not play in a game where there is a knish. But if he is a 21 player, sooner or later he'll have to play with a "knish" because the girls like 21. Then he'll slump and not look left or right, trying to blot out the sight of a "knish" in *his* card game. One of them said to a woman who had just hit a soft 21, "Knish, I have been trying to get a 21 all day and you hit one."

You see there are all kinds: Restless players who never stay at one table long, moving from table to table. Players who won't go to an empty table not wanting to play head-and-head with the dealer. (Yet this is the best way to play 21 because no one can spoil your hand, and contrary to what people say, the dealer does not have the best of it.)

There are bored players, who only play because there is nothing else to do and show how bored they are in their whole demeanor.

Another annoying player is one who is constantly counting his chips. In fact, he keeps them in his pocket so nobody knows how he is doing. Even he doesn't; he holds out on himself.

Yes, there are some pretty eccentric gamblers in the casinos, but the bulk of the customers are just pigeons, normal folk in Las Vegas to have fun and lose a few dollars.

Every once in a while, I'll hear or read of some player who has been barred from the casinos because he has a method of play in which he never loses. Hogwash! Bologny! For the birds!

If there was such a man—and I'd like to see him and will bet my life savings there isn't—the casinos couldn't and wouldn't bar any player who has money and plays within the rules of the club.

If you think you have problems winning here, however, just think what would happen to you in Europe. There, when there is a standoff (a tie between dealer and player, the house wins). Of course here under those conditions nobody wins. If I could run a house here with European rules, I'd be glad to return half of every player's losses at the end of the game. That's how unfair I think their rules are. (Maybe I can't bee too angry because over there in roulette there is only one zero on the wheel which gives players twice the break they have here.)

In all clubs a dealer must draw another card on all hands up to and including 16. The player, of course, may stop anytime he wants to. I bring this up because there are all sorts of rules in home games. If you play 21 at home and pass the deal each time a player gets blackjack, be assured in a casino, the blackjack only entitled you to 3 to 2 odds on your money; unfortunately you never get to be a dealer. I only remind you because players constantly ask this.

A standard rule in Nevada allows players, when they want to hit, to gently scrape the cards on the cloth toward them. When they do not want to hit, they slide their cards under their money. When they go over 21 they just turn their cards over. Actually there is no need for conversation and you are better off if you keep your mouth shut.

I have several people everyday tell me that winning at 21 is purely luck. "Ha, Ha" say I. In 21 a player with skill and a knowledge of money management wins. The other players lose. I've had a woman beg me, "Save my lucky seat at the 21 table. I'm going to pick up some more money." How she figured it was a lucky seat I don't know.

Another man lost several dollars and cursed his bad luck. The next night he won several hundred dollars. "I never played so good," he boasted. "I had those dealers begging for mercy." When he won, it was skill. When he lost, bad luck.

Another woman plays with a rabbit's foot alongside her cards and when she gets a few bad hands gets up and walks around her chair. It's odd the great fascination 21 has for women. Invented back in the 1300's the game was inspired by the bachelor. Its symbolism is built around the attainment of 21, the traditional age of adulthood. The equality of the suits was the symbol of the equality of the members of the family.

I'll tell you where luck enters into the play if you are a skillful operator. If you sit down during a dealer's bad streak you can make the luck pay off. If you meet up with a hot dealer your skill will allow you to ride it out with a minimum of losses. In this case bad luck embraced you.

It's not a bad idea to try and walk into a table when

cards are acting up as far as the dealer is concerned. It's the valuable sixth sense that tells you when you're in a win cycle so you can make the best of it.

I think the fascination for 21 springs from the need of making correct decisions. It is a challenge. "Should I stop?" "Should I hit?" When everyone of your decisions is accurate and correct then you are a good player.

Maybe this is the point where I must state that courage or guts is a necessary adjunct of every good 21 player. When a dealer shows an eight on the board and you have 16 and a big bet on the table, it takes guts to draw another card and take that big chance of going over but take it you must. I watched a player who started playing 21 in two dollar units. He had just this situation of having to draw to a "16"; did it and won. But later in the game he was betting $10 and had the exact situation. He stuck. After losing he explained to me, "I just couldn't draw with $10 in front of me." Nuts! Right? He had guts only up to a certain amount. That's when you need courage when a big bet is on the table.

You may say, "Do you recommend consistency at all times no matter what the betting?" Of course. If a play is right, it's right no matter how much money is involved. If it's wrong, it's always wrong.

Guts also is involved when you are trying to ride out a bad streak of cards. Bet low. Don't chase your dollars. The cards always turn. When they do, press your luck and bet high again. It always takes courage to ride out a bad streak when the cards are doing nip-ups.

If you have eliminated all guess work in the play, it will be easier to play confidently and expect and handle loss streaks. It's the pressure that often makes you pile up mistakes.

I think the villains most responsible for the poor 21 players are the high money players. I've seen them over and over again. They have big piles of $25 chip in front of them, several hundred dollar bills and a Scotch. A cigarette dangles from their lips. They are the epitome of the confident, big money gambler. And they often play like dopes.

35

They'll split pictures, and fives and not split aces. They'll make mistake after mistake and the curious and admiring (admiring because he's gambling with so much money) believes everything he does is correct. After all, look how rich he is. They don't figure he made his money in a coffee plantation or in the garment business.

So a few more suckers are turned out who will lose their money aping his mistakes and tell their friends, "I had the worst luck in Las Vegas."

5

HITTING AND STOPPING AT 21

A woman player once said to me, "I found out the only time I play well is when I have good cards. I don't know what to do with bad cards." How right she was! Anybody can play with good cards, but you will notice as you play this game that most of the time you have to make a decision. You will receive more hitting hands than stopping hands, so you have to know how to hit them or what to hit them against.

If the dealer has a 7, 8, 9, 10, or ace showing—by showing I mean the card the dealer turns face up—and you have any combination of 12, 13, 14, 15, or 16 you must hit the hand. These are bad hands and we call them stiffs or breaking hands. You may get these combinations from more than two cards, but it doesn't make any difference. You must still hit any hand from 12 through 16 if the dealer has a 7 through an ace showing. For example: If you have 7 in two cards—get hit with an eight, you now have 15. It is still a stiff and you must hit again. You may have an 8 and a 4 in two cards which is 12. You hit with a 4 and now you have 16. This is still a bad hand against a 7 or better, HIT AGAIN. In other words you must hit these breaking hands until you have a 17 or better. Remember, don't be afraid to hit these bad hands against 7, 8, 9, 10, or ace. If you don't you cannot win. If you do you will have a chance for your money. The strong point of hitting your stiffs or bad hands is the strength of playing 21.

A player said to me, "You have to have a lot of nerve to hit a 15 or 16 when the dealer has a 7 or 8 up." I told him, "If you have nerve enough to sit down and play like you do, you should be able to hit anything."

Do not let the size of the bet change your method of playing. In other words don't play "scared pool". Hit when you have to. The bet doesn't belong to you anyway—it is in action. It is on the fence and it is up to you to make the bet fall your way. The wind or you guessing won't help one bit. Remember, your money is in escrow and it doesn't belong to you or the club. Just play your hand the way it should be played—the right way.

Now let us talk about what you should stop against. You know now what I mean by a "stiff" or bad hand—12 through 16. If the dealer's up or face card is a 2, 3, 4, 5, or 6—you stop your stiffs or bad hands. Just slide your cards under your bet—that means stop. Now that doesn't take too much concentration, does it? Hit all your "breaking hands" against 7, 8, 9, 10, or ace. Stop all your bad hands against 2, 3, 4, 5, and 6.

I find this the most advisable way to explain about hitting and stopping your stiffs or breaking hands to the public that comes to Vegas, as it will not confuse them and also give them a chance to win. There may be a few professionals that claim some variations to the above rules, but believe me in all the years I have been around 21 games, if you follow just these simple rules, it makes gambling enjoyable and more profitable instead of frustrating. Countless number of times I have seen the player straining his mind to decide what to do with a hand that is simple to play and can't decide what to do with it. He will study the hand, then take a guess and hope it works out O.K. A deal or so later, will receive the same cards under the same circumstances, go through the same ritual, and do the exact opposite of what he had done before.

Splitting Pairs

A twenty is pretty hard to get in two cards, contrary to what you hear or read. There are 136 two card combinations to make 20. The odds are a little over 8½ to 1 against you having 20 with two cards. Not so easy to get 20, is it? The odds against you to have a pair of fives, fours or nines are much, much larger. These are good hands, so why split them?

Some players will split eights against any card the dealer has up, hoping that the dealer will have a small card underneath or in the "hole" as we call it. It is like betting into the high card with the worst of it. Why gamble and put up more money just to find out if you have guessed right or wrong. It's not worth it. That's exactly what it comes to—guessing which we are eliminating from the game of 21. So when you have a pair of eights, and the dealer has 8, 9, 10, or ace up, just hit your sixteen—don't split them. It is a bad hand and you could make it into a good hand. If you should lose it, you are only losing one bet instead of two by splitting them. Only split eights against dealer's 2 through 7.

Sevens are a good split against the dealer's 2 through 7 showing, because fourteen is a bad hand and there are 32 cards to improve it. For example you can catch 1 of 16 pictures, which will give you 17, one of four aces which will give you 18, a two, three or four which will give you 9, 10, or 11 which will give you a chance to draw a high card for a winning hand.

The reason you only split sixes against the dealer's 5 showing is because there are only five cards that can help the 6. When the dealer has a five up, it is the biggest disadvantage for the dealer and the best advantage for the player—at all times. The only five cards that can help improve splitting sixes, are ace, two, three, four or five. Some players will also split sixes against the dealer showing 2, 3, 4, and 6 thinking they have the advantage, because the dealer has a small card up and must hit. They forget that the dealer had more ways of helping his hand with a small card up than the player who splits sixes against the small card. Example: You split sixes against dealer's up or face card of a 6. You receive a 7 on the first 6 and stop. You hit the next 6 and receive a picture. You also stop as the dealer has a 6 showing, saying to yourself, "The dealer must hit his six." But what if the dealer has an ace in the hole. He now has seventeen and must stop in some clubs. In the clubs where the dealer has to hit the soft seventeen, he has more of a chance to improve the seventeen. When a dealer has a deuce or three showing, believe me, it is very dangerous for the player. He is taking much, much the worst of the bargain. The player is splitting sixes, putting up more money and the dealer has almost twice as many chances to improve his hand than the player. That doesn't make much sense, does it? In splitting sixes, when the dealer has a four showing, it is still in the dealer's favor as he can improve his hand more ways with a 4 and a 6. So let's not take the worst of it. Give yourself a chance. Remember the minute you step into a gambling club you have the worst of it and haven't even made a bet yet. So remember, don't split sixes against any card but the five. Just play your hand according to the rules.

In splitting two's and three's when the dealer has a 2 through 7 showing, your chances of improving your hand are as good as the dealer's, if not better. The dealer must hit on 16 or less—you don't have to.

As I have said in the rules, splitting aces is a must no matter what the dealer has showing. You must remember that in most all clubs you only receive one card on each ace—that's all ... The dealer will place two cards next to the aces and go right on to the next player without even hesitating. You might receive two low cards and have two bad hands, but you can't do anything about it. When splitting any other pair, however, you can hit with as many cards as you want to until you are "good" or "over." That is the rule in Nevada. But it is still to your advantage to split aces. The odds are a fraction over 2 to 1 against you receiving a ten or picture, but you don't have to have 21 to win. You can also receive a 7, 8, or 9 which will make a "stopping" or "good" hand. The percentage is a little in your favor that you will have a stopping hand after being hit with one card. So keep right on splitting aces—it is the best of any pair to split.

By following these rules on splitting pairs, you will not get into any trouble with playing your pairs and won't throw your money away on stupid splits where you are a "dead fish" the minute you make the wrong split against the dealer's up cards. I have seen players split sixes and sevens against the dealer's picture or ten. That is like walking into a den of rattlesnakes barefooted. In face I have seen players split pairs regardless of what the dealer has showing.

They are told to split pairs so they think you split them all the time against anything. That is how a player gets into trouble and loses two bets instead of sometimes winning one bet. Remember when you have a pair and the rules don't call for a split, just hit the pair and play the hand the way the rules say.

In all clubs on the "Strip" in Las Vegas, the minimum bet on 21 is $1.00. In downtown Las Vegas, the minimum bet on some clubs is 25¢ I suggest that you go downtown and practice your rules in the clubs that have the twenty-five cent minimum. This might save you a tidy sum.

Double Down

For the benefit of the many that don't even know what

41

doubling down means, I'm going to explain the meaning as simply as I can. Let us say that you are betting $5.00. You are dealt two cards and you have a combination of 10 or 11 in these two cards. You turn your cards up and add another $5.00 to the $5.00 you have bet. You are now trying to double your money—hence the saying "double down." Now remember you only receive one card when you double down. Good or bad, that is all you receive. You cannot hit anymore. There is many a time a player will double when he should not, lose their bet, whereas if they didn't double they would have a chance to win the hand. I will now explain how and what to double against and what not to double against.

ALWAYS double down on your two card combination of ten or eleven when the dealer has 2, 3, 4, 5, 6, 7, or 8 showing. NEVER double down when the dealer has 9, 10, or ace showing. ONLY double down on your combination of 10 or 11.

When only doubling on ten or eleven, according to the rules you are playing the game of 21 the way it should be played. Please do not double on eight or nine as quite a few players do. You are trying to keep the percentage down and you cannot do it by doubling on 8 or 9. They are a tough double as many a time during the course of your playing you will receive a 2 or 3 when doubling on 8, or a deuce when doubling on 9. You now have ten or eleven, and cannot do anything about it because you only receive one card when doubling down—no more. So now you are stuck with a good hand and pray that the dealer will "go over" or "break" as that is the only way you can win your bet. As I have said before, praying does not help in this game. You have to get by on your playing ability. By *not* doubling on ten or eleven when the dealer has a nine, ten, or ace showing, you are giving yourself a chance to win a bet instead of losing twice as much money. If you just hit your tens and elevens against these high cards you will be able to hit again if you receive a small card on your first hit. You have a chance to better your hand because in all probabilities the dealer has a stopping hand with a nine, ten, or ace showing. By not doubling you will be playing a much "tougher" game of 21 and won't be sticking your neck out.

I have seen players double-down on twelve and thirteen and I wonder where they get their money to play with. I just chalk it up to the ignorance of the player not knowing the game. I am giving them the benefit of the doubt.

I feel more comfortable doubling on ten than eleven as many a time when doubling on eleven there is that lovely ace staring you in the face and you have a fat twelve, but when doubling on ten that lovely ace makes your hand a 21. As I have said, you don't have to have twenty-one to win. By doubling on ten, when you receive a picture of ten, you have twenty. A pretty good hand in any man's country.

There are some clubs in this state that will let a player split a combination of ten or eleven. Now isn't that nice of them? They are letting you take a good hand like a six and a four or an eight and a three and break it up to make two bad hands. If you are playing in a club and a dealer should suggest that you can split a ten or eleven, just get up and quit. He is taking advantage of your ignorance of the game, and some of the bosses of these clubs that allow it should be run out of the gambling business. The game is strong enough for the clubs by the way the players throw their money away without resorting to such tactics against a player that can't match wits against some of these morons. I have found out that the player is very gullible and trustworthy when gambling. He will believe most anything about the game he is playing—hoping that it will help him win. I am telling you now. Don't believe everything somebody working around a club tells you. Know who you receive information from. There are new dealers that are breaking in all the time. They work in a club a few months and now think they are smarter than the bosses. Most of them never saw a deck of cards or been in a gambling club in their lives. These are the type that will try to tell a customer how to play.

A dealer that works for me in the club I am at went downtown (where most of the new dealers work) to meet a friend of his. While waiting he started to play 21—lost eighty dollars so went across the street to another club. He only had $20 left so he bet four dollars and picked up two pictures. This new dealer said to him as he put the cards under his money face up, "Do you want to split them?" This friend of mine looked at him and didn't say anything. He was a little "hot" as he was eighty dollars loser. The next hand my friend bet the eight dollars and had two kings. He did the same thing—turned them up and slid them under his money. The dealer said again, "Do you want to split them?" But this time he took the kings and spread them apart like it was the right thing to do—split pictures when you get them. My friend reached over and slapped him right in the nose and said, "You are paid to deal the cards, which is a hard enough task for you, not teaching something about a game you know nothing about."

In doubling down, as I explained earlier, you put up the same amount of money that you have originally bet. Now if you feel that you don't want to risk all of the money on one bet, you don't have to. You can put up as much as you want up to the amount you have first bet. Example: You bet six dollars and you receive a ten or eleven and the hand calls for you to double. Ordinarily you would have to put up six more dollars to cover the "double" or "down" bet. That would be a total of twelve dollars invested. If you feel, however, that you don't want to put up six more dollars, you can put up any amount below six dollars—two or three dollars, or even one dollar.

That is acceptable in all clubs. Remember it isn't even necessary to double at all if you don't want to. If your hand calls for you to double on ten or eleven, and you don't want to—just hit the hand and play it like you would any other hand.

Simple rules to remember:
Always—split aces
Never—split tens, pictures, nines, fives or fours
Only—double on the ten or eleven
Never—double when dealer has a nine, ten or ace face up
Hit—all soft hands from soft 13 to soft 17 regardless of

what the dealer has showing.

Only—split eights when the dealer has a 2-3-4-5-6-7 face up

Only—split sevens when the dealer has a 2-3-4-5-6-7 face up.

Only—split sixes when the dealer has a 5 showing

Always—split twos or threes when the dealer has a 2-3-4-5-6-7 face up

Hit—all your breaking hands from 12 to 16, when the dealer has a 7-8-9-10 or picture and ace face up.

Stop—all your breaking or bad hands from 12 to 16 when the dealer has a 2-3-4-5-6 face up

Bet—more when winning, less when losing

Study—*Practice* and play this way always. The right way is the best way in the long run.

6

SOFT HANDS IN 21

It seems that the ace in the game of 21 is the most confusing card in the deck. I am sure if there was a way to eliminate the ace the game of 21 would be much easier to play. Millions of dollars a year are lost by players that butcher a hand with an ace in it. Especially when they have to hit. I have seen good players hold up the game and add up the hand after being hit with an ace, or having an ace in their hand and being hit with a small card. Many a player will say out loud, "Oh God, what do I have now?" after being hit with an ace. So don't be perturbed if you are one of the thousands that have trouble with an ace. You are not alone. You have plenty of company.

The ace is a very important card only when you know what to do with it and how to use it. There are only four aces in a deck, but you will see them quite a bit during a play at a 21 game. It will seem to you like there are twenty aces in the deck, especially when a player doesn't know how to use them. I have heard many a player say out loud, "Another ace. How many are there in this deck?"

A poor player doesn't realize that an ace is a strong card in their favor when it is used in the right spot. The most difficulty a player has is when he receives an ace and a small card in his first two cards. For example: An ace and a 4. That is what we call a soft hand—when you receive the ace and a small card in the first two cards.

These two cards can be used as a 5 or a fifteen. Why? Because the ace in the game of 21 can be counted as a one or an eleven. That's all! The minute a player is told the ace is one or eleven a mental block develops in his mind against all aces, and whoever told them the game of 21 was easy to play!

Here are all the soft hitting hands that you will receive in two cards. Ace and 2, ace and 3, ace and 4, ace and 5, ace and 6. Upon receiving any of these two card combinations you count the ace as eleven, i.e. ace and 4 are fifteen, ace and 5 are sixteen, ace and six are seventeen, ace and three are fourteen, ace and two are thirteen. HIT these hands all the time regardless of what the dealer has showing. They are bad hands, but by hitting these hands you are receiving a FREE card, so to speak. You CANNOT GO OVER when you ask for the first hit—so the expression "soft hand" is derived. You can, however, improve the hand with a good card.

The saying is, "You can hit it, but can't hurt it." (Applying to these soft hands). I have seen hundreds and hundreds of players stop on soft 16 (an ace and 5)—like throwing their money down the drain. I have seen thousands stop on soft 17 (an ace and 6). I asked a player why he stopped on soft 17. He answered, "Why spoil a 17?" What's so good about a soft 17? It's a bad hand. How can you spoil a bad hand? I have seen players stop on soft 13 and soft 14.

I won't even waste my breath and ask them why. It's very simple—they don't know what a soft hand is and it is not easy to explain to a person during a game. I have seen countless number of players hit on soft 18, 19, 20 and 21. Why? They can't add. The ace confuses them. Example: You have an ace and 4 in two cards which is soft 15. You hit with a four. You now have 19. Why hit again? Plenty of players do. You have an ace and 3 in two cards (soft 14). You hit with a 7—you have 21. Players still hit. Why? They can't add.

These are common occurrences. They happen all the time. If you are a player that can't figure out the ace, please ask the dealer what you have. He will tell you. Don't be ashamed or embarrassed. It is better to ask before you make the mistake. Once you hit, the dealer cannot take the card back. You can't say "misforgiving". Your mistake is the club's benefit. Thousands of players are making benefits for the clubs. Believe me, the clubs don't need them.

These are the soft hands you do NOT hit in two cards. Ace and 7, ace and 8, ace and 9, ace and 10 or picture. They add up soft 18 (fair hand), soft 19 (pretty good hand), soft 20 (good hand) and a Blackjack (can't be beat). There are much too many ways to make a soft 18, 19, 20, or 21 in more than two cards to put down here. It really isn't necessary. All you have to do is use a little common sense when hitting your soft hands.

Now let us talk about hitting your soft hands with a high card. Let us say you have a soft 14 (an ace and 3) in your first two cards. You ask for a hit or card and the dealer hits you with a nine. (Remember, you are never over when asking for the first hit). The ace now becomes a one, so an ace, 3, and 9 are 13. That is what we call a hard hand, because now if your hand calls for a hit, according to the rules, and you receive a 9 or 10 you are over. You have lost your money. You have an ace and 6 in your hand (soft 17). You are hit with an 8—you are not over. You have lost your money. You have an ace and 6 in your hand (soft 17). You are hit with an 8—you are not over. You have ace, 6, and

8—a hard 15. Now if the dealer has a high card up you hit. If the dealer has a low card up, you stop. Remember, ask the dealer what you have if you are in doubt. This applies to any hand. Don't outguess yourself.

As far as doubling down on soft hands, contrary to other opinions, there are only two that I advocate. If you receive a soft 17 or 18 in two cards, and the dealer has a five or six showing, you can double down. Top players will double on these hands as they have the best of it. The odds are in the players' favor. It isn't necessary, however, and it would probably be wise to wait until you know what you are doing with your "soft hands." Also if cards are going your way.

Here is an instance that happened in the club recently. There were six players at a 21 game—all small bettors. A player playing in the middle of the table had an ace and 3—a soft 14, hit with an 8 and showed it to the player on the left of him and asked him what he had. The player answered, "I don't know." So he showed it to the player on the right of him. She said, "I don't know." He then showed the hand to the other four players. Finally one of them said, "You are over—you have 22." Six players and not one of them knew. God save the 21 players!

In most clubs in Nevada, the dealer must hit on soft 17. By doing so it adds a little more percentage in the clubs' favor. This is for you players that stop on soft 17. If it's good enough for the club to hit a soft 17, it should be good enough for you.

Here are all combinations of soft hands that must be hit *regardless* of what the dealer has showing:

Two card combinations: Ace and 2; ace and 3; ace and 4; ace and 5; ace and 6.

Three card combinations: Ace, 5, and ace; ace, 2 and 4; ace, 3 and 3.

Four card combinations: Ace, 2, ace and 3; ace, 2, 2, and 2.

Five card combinations: Ace, 2, ace, ace, and 2; ace, 3, ace, ace and ace.

Everyone of these combinations total to a soft seventeen. As you will notice, you can only make a soft 17 with small cards, six or below. On the other hand if you have a 7, 8, 9, 10 or picture with your ace—it is an automatic STOPPING hand.

This is something very few people know. You, or the dealer, can hit with a total of 10 cards and not go over. They are: 2, 2, 2, 2, 3, ace, ace, ace, ace, and 3 in rotation. It has been done, so be alert.

Insurance in Blackjack

We come to the part of the game of 21 that is called insuring your bet. I will explain how it is done and why most players take insurance on their bets.

The *only time* a dealer can give you insurance is when he has an ace showing. He cannot give you insurance with any other card showing.

When you sit down at a 21 table to make a bet you place your money in a square box about 4" by 4" marked off on the table. Directly in front of this square in some clubs is a smaller box which is about 2" wide and 4" long. In this box are the words "insurance 2 to 1." In clubs that don't have the insurance box, you place your insurance bet directly in front of the box you have made your original bet in. This means when the dealer has an ace showing, he will say, "Does anybody care for insurance?"

That means, do you want to protect your bet? Which is what any kind of insurance means—protection against a loss. This means that the "dealer" will bet you or lay you the odds of 2 to 1 that he does not have a ten or picture in the hole. If he does have a ten or picture in the hole or down card, that would give him a Blackjack and he would take the player's money unless the player also has a Blackjack and it would be a tie.

If you, the player, thinks that the dealer has a picture or ten in the hold (an ace showing) you are allowed to put up half the amount of your original bet in this little box that says "insurance 2 to 1". Then the dealer will look at his hole card and if he has a ten or picture he has a Blackjack.

If you had taken insurance, you would not lose your money.

You have a standoff or push. If the dealer, after looking at his hole card, does not have a ten or picture in the hole, he will then take your insurance bet and will put the money in his rack. You now play the hand as the rules say. I will give you an example. Your bet is four dollars and the dealer turns up an ace. You think that he has a ten or picture in the hole so you put up two dollars in the little box that says "insurance 2 to 1". If the dealer turns up a blackjack he will take your original bet of four dollars and pay your bet of two dollars which you have placed in the insurance box. You have broken even. You have put up a total of six dollars. Four dollars that you originally bet and two dollars for insurance and received a total of $6.00 back, so you have just what you started with.

The dealer had bet you or "laid you" 2 to 1 that he doesn't have a blackjack. But having a blackjack he must pay you 2 to 1. Remember this, however, the dealer doesn't lose a penny with all this transaction. He uses your money all the time. He has invested nothing, so he has nothing to lose—but much to gain. Just like a banker—you put up your own money to insure your own money, and the dealer takes a commission on your money.

Now let us say that the dealer after looking at his hole card doesn't have a ten or picture, so he takes your insurance bet and puts it in his rack. You now play your hand like any other hand. Insurance betting is over with.

The funny part of this whole wager is that you cannot win any money. You either break even, or lose half of your original bet.

Most players that take insurance have various misconceptions of what insurance means. I will try to explain some of these: Some players take insurance when they have a good hand, like a nineteen or twenty, figuring that if the dealer DOES have a blackjack, they will break even, and if the dealer doesn't have a blackjack, they might win the bet and the insurance money they had just lost. That's fine. But nobody has yet shown me where you must win with nineteen or twenty. There is no guarantee. The dealer can also have or make a nineteen or twenty. He can also make a twenty-one if he has to hit his hand. You do not have a sure thing or "cinch hand" (which means you cannot lose). The ONLY guaranteed winner in a 21 game is when you, the player, have a blackjack in two cards and the dealer doesn't have an ace, ten or picture card showing. He cannot tie or beat you. He must pay—which incidentally is a State law. The dealer must pay you when he loses, and take your money when he wins.

There are some players that take insurance regardless of what they have. Good hand or bad hand, it doesn't make any difference to them, as long as the dealer has an ace showing they take insurance. I guess somebody told them to take insurance all the time—so they do. Some players with a bad or "breaking" hand take insurance, hoping the dealer will have a blackjack and they will save their money.

Good thinking, if you are a moron. Why take insurance on a bad hand? If the dealer doesn't have a blackjack you have lost half your bet. Now you are fighting to make a bad hand into a good hand, as you must hit it against an ace showing. If you should win, you only won half as much as you should have.

Example: You bet $4.00 and the dealer has an ace up. You have a "stiff" so you take insurance for $2. The dealer doesn't have a blackjack so you have lost two dollars. Now let us say you hit the stiff and win the hand. The dealer pays you four dollars. You have a total of 8 dollars but you have invested $6 so you have only won $2. That's a tough way to win half a bet.

Now what to do when the player has a blackjack in two cards and the dealer has an ace showing—Example: The player looks at his first two cards and he has blackjack. He turns the hand face up. Now the dealer has an ace showing. The player, who has bet $6 will now put $3 in the insurance box. That is what you will hear dealers and other players tell you is a cinch bet—you cannot lose.

If the dealer has a blackjack you have tied him as you also have a blackjack, so he cannot take your six dollars. He must pay you 2 to 1 on the insurance bet you made of $3. You have won $6. You have invested a total of $9 and received a total of $15. If the dealer after looking at his hole card doesn't have a blackjack, he will take your insurance bet of $3 and put it in his rack.

Now he must pay you for the blackjack you have turned over. You receive a bonus of an extra dollar for every two you have bet. We call it 3 to 2. The dealer will give you $9 for the six you have bet. A total of $15—you still win $6. This 3 to 2 applies to any amount you bet. It could be $1 to $500. A dollar blackjack would be $1.50 in return. Ten dollars would be $15 in return, $25 would be $37.50 in return and so on.

What's the cinch about giving away a third of your bet? That's exactly what it comes to, a third of your bet. When you turn up your blackjack, you have it and the dealers "got his to get". When you sat down to play, you were gambling. So why not gamble that the dealer doesn't have a blackjack? The odds on the dealer having a blackjack are a fraction over two to one and in the long run the club will wear or grind you out. The odds are in the clubs' favor that the dealer will not turn a blackjack with an ace showing. If the club didn't have a little "edge" or percentage going for them, they could not stay in business. They are entitled to that. If they didn't have the best of it, the 2 to 1 on insurance wouldn't be on the table for you to read.

So I am taking it for granted that by now you should know that you MUST NOT TAKE INSURANCE. You are taking the worst of it. But I will say this. If you are the player that comes to Nevada once or twice a year and you should have a blackjack you can take insurance if you want to. Even saying this goes against my grain, but it doesn't mean much to the once or twice a year player.

If you, however, are the player that comes quite often— that is five or six times a year, DON'T TAKE INSURANCE ON ANYTHING. You are a continuous player and it will tell on you without you knowing.

We had a very "tough" 21 player who would come in a few times a year—a big bettor. When he would sit down to play we knew we would have a struggle on our hands. We had one strong point in our favor. He always took insurance on anything he had in his hand. He would play three hands at a time. We always liked to see the dealer have an ace showing for the insurance bet. That is the only mistake he made—taking insurance. Many a time he would finish winner at the end of a play, but most of the time we would beat him. How? By his taking insurance. I kept track a couple of times. The time he beat us for $6,000 he would have won $13,000 by not taking insurance. He bets $500 a hand—that is $750 insurance everytime. The other time he lost $10,000 and $6,000 of it was by betting on insurance. I have this to say to you—some of the richest companies in the world are insurance companies.

Remember, the only time a dealer is supposed to look at his hole card is when he has an ace, picture, or ten showing. He has no other reason to look unless he has other thoughts on his mind. This warning applies to wherever you are playing. QUIT. Take it on the duffy. Run!

7

MONEY MANAGEMENT IN 21

One fine evening, a few years ago, a fellow with a foreign accent came up to me and said, "You work here?" I replied, "Yes, I do." He said, "What's it all about, this game of 21? I win hand and hand and hand—win all the time. At the end I'm broke. How do you win?"

That's where management of your money comes on the game of 21. How to bet, how much to bet, and when to bet. I don't care how good you play the game—you have to know where your money is going and why. I have seen good 21 players mismanage their money and finish loser where they should have quit winners, and then wonder why they have lost their money. I have also seen good players quit winners with one-fifth of what they should have won if they had bet and managed their money the right way.

Playing and knowing the game of 21 is fine. It is a good feeling for a player to know that he can walk into a club and play the game without making a fool of himself. However, by not knowing how to bet the right way, your playing ability will only keep you in the game a little longer. You also have to have a betting ability to make you a winner.

When playing 21 you must give your money and yourself a chance to win. I have seen players come into a club and start betting five dollars at a time. Their biggest bet during the whole play would be ten dollars. At the end of the evening they would be four or five hundred dollars loser. They can't understand how they lost that much money by only betting such a small amount. They were what we call "ground out of their money."

Slowly but surely the club was taking its pound of flesh and the longer the player sat and played the worse it would get. Once you are hooked a few hundred dollars playing five and ten dollars at a time, the harder it is to get out even. Do you realize how many hands you have to win to get "even" or how long you have to sit at a 21 table to try to win back your money if you are four or five hundred loser? Believe me, it is very difficult to do.

The strength of gambling is to bet more when you are winning, not when you are losing. That is the secret of gambling. Bet with the House's or Club's money. Why keep betting more when you are losing? Only idiots do that and there are plenty of them around. I have seen players that keep on winning, but bet less and less as they win hand after hand. I have seen dealers "go over" ten and fifteen times in a row. I saw one woman win 22 consecutive bets in a row. She started with two dollars and finally got all the way down to betting one dollar. A very rare feat, but she accomplished it. (And players wonder how the clubs win so much money?)

Follow these simple rules on how to bet and manage your money while playing. You will see how easy it is to eliminate the guess work of when and how to make the right bet at the right time.

You must progress when you win—not keep on doubling your bets till they are out of proportion. You must take a little and leave a little as you sin.

The player himself must set a limit in his own mind of how his biggest bet should be. It is very difficult to tell a small player that he must reach the limit before he can win money. That is impossible for the small player to do. Some clubs have a $500 limit. How does anybody expect a two, five, ten or even twenty-five dollar player to bet until they are betting $500. We would have to have a doctor and nurse at each table to take care of the fainting spells that the customers would have betting to reach the limit.

When you are progressing as you are winning, and you should lose the next bet, you must start all over again—bet the same with the same size bet that you originally made. Don't get ambitious or excited—just revert back to your original bet every time you lose.

The downfall of most players is "chasing their money". We call this type of player a "steamer". One that gets mad and starts to bet more and more as he keeps losing—thinking or saying to himself, "I must win the next bet." Well, you don't have to win the next bet. You can lose the next ten in a row. There isn't a person in the world that can prophesy or guarantee what will happen in the next hand. The player soon finds that out after he has lost his money and is broke.

There are millions of players that come to Vegas every year—sit down at a 21 table, bet one or two dollars at a time (never more), just having a ball. They spend two or three days enjoying themselves and then wake up to the fact they are two, three, or four hundred dollars loser, and only betting one and two dollars.

How could that happen? After all they were playing very small, to enjoy themselves.

How could anybody win betting one and two dollars all day long? It is impossible to get "out" or even after being "hooked" or loser a couple of hundred dollars, by still betting one and two dollars. Gambling clubs in the state of Nevada win millions and millions of dollars from these small players that don't have the slightest chance in the world. Their money isn't worth a nickel on the dollar the minute they step into a gambling club. Don't get the wrong impression of what I am saying. I am not criticizing the small player. After all, a player must play according to what they can afford to lose. I am only criticizing the way they bet.

Believe me, most of you small players can stand plenty of criticism.

The average players who gamble in Las Vegas are not big or fast players. They don't come with thousands of dollars just to try to make a fortune. They are what we call "pleasure" players. They come into town with a few hundred dollars hoping that they will survive all the hazards and pitfalls that they have been told about at home or read about by some columnist that never left his hotel because the whiskey was free. Nobody has to set a trap for these type of players. They set the trap and fall into it themselves—as soon as they sit down at a 21 table.

It doesn't make any difference how small a player you are. The one and two dollar player must be able to manage his money as well as the bigger player. The amount has nothing to do with managing your money. This is the best way to bet and manage your money at a 21 game:

YOU MUST PROGRESS AS YOU WIN. If you don't you don't have a chance. You cannot stay at the same level bet after bet. That is what grinds you out of your money. Example for two dollar bettor: Your original bet is two dollars. If you win the bet, bet 4 dollars. If you win the next bet, bet 6 dollars. If you win the next bet, bet 10 dollars. As you notice, you are leaving a little and taking a little. That is what we call a slow progression. If you win the 10 dollar bet, just bet 10 dollars. Stay at the same bet. Then it is up to you, the player, to determine how much higher you want to progress. Actually, a two dollar bettor should stop at $15, which is a pretty good bet for the one and two dollar bettor.

Some players wait until they start to shake and that gives them a warning that they have reached their limit of betting. It is very hard to tell a player how much they should bet or how much they should win. Do you know that one percent of all the people that gamble will reach or bet to a $500 limit? A small player is not supposed to gamble that high or win thousands of dollars. The average two dollar player would be happy and grateful to win a hundred dollars or two now and then. This is pretty good and it could be done if the money is bet and managed the right way.

Now let us say you bet the two dollars and lose. Just continue to bet two dollars—no more— until you win a hand. Then start progressing and if you keep winning progress until you reach your limit of 15 dollars. Stay at this limit until you lose a bet. Then revert back to your two dollar bet. Continue to play this way all the time wherever you play, and you will be a "tough" bettor.

You are a two dollar bettor when losing, and a fifteen dollar bettor when winning. Believe me, it is much better on the nerves and ulcers. You are more relaxed playing this way than betting $50 when losing and a two dollar bettor when winning. Remember, every hand is a new hand. Forget about the last hand—win, lose or draw. It is like yesterday's news. If you have made a mistake forget about it. There is nothing you can do to rectify the mistake. Don't let it interfere with playing the next hand.

By playing a slow progression, you will notice that after winning two hands in a row your profit takes care of the third bet. The next winning hands in succession are all gravy hands—you are getting a free roll and you are not supplying the money. You are now playing with the club's money and are now considered a tough bettor. I will make it more simple for the non-college graduates. Your first bet is $2, next $4, next $6, then $10. You can stay at the $10 bet once to give you a little more bankroll, then jump to your $15 bet and stay there. Don't "drag down" as long as you are winning.

Don't guess when you will lose a hand. You can't. If you

start guessing, it will be your downfall.

This way of betting applies to a $5, $10, $25, $50 and $100 bettor. The player that comes in and bets $500 "right off the shoulder", which means his first bet is $500, doesn't need any advice on how to manage his money. All he needs is more money. Believe it or not, you the player that bets his money with a method behind it, is a much tougher player than the big bettor that comes in cold and bets $500 immediately. Why? Because a player betting $500 on a hand is like a one-dollar player. He has bet the limit as soon as he sat down. In order to do that he must have plenty of money. He cannot bet any more because he has bet the limit. What happens if he should go bad and be 15 or 20 bets loser? It comes to a lot of money.

Fifteen bets loser is $7,500. 20 bets loser is $10,000. A one dollar bettor that bets a dollar at a time and gets to be $15 or $20 loser is in the same predicament only on a much smaller scale. He has a tough struggle trying to win his money back, a dollar at a time. The same way applies to the $500 bettor. He has to win his money back $500 at a time, and that takes a lot of winning bets to do. Whereas you, the "tough" player are playing the scale. You are going up when winning and down when losing. You are not getting into any trouble while losing as you are staying at your minimum bet, but once you start to win a few hands in a row you are now playing with someone else's money—the club's—and I assure you they won't like it one bit.

It takes plain "guts" or fortitude to bet when you are winning. When you see a player betting small then bet higher while losing, you often hear people standing around remark to each other, "He's got plenty of courage betting that high." I laugh when I hear somebody pass a remark like that. They don't know that this player is playing in desperation, as we say. He is trying to win a bet so he can break even. If he wins the bet he runs like a whipped dog. These type of players every club would send a limousine for. These "steamers" are what we call "red hots" cooked before they play.

I am going to explain how different types of bettors

should bet, so if any reader should be in one of these categories, they will know how to manage their money.

A $5 bettor should not be afraid to reach a limit of $50 as he keeps on winning. He should progress at the rate of $5-$10-$15-$25-$25-$35-and $50.

A $10 bettor should not be afraid to reach a limit of $100. He should progress at the rate of $10-$20-$30-$50-$50-$75- and $200.

A $50 bettor can reach a $300 to $500 limit. That depends on how much guts he has. $50-$100-$150-$225-$225-$300 and further if he wants to. A $100 bettor should reach the limit without any hesitation at all. $100-$200-$300-$400-$400-$500.

You will notice on the fourth and fifth bet you bet the same amount. That is to give you a little leeway. A sort of cushion if you win both of these bets. If you should lose the next bet you will be in a comfortable position when you start with your original bet. That is called "playing money."

In playing this progression, if and when your hand calls for you to double down or split pairs do not hesitate one bit regardless of what amount you are betting you must play the hand—not the money. Please do not let the size of the bet make a coward out of you. Remember the bet must not interfere with the playing of the hand. I don't care if the bet is one dollar or five hundred. It will not change the spots on the cards. If your hand calls for you to double down or split a pair, and you have a big bet staring you in the face, just remember how you accomplished this—only one way. By playing and managing your money according to the rules. So what have you to fear—nothing. You got this far on your ability so continue to use it, even if you should lose the bet you didn't go down with the worst of it. The same play will come up many a time while playing and who is to say you must lose the next one. When betting someone else's money be brave, when betting your own be a coward.

I had a New York stock broker say to me one day, "I have been coming to Las Vegas for the last four years at least twice a year and haven't won once in all these trips. I can't even come close to a winner. I am very successful at my business, good at figures and I am very disgusted at myself. I guess there is more to the game of 21 than I thought."

He then asked me if I could give him any advice as to what he was doing wrong. Here was a millionaire investment broker asking for advice. Why? Because it hurt his ego not being able to at least win once out of 15 trips to Las Vegas which amounted to quite a bit of money as he would lose 4 to 5 thousand dollars each trip. He said it wasn't the money as much as not being able to win once out of fifteen tries. I had known him casually at first but as he would come to town we would converse more each trip. In fact he had given me a couple of leads on some stocks that right now I wish he had instead of me. He also told me that he had asked three or four men in the gambling clubs what was wrong with his playing but never did get the right answer. I told him that he must have been talking to a couple of porters or relatives that worked in the clubs he had asked for some friendly advice.

Anybody that had been in gambling would have given him the answer in one second. He was a "steamer". I took him to lunch and gave him the "facts of life" about gambling. I told him about progression in betting his money and that he wasn't a good player only a fair player, but if he manages his money he will have a better chance to win. He'd been chasing his money for the last four years and never caught up with it yet.

I also told him that believe it or not, a gambling club doesn't like to see a good customer lose continuously. They would like to see them win once in a while, (but not too often).

Even a small player that comes to Vegas with four to five hundred dollars but comes six or more times a year is a good customer as it amounts to a lot of money and there are thousands of small players. I told him that there is no guarantee that he must win playing this way—just like the stocks he gave me. Well, he started to play and played for 2 hours up and down but never was in trouble. Finally the cards started to favor him and he would be winning four and five hands in a row. Lose one and win four or five more. As he was a $50 bettor it didn't take long for him to be a couple of thousand winner. He quit, came over to me and said, "You saved my life. I now know what a bad player I was and am leaving town as soon as I can—just to go home a winner once." The best compliment was when a couple of floormen watching him play said to me, "This fellow is a pretty tough player." I said, "He sure is." He could have lost just as well but he would have gone down fighting. The other way he would have lost his money and still be wondering why.

I had a columnist that came in for most of the opening night shows. She played 21 like I would ride a horse—and I have never been on a horse in my life. She would lose $600 to $800 every trip she made. Lucky for her that she didn't come to all the openings as she never had a chance. Her money was worth less than some of the worthless oil stock I bought some years ago.

Let alone striking oil, we can't even strike water, and still my chances are better than hers when she plays 21.

One day while playing she said to me, "All I have been doing is writing checks. Every time I come to this so and so town. Right now I am $600 loser and expect to lose more. What's the trouble with my playing?" I answered, "As long as you asked me for an honest opinion I will give it to you. My 9 year-old son plays better than you do. You bet to lose. You bet 5 and 10 dollars all night long—afraid to double down. A couple of times you wouldn't even split aces because you were betting $10 and would have to put up $10 more. You are playing "scared pool". Your collar gets tight the minute you bet $10. Any player that walks into a club and can lose from $600 to $800 should be able to win a few hundred dollars without being afraid. To do that you must bet more than $10 when winning. My advice to you is to just bet small—in face one dollar at a time would be just right for you. The day and one half you spend here will cost you less money and your checks would be for less amounts. Now I am going to prove to you that I am not talking out of my hat."

I told her to bet $10. She won the bet. I said, "Bet $20." She did and won the bet. I said, "Bet $30." She looked at me and her hands started to shake, she couldn't back down. At that moment I was called to another table for credit and walking back past her table I saw she only had $10 bet.

As soon as I was called away and before the dealer had dealt the cards she grabbed $20 off the bet. She was fooling me, but she forgot one little thing. She was writing the checks, not me. I never went back to her table again as she knew exactly what I meant by proving a point.

I am not like other so-called experts that tell you how to play and do just the opposite when playing themselves. I won't tell anybody anything that I won't do myself when gambling. When I walk into a gambling club and decide to play, I make up my mind as to how much I am going to lose first—which is usually around $500. That is all I will lose, come hell or high water. However, I don't set my limit on my winnings! As I have said, I will play for three days if the dice are passing or I am going good at a 21 game. I play and manage my money the exact way it is written in this book during a "play". If I am winning I will raise my original to a higher level so it will give me a chance to win more money. I usually start with a minimum of $20 when playing 21 and progress the way I have told you. If the cards are going my way and I am winning, I will jump my original bet to $30 or $40. If I start losing a few bets, I revert back to $20 and stay there. I have even bet much less if I am going bad. When I walk into a gambling club I am known as a tough customer. The bosses aren't too delighted to see me play. They respect my playing ability knowing that they can't beat me out of much, but if I should walk to the right table—they do the sweating, not me.

I don't play too often as it isn't good for the blood pressure. Besides it's here whenever I feel like playing or "taking a shot" as the saying goes.

If you the player, small bettor or big bettor, follow these

simple rules and use common sense, clubs will have a little more respect towards your playing ability when you play at a 21 game. Also you the player will have a different attitude towards the game knowing that if you lost your money you at least had a chance. The club had to fight for it.

Don't be afraid to quit winner. You are not bolted to the chair. If, during the play, you are winning and you should start losing don't be afraid to get up. Either quit for a while or go to another table. There is nothing wrong in moving about. It is also good for the circulation. You might find walking around will shake some of the cobwebs out of your brains. When winning, don't chase your money after losing a few bets. Put your shoes on and take a walk. Dealers in clubs deal for 8 hours. so they must go good or bad and it is up to you to catch the dealers that are going over and you are making your hands good. You know what doctors say, "Walk—it will do you good."

Quite a few clubs in Nevada are using shoes at some of their 21 tables. The dealer uses four decks of cards instead of one deck. All cards but one, the dealer's hole card, are dealt open as usual. The reason for this change is that the so-called counters who are good at it could beat the 21 table and four decks make for faster games.

In Europe many deal with open cards and one deck and you still have a chance if you have a good memory and are a good counter, you can beat the game.

The game is played exactly like you are playing at a single deck game. The play is much faster and you can lose faster or win faster, whichever way suits you. There is only one slight difference. The shoe helps the poor club. It raises their percentage a little higher.

I have seen many a strange thing happen in a gambling game. You will always have a chance as long as you have money to play with, regardless of how small the amount. One incident I recall very vividly in my mind is of a player having six dollars left after losing $700. Four hours later he walked out with $17,000. It could happen to you. Full speed ahead.

I have one last warning to give you. The dealer can give you an automatic 18 and break you in the long run. So hit your "stiffs" against high cards and let the chips fall where they may.

8

INSIDE POKER

Is poker a game of skill or is it just chance? One time a court tried to decide this question and the jury asked for a deck of cards and played far into the night.

At the end of the game, eight said it was chance and four said it was skill. Coincidentally, the four had won and the eight had lost. It was a hung jury.

Our guess is that a good, skillful player will win over a period of time. What is skill? It's the knowledge of the game, the play and the odds.

Take this my favorite story about poker:

Five years ago, a friend of mine who was a chief engineer at Lockheed (he will be nameless because of the nature of the story) used to bring the boys home once a week for a poker game. He is married, has four children, the oldest is 12, and his mother lives with him. Grandma was bored stiff. Her husband had died and her son and daughter-in-law weren't the most interesting people in the world. But she did enjoy peeking in at the weekly poker games. However, after a while, the boys looked upon her as a pest and her son told her to go to the movies instead. The 68 year-old grandmother didn't like movies but she did like poker. So she began drifting over to Gardena, a city in California where poker is legalized and where games go on all day and night.

When Grandma was permitted in the room with her son's poker game, she was quite critical of the play. She felt for instance that players held kickers with pairs too often and at the wrong times. She started studying a couple of handbooks on poker. She learned for instance that the odds against providing a pair was 2½ to 1 against you and with a kicker wasn't equal to the reduction of chances to win. In Gardena she watched faces and associated them with their method of play. She would lay out hands at home and spend tedious hours learning the odds on every play.

Then she got her feet wet and entered a 25 cent ante game. She lost $7 her first day but her first week she won $45. She plays every day for a minimum of four hours. The first year she averaged $75 a week profit. The second year she boosted her winnings to $100 a week. Not a million, true enough, but a nice conservative sum with a conservative investment. And think that a few years ago she was just a pest!

Frequency of Poker Hands

Let's analyze an "honest" poker game—one in which there are no marked cards, no sharpers, no cheating, no false dealing. The "hands" are those obtained by the average player in an average game with 52 cards.

First, let's determine the chance of obtaining certain types of "hands" when five cards are dealt out to each individual. (Later we can analyze draw poker, the game in which several of the original five cards may be discarded and replaced by the drawing of additional cards from the remainder of the deck.)

There are 2,598,960 different poker hands possible in the random selection of five cards from a deck of 52. Of these hands, there are 1,302,540 different ones—more than half the entire number of hands—with no pair or higher (called busts). Other hands contain one pair, two pair, etc.

The following table indicates the chances of a poker player receiving the types of hands listed:

ODDS FOR POKER HANDS

Hand	Number of Such Hands	Odds Against Getting
Royal Flush	4	649,789 to 1
Straight Flush	36	72,192 to 1
Four of a kind	624	4,164 to 1
Full house	3,744	693 to 1
Flush	5,108	508 to 1
Straight	10,200	254 to 1
Three of a kind	54,912	46 to 1
Two Pairs	123,552	20 to 1
One Pair	1,098,240	1.37 to 1 (4 to 3)
Busts	1,302,540	1 to 1
Total	2,598,960	

If you want to determine the probability of getting a hand higher than a specified value—that is, the probability of getting a hand higher than two pairs (three of a kind, straight, flush, etc.) Do as follows: Add the numbers of such hands occurring in the 2,598,960. The total of hands higher than two pairs is 74,628. Then, upon dividing 2,598,960 by 74,628, you obtain the number of hands which must be dealt to give one hand higher than two pairs, namely, 34.8 which is rounded off to the nearest whole number, 35.

Thus, one hand higher than two pairs occurs once in every 35 hands, meaning that the odds against getting such a hand are 34 to 1.

Similar computations give the probabilities and odds for other specified hands.

Draw Poker

There are so many variations of poker involving different rules that it isn't possible to discuss all of them here. However, let's consider draw poker in view of its popularity.

Five cards are dealt to each player. In proper rotation sequence, any player holding a pair of Jacks or better hand may initiate a procedure whereby each player is permitted to discard one, two or three of his cards. The player who initiates this procedure is said to "open" the draw.

Each player has one chance in five of getting a pair of Jacks or higher hand in the original five cards. As noted in the previous table, there are 198,180 hands which are higher than one pair. Of the 1,098,240 one-pair hands, four-thirteenths of them are Jacks, Queens, Kings or Aces—a total of 337,920 hands. This latter figure and the number of hands above one pair add to 536,100 hands of Jacks or higher.

If the 2,598,960 possible hands are divided by 536,100, the result is the number of hands which must be dealt to give one hand of Jacks or higher, namely, 4.85 hands. Rounded off, the nearest whole number is five, which means that one out of every five hands will be a pair of Jacks of higher.

In draw poker, the player is necessarily interested in knowing what chance he has of improving his hand.

Suppose he holds one pair and draws three cards. The odds against bettering the hand at all are 7 to 3, or in simpler form, 2-1/3 to 1. The odds against his making certain combinations are as follows:

Against making two pairs	4.9 to 1
Against making three of a kind	7.8 to 1
Against making a full house	89 to 1
Against making four of a kind	359 to 1

If the player holds one pair and an additional card, an Ace for example (generally referred to as a "kicker"), and he draws only two cards, then he has the following odds against bettering his hand:

Against making two pairs	4.7 to 1
Against making three of a kind	11.9 to 1
Against making a full house	119 to 1
Against four of a kind	1080 to 1

The odds against bettering the hand at all are 2.8 to 1, or 14 to 5.

A comparison of the above tables indicates that there is no over-all advantage in holding a "kicker". Notice that with a "kicker" the probabilities of getting three of a kind, full house, or four of a kind decrease while the chance of two pairs increases only slightly.

Accordingly, it is not advisable to hold a "kicker" to a pair in a draw poker game.

If a player has two pairs and draws one card, the odds against bettering the hand for the only possible higher hand are 10.8 to 1.

The question of whether to discard the lower pair of two pairs in an attempt to improve the hand has caused considerable controversy. Actually the circumstances of the moment and the actions of other players have much to do with the decision.

If you are interested in determining whether you should draw a single card to two pairs or discard the lower pair and draw three cards, consider the probabilities against bettering two pairs as against getting a hand higher than two pairs when you draw three cards. In a one-card draw the odds against making a full house are 10.8 to 1.

The probabilities in a three-card draw are as follows:

Odds against bettering the pair	2.3 to 1
Odds against making two pairs	4.9 to 1
Odds against making a hand higher than two pairs	6.8 to 1

Thus, if you discard one pair, you have 3 chances in 10 of getting either two pairs, or three of a kind, or a full house, of four of a kind.

Actually you have 1 chance in 8 of getting a hand higher than two pairs, as against 1 chance in 12 of bettering the two pairs when you draw a single card. However, it must be remembered that a sacrifice was made in discarding the lower pair—that is, after starting with two pairs, say aces and sixes, the decision was made to discard the sixes and reduce the hand to a pair of aces before the draw.

Thus if you were convinced it would take more than two pair to win the game, you would be justified in discarding the lower pair. If you were convinced two pair would win the game, you would not consider breaking up the original two pair since a hand of two pairs occurs on the average once in 21 hands.

Suppose you have three of a kind and draw two cards. Here are the odds: against making a full house, 14.7 to 1; against making four of a kind, 22.5 to 1. The odds against bettering the hand at all are 8.4 to 1.

If you hold a "kicker" with the three of a kind and draw only one card, you have the following odds: against making a full house, 14.7 to 1; against making four of a kind, 46 to 1. The odds against bettering the hand are 10.8 to 1.

It is obvious that no advantage is gained by holding a "kicker". As a matter of fact, the chance of getting four of a kind is decreased considerably, while the chance of getting a full house remains the same.

Straights and Flushes

The odds against drawing one card to four of a single suit to make a flush are approximately 4 to 1 (1 chance in 5). You have less chance of drawing a single card to fill straight than a flush.

Suppose you are drawing one card to an "outside" straight—that is, you have a sequence of four cards (say 5, 6, 7, 8)—and are trying to get the 4 or the 9 to make a sequence of five cards. The chance of getting a 4 or a 9 in a single draw is approximately one in six. This means that on the average you may expect to get the card you need to make an outside straight only once in six attempts.

If a single card is drawn to an "inside" straight, trying to get a 6 when you hold 3, 4, 5 and 7, the straight is successful only once in 12 tries. This is the reason why "smart" gamblers never draw to an "inside" straight.

Considering these probabilities and the odds against drawing a single card to make a full house out of two pairs (approximately one in 12), it is advisable to match one wager by an opponent who draws only one card, but not to go beyond that point.

Suppose, for example, you hold three of a kind, say three Jacks. Your opponent draws only one card. First you try to figure out whether he is drawing to a straight or to a flush or whether he is trying to make a full house out of two pairs. After you draw, you still have only three Jacks. Your opponent makes a bet and you must decide whether to meet (or "call") the bet or drop out. This is always a hard decision, especially if your opponent keeps a "poker face".

On the basis of mathematical chances, your opponent has one chance in six of success if he is drawing to a straight. If he has two pairs and is drawing to a full house, the chance of success is about one in 12. If he is drawing to a flush (five cards of same suit), the chance of success is about one in five.

If your opponent had three of a kind to start with, he would not be drawing a single card—unless, of course, he's a novice at the game.

Thus, knowing that your opponent has a relatively small chance of successfully filling his hand, you are justified calling a bet.

HOW TO WIN

Jokers and Wild Cards

Introducing a Joker into the game changes the number of value hands while the number of "busts" remains the same as in the game without the Joker. Therefore, the probabilities of higher hands increase. The number of specific value hands and the odds against occurrence are shown in the table on the next page.

Introducing two Jokers increases the number of value hands even more while the number of "busts" remains constant.

If certain cards in the deck are designated as "wild" (deuces, etc.) then the probabilities of high value hands increase considerably while the number of "busts" decreases.

POKER HANDS WITH ONE JOKER

Hand	Number of Such Hands	Odds Against Getting
Five of a Kind	13	220,744 to 1
Royal Flush	24	119,569 to 1
Straight Flush	180	15,942 to 1
Four of a Kind	3,120	919 to 1
Full House	6,552	437 to 1
Flush	7,804	367 to 1
Straight	20,532	139 to 1
Three of a Kind	137,280	20 to 1
Two pairs	123,552	22 to 1
One Pair	1,268,088	1.2 to 1
Busts	1,302,540	1.2 to 1
Total	2,869,685	

The effect of introducing Jokers or designating "wild" cards is to wipe out any advantage that an experienced player or one acquainted with the normal probabilities might have over others.

An odd fact that may be noticed in examing the table of possible hands with the Joker in the deck is that the probability of making three of a kind is greater than the chance of making two pairs.

The introduction of the Joker does not change the number of possible two-pair hands while it does increase the number of three-of-a-kind hands.

Drawing cards is only a part of poker. Every play and every action by every player is significant. Some players are natural bluffers; others are very conservative. The size of the wager and the manner in which it is made often provide a clue to the player's hand. But invariably the highest hand is the winning hand, for few players allow themselves to be "bluffed out".

In Gardena, California, which has legalized poker, the clubs are open 24 hours a day, except for one day a week, when they are closed for a few hours so the place can be cleaned up. It is a haven for insomniacs.

I know one fellow who passed away recently, a TV writer named Bert Richman, who played every night and did his TV writing starting at dawn. He couldn't sleep and he loved playing poker through the night.

9

THE SLOTS

The backbone of many a gambling club in the State of Nevada, and perhaps eventually in Atlantic City, is the slot machine.

There are clubs that would have to close their doors, without a slot machine. In some clubs the gambling games like craps, 21, and the wheel are put there for accommodations only and if the club could take them out they would. There are clubs that have slot only and don't want anything else in the club to disturb the addicted slot players. The only sure thing in a club, for the house, are the slots.

A slot club will try all kinds of gimmicks to draw the slot "drunks" to the club. They will give away balloons for the mothers to give to children—and the mothers don't have to walk very far, just outside the club where their offspring are watching them with their noses pressed against the windows—also free key rings, free buffet cart, and above all free whiskey. All this just to play the slots. I also forgot to mention the bells that are ringing all the time—that alone is enough to drive anyone crazy. But these little noises are music to the slot player's ears as it means that some idiot has hit a $2.50 jackpot and only invested $10.00.

A prize fighter would never have a chance in there with all those bells ringing. Did you ever see a slot player playing two and three machines at a time? It is like a three ring circus. They jump from one machine to another—never off balance—every move in rhythm. They would put a ballet dancer to shame. The only time they are off balance is when they are out of money and have to get more change. If there isn't a change girl around, a player will put a paper cup on the handle of the slot or slots they are playing. That signifies that the slot is in use and the player will be right back. Woe to anybody that uses any of these slots. There has been many a fight over a slot machine where the paper cup was brushed off or knocked off accidentally on purpose.

Did you ever see two of the weaker sex go at each other to see who loses their money first? Such language, like two truck drivers. Most all clubs have chairs so the players won't get too tired and some clubs will even furnish you gloves so your hands won't get dirty handling the coins. Did you ever see a player's hands after playing for a couple of hours? They look like they had just come out of a coal mine. Some players will only wear one glove just to put the coins in. The other hand must be bare so they can get the feel of the slot machine—like at a seance. They are trying to convey a message to a piece of iron.

A player will pull the handle all different ways to try to change their luck. They will pull it slow, fast, medium, very slow, jerk it very fast, give it two jerks, hold the handle down while the reels are spinning, let the handle go back fast as soon as the reels start spinning, bang the slot, kick it.

I have even seen a player break his wrist after two bars showed and the other one just slipped by. He took a punch at the glass. As most of the slot players are women, who don't know how to play any other game, and as there isn't much thinking to a slot machine, all you need is money and a good right hand to pull the handle. There are many more nickel slots than any other as women like to play where their money can last longer. There are all kinds of slot machines from a penny to a silver dollar. Penny, nickel, dime, quarter, halves, and silver dollars. Years ago before the gold was called in, one club had a $2.50 gold piece slot machine. It didn't last long. Somebody stole it.

Players at a slot are obsessed with the idea that the slot belongs to them. They put money in and are going to play until they hit a jackpot. Money be damned, the object is to beat the machine. They will put in five times as much as the jackpot will pay just to hit it and are satisfied that they have beat their mortal enemy, the slot machine. When they do hit the jackpot, they holler "Jackpot" at the top of their lungs so that everybody around can hear them and smile at the disheveled player, hoping it is their turn next to holler "Jackpot". That is the war cry of all slot players, "Jackpot!"

I will say this. It is nice to come to a state like Nevada where a person can enjoy themselves at any game they like to play and as most tourists that come to Nevada with the knowledge that they are going to lose a few dollars. I certainly agree with them whole-heartedly, as that is just what is going to happen to them. But why they have to get mad at a slot machine and play until they are broke is beyond me. Is it possible that when a tourist comes to Nevada they lose all their perspective and are like a bull in a china store—just run helter-skelter from one club to another and one slot machine to another. Money runs through their hands like water.

We have a Western Union office in Las Vegas which I wish I had stock in. I'll bet it does more business than any other Western Union in the world when it comes to sending home for more money, or to get bailed out of town. No way to get home, no friends, "Please Maw, send me money so I can get home."

There is a gasoline station in Barstow, California. It is about half-way between Vegas and L.A. Some players leave a $5 or $10 bill there and receive a receipt. And as soon as they arrive in Vegas, gas up immediately, then check into a hotel or motel and pay their bill for the room in advance. Now they are ready to do the town—no worries at all. Their room is paid for and if they should go broke, which they do, they are all prepared when leaving town, drive to Barstow and fill the tank with gas and pray that nothing happens to the car. Also they have to be at this gas station before 6 P.M. It closes at 6 o'clock. Most of these type players are slot players. I at least give them credit.

They prepare themselves as to what is going to happen to them, because if they didn't leave some money in that gas station it would be a long push back, as most slot players have no control over their money. They must hit the jackpot, regardless of the cost and "regardless" is what breaks them.

Let me tell you that a slot machine is sometimes called a "One-armed Bandit". And whoever gave the slot machine that name should get the medal of honor. He hit the name right on the head. This one-armed bandit takes your money and to make you like it he laughs right in your face, but you can't do anything about it. He has a license to steal, and after all nobody dragged you into the club. You came in of your own free will.

Years ago when slot machines were plentiful around the country there was many a bar or club that had slot machines that never stated on the machine what you could win. The slot machine mechanics would adjust the slot any way they wanted to. If you didn't like it, you didn't have to play. Many a time the machines would be adjusted to a high percentage for the house on a weekend when they knew they would get a lot of transient business, but would change the percentage back during the week for the locals. A slot can be adjusted any way the club wants to and would never pay off a jackpot if they wanted to.

This had been done to many a slot years ago, but today

in Nevada on all machines it states on the slot what you can win and what type of jackpots. When a state inspector comes around (and you never know when) you had better have on the reels exactly what it states on the outside. The inspector will just walk up to any one and say "Open it." A club would be very foolish to try to beat the public. It isn't necessary. All a club has to do is open the doors and keep the bells ringing and the flock will follow.

An old friend of mine that has been a "slot man" for 35 years, once told me, "In the first place a slot was built never to be beaten, just to play at."

Do you know that there are about 40 different size springs and about 550 parts counting all equipment on a slot machine, which makes them susceptible to breaking down or parts wearing out, or somebody trying to cheat a machine—which is happening all the time. Any fair-sized club will have a slot mechanic on hand at all times to handle any breakdowns, as all machines in the state of Nevada must be licensed and a machine cannot make any money back in the shop.

It must be fixed as soon as possible and put back on the floor where it will earn its keep. A good slot mechanic can dismantle a machine, clean it and put new parts in and put it together again without hesitation. If you ever saw the inside of a machine, you would be amazed at how he does it. He cannot make any mistakes either. One little mistake and the machine is paying off to the wrong person—the player. Sometimes it is quite a while before it is detected.

No two clubs have the same percentage on their machines. An owner determines how much the traffic will bear, and it also depends where the club is situated and what kind of clientele it handles. Some clubs, where their players are small bettors (nickel or dime slots) and do a large volume, will work on a 7 or 8 percent markup, so they say. Other clubs that have tourists who are a little bigger bettors and less volume will work on a 10 to 15 percent markup, so they say. Nobody but the owners of a club and the slot mechanic who makes the adjustments know how much percentage a machine earns. That is strictly up to them and it is entirely legal. A club must earn what it thinks it could. After all they give you free souvenirs, free food, and free whiskey.

Fifty and sixty years ago, as slots were being put in clubs and bars around the country, somebody always was devising a way to beat them. Even newsboys who delivered papers to some of these clubs would stuff a small wad of paper up into the trough or chute where the money comes out and when a player would get a hit, nothing would come out and they would go to the bartender and he would give them the coins they had coming. Then the newsboy would take the wad of paper out of the machine and the money would fall out. But in later years there were better ways to try and beat a slot machine.

These ways were concocted by men that knew the inside of a slot machine. Usually by former slot mechanics that would show somebody a way to beat a machine, but would tell them not to do it in the club where he worked. It would backfire as it would be told to another friend and this friend would tell it to another and so on. Until somebody would try it in the club where the slot mechanic who had originally given out the way to beat the slot would be working. Now he would have his hands full trying to stop what he had created.

There are quite a few ways to beat the slot machine. Here are a few of them that are still being tried in clubs that have old machines or have not done anything to counteract these gimmicks. Years ago a slot cheater found out that the trap door that releases the jackpot money could be sprung by sticking his hand into and up the trough where the money comes out. There was one catch, however, when the trap is sprung the door snaps back immediately and your hand better not be in the way.

So he had a hand made of plastic to fit over his hand and he did very well until he was caught. One time a player who saw him do this at a club, but didn't know that he used a plastic hand, tried it and when the trap door sprung his fingers were caught in the trap door. It took the slot mechanic three hours to get this player's hand out of the machine. He had to take it apart to do it. The spring is very powerful. It broke three of his fingers and I'll bet he never did that again.

Anyone caught tampering with a slot machine in the state of Nevada is subject to arrest. The courts are pretty strict when it comes to cheating at a game or slot machine. Do you know that even if you put in coins from a foreign country you can be arrested. It is just like putting slugs into a machine as they are just as worthless. I knew a slot mechanic that worked on an army base fixing slot machines. They used to give meat tokens to the soldiers and they would put them into the dime slots as they fitted perfectly. This mechanic went through the war without having to pay for any meat bills. He used the tokens he took out of the machines.

The employees that take care of the slots in a club have to be on their toes all the time. If they are not trained to look for certain gestures and moves the club will be taken like Grant took Richmond. One cheater will tell another about a soft spot where the clerks are "stiffs" and don't know what to look for. One cheater was beating a club for months. He had a key to open the back of the slot machines.

Every now and then he would beat different machines in this "soft" spot. He spread his business around, as we say. He didn't work on one slot—gave them all a little of his business. He and two girl friends would get around a slot and play it. When the right spot showed he would open the back of the slot and one of the girls would put a coin in and pull the handle, but wouldn't let go. He would stop the timer, line up the reels on the jackpot. close the back, then walk out.

The girl would let the handle go as soon as he closed the back and the timer would click off the reels in rotation just the way the cheater had set them on the jackpot. This has to be done very fast as it only takes a few seconds once the timer is let go. There isn't anything the club can do about a gimmick like this as it looks perfectly legitimate. The coin is in the machine and there is no way to find out if the machine has been tampered with. The only way to stop this is if you can catch them in the act. If you don't you have to pay the jackpot. Most of the time they are the big ones. The old saying is, "If you are going to get caught, it might as well be while you are taking the big one off."

Probably very few of you have heard of the "rhythm" players. If you think they are a group of singers, you are wrong. They are a group alright, but their job is cheating slot machines by using rhythm on the handle. A rhythm player will put a coin in the slot, pull the handle back slowly until he hears click that he is trained to hear. Then he will pull the handle down and go through the same routine over and over. That is called getting a free play. As the "pays" show, they drop, and if a jackpot shows they let the handle go and use the standard war cry, "Jackpot." Most clubs today use what is called a cheater's bar. This prevents the clicking and when the second coin is put into the slot the cheater will lose it. So he will try another one or leave and give some other club his business.

Another style is called, "Walking the reels". The reels are connected to what is called a ratchet which has teeth around it. A cheater will look for a machine where the teeth are worn or will sometimes try to jerk the handle a certain way to break some of the teeth. When that happens they put a coin in and slowly turn the first reel step by step until the bar shows, wait until they hear the clock which means the reel is locked in, then walk the second reel the same way, bring the bar up, wait for the clock and do the same thing to the third reel—let the handle go and the favorite war cry, "Jackpot!"

There are some cheaters that are called "drill men." They carry a small drill and actually drill holes into the machine, but like safe-crackers they know exactly where to drill. These holes are very small and are hard to detect. One method is to drill a hole directly in front of the firing pin. This pin sets the slot to working as soon as the coin hits it. After the hole is drilled, a small wire is inserted into the hole and now all the cheater has to do is push the wire into the firing pin and they can play as long as they want to, for nothing. The drinks are on the house.

Another method is to drill a hole in front of each reel, push a wire into each hole, and when the bar shows, stop it with the wire. You start with the first reel, when you hear the click, start on a second reel. When you hear the click, start on the third reel, then pull the wires out and lo and behold, the safe is open—Jackpot!

Another drill and wire method is a little more difficult, but not for the expert. The tougher the better, the bigger the challenge, the more fascinating the job. They take the top or head off the slot, insert a wire into the back, put the top back on, then work the wire down to the timer. They then put a coin in, pull the handle, put the wire on the timer. That stops the first reel from clicking to a stop, and the only time the reel will click to a stop is when you take the wire off the timer. You do that when a bar shows, then after the click, put the wire back on the timer and do the same to the second and third reels. You can do this to a four or six reel machine as well. You must remember that the second reel will never click into place until the first reel is locked in. The reels must go in rotation and if the timer is held, the reels will spin all day. After playing and winning a jackpot, a "drill" player will plug the holes with gum or rubbery substance, leave and come back when he is short of funds and continue the same procedure.

Believe me when I tell you these little holes are hard to find and many a cheater has played a club for months without being detected. Today most clubs have a way to stop these drill master-minds if they think they are being taken or find some of the holes by holding the shell of the machine up to the light and see the light peeking through the holes. They use a piece of boiler plate and put it next to the firing pin, as it can't be drilled through, and they also put what is called a stopper next to the timer and it kicks the timer off. They also put a piece of boiler plate by the reels and that stops the drilling for "oil" at that position.

One of the oldest gimmicks known to cheat a slot is called "spooning a slot." The name fits the subject as you shall soon see. A cheater will have a hard piece of metal shaped into a spoon and will stick it up the inside of the chute or trough where the money comes out. He will feel for the trap door slide underneath the jackpot. He will then play the slide up and back and in doing this two or three coins will drop out. He will continue to do this until the jackpot is empty. Sometimes if there is a weak part in the trap the pressure of working the spoon back and forth will spring the slide the the whole jackpot will fall out. Now on most slots they have a protector on the trap to prevent this from happening.

The inside of the first type slot machine was built like a ferris or spinning wheel or like a big six-wheel you see in the clubs today—only on a much smaller scale. You put your nickel in and it spins around and where it stops nobody knows. They had five different colors, like yellow, purple, green, red and black. Each one paid a different amount up to five nickels. You also could put up to five nickels in at one time, but the most you can get paid is five nickels if the black number showed. That is what I call giving the sucker an even break. He might break even IF the black showed.

Today on our modern one-armed bandits, there are 20 ribbons or decals on each reel, and a few machines have 21. Of course 20 decals aren't strong enough for some clubs, as the odds are 8,000 to 1 that a jackpot won't show on a 3 reel machine, i.e. the odds are determined by how many bars are on the 3 reels. On reels that have 21 decals the odds are over 9,000 to 1. That is what I call a pretty even bet.

About seven years ago, a big doctor came to town and all he would play was the dollar "Buckaroo", a four reel slot that paid $5,000 for the big jackpot. He played for one week at a club. I don't mean continuously. He would play for a few hours, rest awhile. All in all he would play about 12 hours a day. When he didn't play, the club would turn the machine around so nobody could play it. Just like the Doc rented the slot. After seven days the Doc lost $25,000 and never hit the jackpot. They even opened the slot to show him that the four bars were on the reels and that satisfied him. The odds were right—only 160,000 to one against hitting a jackpot.

Do you know that some idiots have even taken moving pictures of a slot machine in action? They do this for hours, spend God knows how much money on film, study the developed film at home for hours, then come back and tell the owner or slot managers that they can beat the machine and also can tell when the jackpot will hit. They are told to go ahead, play as long as you want to or as long as your money will hold out. I have never yet heard of anybody being barred from playing a slot machine legitimately. Nobody ever will hear of it. Yes, I have heard of players being stopped from playing a slot when it goes haywire, as some part is worn or broken.

If you, the player, find one just keep right on playing until you are stopped. It is not your fault, so take advantage of it. You are not doing anything wrong—finders keepers. Let me tell all you "picture takers" and smart alecs that think that they can foretell or guess when the jackpot will fall or show, that it is IMPOSSIBLE. Not even the slot mechanic, who knows the machine inside and out can tell what will show in the little glass windows.

In fact nobody in the world can tell or foresee when the reels stop spinning—they may guess, that's all. There are hundreds of players that watch people playing the machines for a while and if they don't hit a jackpot and leave, the "watchers" as we call them, will now start playing the slot that hasn't hit—thinking that it is due for a jackpot. Much to their sorrow they find out it doesn't always happen that way. Just because the odds on a 3 reeler that has one bar on each reel are 8,000 to one, doesn't mean that the jackpot must show. The law of averages says that is what is supposed to happen, but the law of averages doesn't always work that way. A jackpot could drop in 100 spins or 10 spins or 2,000 spins, 4,000 spins, 8,000 spins or even 15,000 spins. Nobody knows when Lady Luck will smile on the law of averages when they are playing. Many a time a player will put one coin in a slot and a jackpot will fall. According to the law of averages, that was the time for the jackpot to fall and whoever was playing the slot was just lucky to be at the right machine when it happened.

A club will fill up the tube with coins when the slot is first put into use. The reason for that is if there are some pays at the start of the play, but after that, as the slot begins to get some action the pays and jackpots come out of the player's pockets because the slot now begins to earn its keep. If a race horse doesn't earn its feed bill or gets a little old, he is gotten rid of, but when a slot machine gets worn out all they replace are the parts and the public feeds them all the time. So they earn their keep and are never put out to pasture.

Do you know that there is about 5 million dollars lost a year by the slot players who forget or don't see a jackpot when it shows on the machine. Sounds silly but it is so true. They are called "sleepers". It means somebody fell asleep.

Who do I blame for this? The generous clubs. It is tough enough to hit a jackpot when it is hit, i.e. a machine will say "Three bars in any position pays a jackpot." This is the most common mistake by the player. Most of them think that to hit a jackpot the bars or stars or whatever constitutes a jackpot in clubs must be straight across and that is where the catch comes in. Most slots in clubs will drop the jackpot hits but on a "3 bar in any position" slot the jackpot *does not drop*. It must be recognized by someone working at the slots—a change girl or runner or mechanic.

Now if the player can't read, and there are many that can't, they will put another coin in the slot and continue to play. The second the handle is pulled—that is the end of the jackpot. Another bonus for the club. Why this is done by the clubs I don't understand. They can't gain anything by it. They have enough percentage going for them as is. Why they don't let these jackpots drop just like the others do. It is just as easy as the other jackpots. Or let the bell ring above the slot so the player will know that something is happening and won't walk away or drop another coin in the slot. What's another bell?

How about the players that hit a jackpot but do not collect all of it. They will run like a scared deer. Some jackpots do not pay the full amount as they cannot put all the coins in the jackpot tray, so the player must claim the balance of the jackpot by calling somebody as most players are either too excited or at one time have been bawled out by some little change girl after asking if they have more coming when a jackpot is hit. They will just take what is dropped and be satisfied.

Let me tell the slot player that they have a perfect right to ask everytime they hit a jackpot, if they have anymore coming. It is your money and make sure you get every nickel you have coming. It will at least let you play a little longer and the husband will have to wait a little longer for his dinner.

Years ago when slots were plentiful around the country and many a slot mechanic would receive a bonus if the percentage was above normal, they had a little gimmick to prevent a jackpot from falling. They would put a jumper or roller on one of the bars in the last reel. It is a teaser. When the bar would show in the first and second reel and the third bar would drop, it would hit the jumper or roller and slide off like the jackpot was just missed. Another bad break for the player, so he thought.

But in Nevada if any club is caught with any gimmick whatsoever or a slot is fixed to beat the played, their license is revoked and the club would now become a beer parlor or roller rink. Consequently clubs are very careful and even some owners that know the slots will check them themselves or send somebody in to check them for them, as they are solely responsible for the welfare of the club.

He will also do this to protect himself against getting beat, as has happened a few times, a slot mechanic will set up a slot machine against the club. They will have a friend come in and take it off, which means "win the money", then adjust the slot back to normal.

Years ago cheaters would beat pinball machines that paid off in cash, like race horse pinballs which are legal in many states. They would use a magnet to direct the steel ball in any slot they wanted to and drain the machine. I was told by a slot mechanic I know who had worked for a large pinball operator years back how some cheaters had drained all the race horse machines on a route and got about $5,000 out of them.

They couldn't figure out how it happened and the cheaters were having a ball around the country. This mechanic took one of the race horse machines apart piece by piece to try and find out what was wrong, but couldn't find anything. One day he was fixing a machine and took out the steel balls and laid them on his work table. Lucky for him he had a magnet laying there that he kept certain type of bolts on it. One steel ball stuck to it and he had the answer. He got a good raise for that.

He stopped the cheaters by having the steel balls taken out of the machines and replaced with brass balls painted white, and the party was over. If the clubs aren't careful this could happen to them on a slot machine. It is very easy to do if the slot mechanic was dishonest. All he would have to do is put a little weight on one bar in each reel and as the reels just spin of their own free will until they are locked into place, just hold the magnet over the glass, line up the bars and wait for the clicks. Presto, the familiar war cry— Jackpot!

Today cheaters don't have to go through all these gimmicks to beat the slot machine. They also improve their methods with the times. Why take the hard way to beat the slot when there is a much easier way? They have keys that fit the back of the slot—no strain or worry with that method. Just line up the jackpot, close the back of the slot and get paid. No tools or any telltale implements on them to give them away if there is any doubt in the club's mind. Just get rid of the key and they are in the clear. Some have even swallowed the key without being seen and you can't convict anybody without evidence—you have to be caught red-handed.

One of the biggest scams in Vegas are shifty-eyed fellows who tell you they have a machine that's fixed. For $20 they'll tell you which machine it is, and you'd be surprised how many tourists fall for it. It's all done with mystery, and you're brought to the machine, and off goes the tipster, never to be seen again.

Yes, machines have been fixed in their day, but seldom, and the fixer is always caught, and anyway is not about to sell a fixed machine to you for $20!

This brings up the fact that a dollar machine in Reno, which hadn't paid off in three months, grabbed a winner of $37,000. Can you imagine the joy, the excitement for that gentlemen? He quickly stuffed the money into every pocket he and his wife had, and off they went.

In some clubs in this state players stand in line on a busy weekend to wait until it is their turn to play. Some have signs that say, "only two slots to a customer". If I didn't see it, I wouldn't believe it. One New Year's a couple of years ago, some college students started a fight in a club and the police had to use tear gas to break it up, but nobody left the slots that they were playing. They were crying and wiping the tears off, but at the same time never forgot to pull the handle. They were afraid to leave as someone would take their place.

One year, a club I was working in decided to remodel the casino. They had to knock out the front walls. This happened in the winter time. People were playing the slots and other casino games and were actually freezing—teeth chattering, put towels and coats over their legs, complaining all the time. Dust, and I mean dust, flying all over the place, hammering going on above us. Not one player left the club. I guess it was very difficult to get up and go to another club where it would be warm. How can you walk when your feet are frozen? I had to stay, and when they would ask me a question, with their chattering teeth, I would answer the same way. The slot players and I had the advantage over the 21 players and crapshooters. We kept walking—I and the slot players—to get change for another bill to keep warm.

There is a woman player in Vegas that has lost about a half million playing slots. She even has somebody with her to pull the handle when she gets tired, but she holds the title for having the biggest muscle for a woman, in town.

Many a machine has been stolen. Some to just take the money out and later are found in the lake or out on the desert. Some are stolen and a few changes are made and sold to small clubs. Slot machines are very expensive today. New ones run from $600 to $1,200 according to coins it takes. Today I would say that 80 percent of the incomes in downtown Vegas is from slots. On the Strip it is the opposite. In Reno it is much higher.

In writing this little chapter on slots, it doesn't mean that I am against a player enjoying themselves playing slots. I know people must let themselves go now and then or life would be very boring. Some people like other games of chance and believe me when I tell you that the way some people play 21 or craps, they would be better off playing the slots. The reason most tourists that come to the state of Nevada play the slots, big 6-wheel, or a chuck-a-luck game is that they know nothing about the other games in a club like 21, dice, or roulette, so they must play some game. After all, how can a person visiting in Nevada go home saying that they didn't play some game? It would be embarrassing. The big 6-wheel, chuck-a-luck and slots are not thinking games, so anybody can play them. Out of these three games, slots is the easiest. Just put your coin in and pull the handle. This reminds me of the time we had a chimpanzee act on the stage of our club and the owner of the chimps would give one of them nickels to play the slots. The chimp would climb up the slot, put the coin in and pull the handle. One day he hit a $5 jackpot and was so excited that he scooped the nickels out of the trough and started to throw them all over the floor. So, dear public, don't give up hope—if a chimpanzee can do it so can you. "JACKPOT!"

10

GAMBLING STORIES

We had a discussion as to whether the casinos are honest and I said they positively were. But how about the patron? There is an axiom all over, that the last check you get is always a stiff. A severely pressed customer chasing his dollars often succumbs to the pressure and loses his sense of moral value. He writes a check and doesn't have the money to back it up. To him it isn't the same as doing this in New York or Los Angeles, at a grocery store or in a garage. But, of course, it is. The bosses are resigned to it even though their collectors do everything legally to collect. Slugs and foreign currency are used in slots. Violators get severe sentences for this. Customers have also been accused and convicted of conspiring with employees to win illegally. Naturally 99-9/10% of the customers are honest but the casinos have better records than the customers.

As for the stars who play Las Vegas and then lose thousands gambling, it is often the case that they are so "hooked" that their business managers or attorneys advise casino managers that their checks are not to be honored beyond special limited amounts. They have just lost too much.

In all gambling casinos there are what is called "nit players." They come to Las Vegas at the same time every year, lose the same amount of money in the same way at the same game and never attempt to change their gambling style. We feel sorry for them, often try to advise them, but they smile sadly and continue on their way.

As I've intimated, the gambling casinos are the stages for amusing and touching incidents. One day a woman of at least 70 was sitting at the 21 table sipping straight whiskey and was pretty drunk. She was enjoying herself but it looked kind of bad. I had known her so I put my arm around her shoulders and said, "You really should be ashamed of yourself drinking so much at your age." She retorted, "I'd rather be drinking so much at your age." It summed up everything.

Another elderly woman was darling about her losses. She came to me and asked, "Where do I get first aid around here?" I wanted to know what the trouble was. "I have a fractured pocket book," she smiled.

Once I worked for a club where one of the owners was proud of all the people he knew—especially those from Texas—especially the wealthy ones. We all knew his boasts were greatly exaggerated. As a gag one of the other bosses told him they expected Daddy Warbucks (a comic strip character) from Texas. "Give him anything he wants," answered the boastful one. "I know him well."

Years ago I loaned $20 to a fellow who I had seen several times in the casino and looked honest to me. I knew he was in some kind of fringe business but it didn't bother me. He went under the name of Curly. About a year later a fellow sidled up to me in the casino, slipped me $20 and said, "Curly told me to give you this." I asked where he was. "I just got out," said the fellow. "Curly is serving life. He didn't want you to think he was beating you out of the 20."

Las Vegas attracts all kinds. I knew a hanger-on who would eat at the same restaurant every day and never pay a check. He knew of an exit that gave him free meals. One day when he told me he was going to eat in our breakfast room I asked him why he didn't go to the restaurant he always went to. "I don't eat there anymore," he said. "The food is not good."

Every casino has a favorite apocryphal story. An incident that never happened but is always told as if it were gospel. This one belongs to the Dunes. One late night a woman with a few drinks in her and a very low-cut gown was playing roulette. She was always putting her chips all oover the layout. As the ball was dropping, one breast fell out of her gown landing right on number 36. The ball had fallen in 36, too. The croupier consulted the pit boss who said, "Give the young lady 35 quarts of milk."

I saw a 21 player win fifteen bets in a row, then lose three bets, get up and say, "This game is too one-sided for me . . . I quit . . ."

One time a 21 player, furious because the dealer had been beating him all evening screamed, "I quit. And you better watch yourself crossing the street because if I see you I'll run you over." He meant it too.

One day a dealer borrowed $100 from another dealer who was a friend of his. He said, I'll give it back to you tomorrow." Seven years later the dealer walking downtown heard a big commotion in one of the clubs, walked inside and there was a big crowd around the crap table. Right in the middle was his friend, Sam, whom he had lent $100 to seven years ago. He had over $20,000 in chips in front of him. The dealer walked up to Sam and said, "Give me the $100 I loaned you seven years ago. I'm broke and I need the money." Sam pushed him away. "Get away from me," he said. With that he picked a big list out of his pocket. He said to the dealer, "I had you on top of the list. You were the first one I was going to pay. Just for bothering me, I'm crossing you off and putting you on the bottom of the list." With that the dealer walked outside to wait for Sam to finish playing. Five hours later Sam came out winning $52,000 so somebody asked the dealer if he got his $100. The dealer said, "No! But he put me back at the top of the list."

11

DICE

When I was a very young boy, I was shooting craps for pennies with the other youngsters. Suddenly a cop turned the corner and we were caught. Everyone else made a run for it. I stood there and pleaded with the policeman, "Just let me see if I can make the four."

Dice games hold a tremendous fascination for the average person and no less for me. It is the game that attracts the most people and the most money in the gambling casino. It is a strong-willed gambler who can resist shooting a few bucks when he passes a crap table. That's why casinos in resort hotels are always ringed by the lobby, restaurants, show rooms and cigarette stands. The hotel wants the traffic through the casino. People cannot resist the pull of the table.

A friend of mine told me, "I just had a shine and it cost me $900. I had to pass through the casino in order to get to the barberr shop." And how true that is.

It is my job to tell you how you can sneak out of the

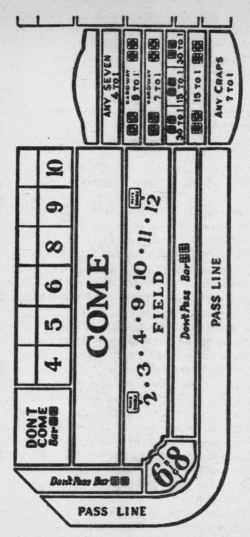

Nevada Layout—Craps

sucker category and show a winning percentage at craps.
That I will do.

If you are a veteran of the tables, you'll recall the
constant chant of the stick-man as "Hard way, field. Play
the field-seven, eleven. Craps." And the like. But you never
hear him implore, "Take the odds on your number!"
Doesn't that make you suspicious? The House wants you to
bet on the field and the propositions. Well, the reason is
that the Field pays the House 5 5/9%. The Hard Way 6 or 8
pays the house 9 1/11% and the Hard Way 10 or 4 pays the
House 11 1/9%.

But if your number is 5 and you take the odds, how
much does the House make? Nothing. That's right, nothing.
The odds are 3 to 2 against you and that is exactly what the
odds pay you, 3 to 2. Of course on your original bet (on
the pass line where your point is 5, you are now only being
paid even money if you make it.)

Then why do people play the Field and the Seven's and
the Hard Ways instead of taking the odds? Because they're
ignorant, stupid. Because they think they're just playing for
the sport of it, when really they're dropping cold, cold
cash.

The player who rolls the dice is known as the shooter.
Players who bet on him to win are betting right or do; those
who bet on him to lose are betting wrong or don't.

The shooter wins if his first roll is seven or eleven (a
natural) and loses if his first roll is twelve, three, or two (a
crap). If his first roll is any other number, that number
becomes the point, and the shooter continues to roll the
dice until he either wins by rolling that number again
(makes his point) or loses by rolling a seven (sevens out).

Craps is the outstanding example of a game in which the
only element of skill is knowledge of the odds and management of money. (I assume that the dice are perfect and that
the roll is honest.)

In calculating the odds, the basic idea is that each die
may land with any one of its six faces uppermost—and that
for each die all six possibilities are equally likely.

Yes, there are shills in every casino. There is nothing

dishonest about having shills. Many players feel uncomfortable when they play alone. They won't go to a table if it is empty. So bosses hire shills who move around from table to table drawing the other players, betting small amounts, and being as unobtrusive as possible.

If you are a loser, can prove it and are nice about it, you can always get carfare home if you don't live too far. (But don't get into this spot.) Casinos are wary because hangers-on have been known to claim poverty after "losing a fortune" when actually they lost a couple of dollars.

No matter how crowded the tables are, if you have money, if you ask, they'll always make room for one more. The adage is all you need is one eye and one arm to play. You just squeeze in sideways and make your bet.

Never, never feel bashful about betting small. Once we noticed in the pit that a young fellow would come in every day about the same time, bet single dollars, lose about $25 and then leave. He played a smart game though, tight and tough. "One of these days," I told the boys, "he's going to make a killing. His game cries out for taking advantage of a good run." Well, one day, he did hit it for $12,000, a nice haul to make up for about $300 he lost. And he was a fellow who was betting single silver dollars among the $5 and $25 chip players.

It is customary for the House to serve free drinks at the dice tables. Warning—be careful. There is no madness to their generosity. The bosses have found liquor loosens some players up. They play more recklessly and therefore the House does better. Don't take more than one drink, is a good rule at the dice table. To be fair to the bosses, though, I'll tell you this. We had a patron one night who was sloppy drunk and who was winning $5,000 on the tables.

When he bet so he didn't know what he was doing, we put his money away safely in the cage and he was put to bed. Next day he was given his money and permitted to gamble again. You could multiply this many times during a year.

There has been many wild stories about how Las Vegas has been victimized by counterfeit check (chip) passers.

Most of it is exaggeration. The Hotels have a friendly agreement with each other to honor each other's checks. When checks are tallied at night and a counterfeit is found (and it always is), then all hotel casinos are warned. It is true there is an occasional counterfeit raid but it is rare. When counterfeiters are caught Nevada law throws the book at them. It is a serious offense and requires severe punishment. If counterfeiters were successful it could throw the entire multibillion dollar gambling industry out of kilter.

Tipping of dealers or "the boys" in any form is customary. Many winners put up bets for "the boys." It is customary but not imperative. It is a nice gesture because as in other professions, the employees need the tips to make their annual income a living one. As pit boss, we never take tips.

There is always a hue and cry at the tables when a dice shooter fails to hit the backboard. To me it is a lot of nonsense. Believe me if the bettor is wagering enough the House will let him get away with most anything.

I knew a little old man, unhealthy but rich, who did not much more than drop the dice six inches for each roll. You have to be a pretty good "mechanic" to be able to call the numbers on the dice even after a roll of a foot or two. I have seen box men plague a woman shooter who just couldn't throw the dice. "What difference does it make?" I asked them. "Just have her toss them as she would a glass of water." She did that and finally she had to be satisfied.

Never play a "grind" game. That means betting the same amount each time you bet. That way the house percentage has to wear you down in the end.

There has been endless talk about honesty in the Las Vegas casinos. Hundreds of times I have been asked by friends, "But is it honest?" I can assure you it is. And if ever a dealer is dishonest, which is beyond the club's control, he is fired immediately if the club finds out.

Wouldn't a casino that makes more than $1,000,000 a year from an honest game endanger its license by being dishonest for a couple of hundred dollars. There's no reason for a casino to be dishonest. Not while the customers play as foolishly as they do.

There's a group in Las Vegas for whom it cost nothing to gamble. Yet, while they gamble constantly, they usually lose, It's a sad part of the gambling scene. Who are the members of this group who are so lucky and then so unlucky? It's the show girls. These beauties are consistently gifted with stake money by male admirers but know so little about the game they usually toss their money away fast. You'd think they'd try to learn the games so they could retire at an early age. But I guess as the axiom goes: "Easy come, easy go." It isn't unusual to see one bearty given $50 ten times over an evening and each time blowing it.

There are a few smart girls who put away part of their gift money but the money that goes into the gambling table goes down the drain. One night a lovely had $20 on a "Don't Come" bet. The shooter had nine for a point and rolled a seven. She walked away from the table. "You won, Miss," I shouted after her. She was amazed. She didn't even know what "Don't Come" was but she was betting it. The girls don't really have the interest in the game. I saw another lovely throw in her cards in a "21" game even though she hadn't lost yet, just to look at a new dress another girl had bought.

I'm often asked, "Is it true that players have lost $250,000 in an evening?" They can't comprehend it. But it is true. Nick the Greek has won and lost more than that during an evening.

And one night an oil tycoon lost $500,000 in and evening. Nevertheless, losses like that for those men is no worse that you or I dropping $500.

Perhaps the most discouraging crap shooter I've ever seen was a young man who hit 17 passes in a row one night and then said to me gleefully "I'm almost even." He won 17 dollars, a dollar a pass. Everyone else at the table won hundreds and thousands of dollars. I hope he learned when he saw some of the players who made it on his roll cash in all those checks.

12

CONTROL OF YOUR MONEY

I have watched thousands of players in the years I have been around gambling be a high winner, keep on playing, and not only lose their winnings but lose all their own money besides. This has happened not only to the ordinary player, but to some of the smartest gamblers in the business. It seems that when a player is in action he loses control of money value. Some players have no idea of the value of the chips in front of them. Some are too busy to even think about winning or lossing—all they know is that they are playing and have money in front of them. I have learned through experience that it isn't easy to quit when you want to. Many years ago I was the type of player that wanted to win the table. I came close, but never could quite make it. What I would do with the table after I had won it, I don't know.

I have been winner many a time and finished loser and bending over and having one of my friends kick me didn't help much. I had to learn the hard way about control of my money. We know that when gambling in a club it is much easier to finish loser than winner. There are quite a few players that are showoffs—when they are winning they have plenty of speech, keep talking all the time telling anybody that will listen how smart they are, tell us how to run the club. We wait patiently until they run out of speech—that is out of money.

One of the classic remarks to anybody watching this after they have lost their money is, "How can anybody win in a gambling club. I am a sucker like everybody else playing this game."

This poor idiot is now blaming the club and everybody in it for his mistakes. He is like most of the winners that don't know how and when to quit. That is the problem When does a player leave a game a winner?

The most important factor is that you must have control of your money. Do not let the money control you. Many a player will say, "I am going to make one more bet and then leave." He will lose the bet and then make another to try to win the bet he has lost.

This is wrong—the money is controlling you but you don't know it. For the benefit of the readers that are just learning the game, here are a few facts about control that you must never forget. This information is from experience that has cost me and many another player quite a few dollars to acquire, so pay heed as this applies to any game you play. In the last 10 years I have never quit loser in any game I have played, *where I have been winner according to the original amount of my investment.*

A player will bet according to the amount of money that they come into a club with. If you come into a club with a couple of hundred dollars and should be fortunate enough to run into a winning streak, you are $300 or $400 ahead.

Now you lose a few bets. You have to quit. You cannot chase the few bets you have lost.

It is very difficult to know when you have enough. A player must make up his own mind as to when he should say to himself, "I have had enough."

Never be afraid to quit any game you are playing winner or loser. A good player is one that can quit winner as well as loser. You have won enough or lost enough. Don't let any remarks from the other players or casino help influence you from quitting a winner. Remember, nobody is going to give you your money back if you lose. All they can do is sympathize with you and listen to your sad story about not quitting winner. I'll tell you one thing though, everybody envies a winner, so wouldn't you rather be envied than pitied? This is something I have been trying to understand for years but can't find the answer—Why do people limit their winners, but not their losers?

If you are winning, keep on playing. Don't quit in the middle of a winning streak—even if you have to sit for two days. Stick and stay. As you keep on winning, keep putting some aside and play with the "overs" as we call it. I will give you an example. This applies to any bettor, regardless of how much money you start with.

Let us say that you are a small player, a 2 or 3 dollar bettor, and you are going good. As you are winning you must raise your bet progressively higher. Before you know it, you have accumulated about $100, which is pretty good for a small bettor, but happens quite often. Put fifty aside and play with the rest of the money. If you keep on winning, put some more aside, but if you should lose what you have in front of you—quit. Take a rest, get some coffee, walk around, or go out and smell the fresh air—it won't kill you. Get the fog out of your head—you probably have been playing for a couple of hours and you could use a break.

There are players that will play for hours without taking a break and the only time they will leave the game is when they are broke. The longer you play the more tired you get mentally—especially if you are losing. Clubs in Las Vegas are open 24 hours a day, but some players think the clubs will close and want to play as long as they can. I knew a few high professional gamblers that never played in a game that had just started. I am referring to card games like stud poker, low ball, pan traveling 21 (where the player who turns over a blackjack becomes the dealer) and fading crap games. These professionals were in no hurry to play. They would wait a few hours until some of the players would get a little groggy, then play and would usually catch some players asleep at the switch—and that's all brother. I don't know how many of you have ever watched a high limit game, but if you ever do, notice how a good player after playing awhile will get up and take a walk or get lost for awhile to shake the cobwebs out of his head.

It all boils down to the fact that it is your money you are gambling with and do not be afraid to quit a game where the cards or dice have been going your way and should change. Nobody's forcing you to keep on playing. Never feel sorry for the gambling club. Most of the time they worry about you. One of the easiest things to do in a club is for a winning player to put the chips in his pocket and head for the cashier's window to cash them out for hard cash. If you do this a couple of times, you will like the idea and will try to do this more often. It is a much better feeling to cash out your winning chips at the cashier's window than to go there to cash another check so you can have more money to play with. That is what I mean by control. You the player have to be your own judge of when to quit a game winner. Don't wait until you have lost all of your winnings back and quit even. You were even when you started to play.

Many a player will sit down and say, "I don't want to win. All I want to do is break even." My answer would be, "You are even before you start to play so why play." Very few people break even when gambling—they either win or lose and the majority are losers.

Most of the 21 players and crap shooters are such bad players they know they are going to lose so would be satisfied to break even after playing awhile. I guess they would call it a moral victory just to break even. The reason for that is that the player doesn't know any better so he is satisfied to break even. What gets me is that most of the poor players are praying to keep their losses at a minimum. How dumb can you be? This is another common remark in Las Vegas. "I didn't come to Vegas to win or lose, I just came to play. All I hope is that I have enough money to last until I leave." Very clever—if it came out of the mouth of a two year old.

13

LIMITS AND RULES

I have watched and listened to someone in the business explaining a point about a game. When they were through, even I didn't know what the explanation was all about.

I also have glanced through a couple of books by some so-called authorities on gambling—also some articles in publications. I wonder where and how some of these authors have the nerve to write about something they know nothing about. They will go out, ask a few questions, do a little research and then write an article or book on the subject three weeks later and don't even know what they wrote about. Not only that, but tell the player about certain rules in Vegas or Nevada that are supposed to be standard rules, which is not so. All rules are not the same in Vegas or Nevada. One author in an article on roulette tells you that on a split you get 34 to 1. This is not true. You receive 17 ot 1. Another author tells you that every club in Las Vegas, the 21 dealer must hit 16 and stop on 17. This is not true. In most of the clubs on the strip, the dealers hit 16 and stop on any 17. Downtown all clubs hit 16 and also hit on a soft 17—this is more percentage for the club.

Another author tells the player to get to the limit as fast as he can. Now does that make sense to a player who is betting $2, $5 or $10? Some clubs have a $500 limit on their games. How can anybody expect a small player to let his money ride until he reaches the $500 limit? Impossible! A fine way to tell people how to gamble. You not only have to have plenty of money to play this way, you also have to have plenty of guts.

Another author tells the player he can ask for a cut in 21 any time he wants to—not so! Once the dealer deals the cards, nobody can ask for a cut. This incident happened at a club recently. A player at a 21 game betting $20 and $30 a hand asked the dealer for a cut. The dealer called over the floorman and told him what the player said. The floorman said to the player, "You can't ask for a cut once the cards are dealt." The player said, "I'll bet you $500 I can ask for a cut." The floorman said "You have a bet." He called one of the bosses over and explained the situation to the boss. The player spoke up and said, "You have explained the situation perfectly, but I can ask for a cut—that doesn't mean you have to give it to me." The player won the bet.

Another author tells you that you only receive one card on each if you split aces. This is not so. In some clubs downtown, if you split aces and receive another ace or two you can also split them. One card on each. A few authors tell you that the limits are the same in all clubs in Vegas and Nevada. That also is not true. Every club has its own rules and limits on their games. The limit of a game is determined by the owners of a club—also by the size of the club. Some clubs have $100 limit, some $200 limit, some $500, and some even have $50 limit.

Some clubs deal to the faces. By that I mean if the club's limit is $200—that is to the public, but if a high bettor comes in that the club knows they can win a lot of money from, they will raise the limit for him, as they have a chance to win something. Also they don't want to lose him to some other club where the limit is higher.

Another author tells of a big player that walked into a club downtown, bet a thousand dollar bill on red on the roulette wheel, won the bet, let it ride four times and had $32,000, but didn't quit and bet it all and lost. All wet. In the first place you can't win that amount if you let it ride 4 times, second no club had ever let anybody bet that kind of money on one single bet (and probably never will). There was only one owner in Las Vegas that I know of that would deal a high game. He owned the Horseshoe Club downtown a few years back. He was a multi-millionaire. A couple of high gamblers walked into his club one day, started to play and asked him what the limit was. He said, "The next bet you make is your limit. Did you bring it with you?" Meaning whatever wager they made regardless of what it was would be their limit for that play. "Bring it with you" means cash only—no markers. That was the end of that conversation. These gamblers became normal players after that remark.

Another wise gambler walked into his place, and walking by a 21 game threw a package of $100 bills on the table ($5,000 worth) knowing that the limit was $500. This boss happened to be standing near by, saw it and said to the dealer, "Deal the cards." The gambler picked up his money and walked out. This owner barred nobody as long as they showed him money. I know of one big hotel owner he beat out of a few oil wells. He had to sell them to pay off. Another gambler years ago after playing cards with an oilman took some oil leases instead of money for what he had won. Today he is a millionaire.

These occurrences are very rare in clubs today. Most clubs have a limit and don't care who you are or don't care if you get mad and tell them you will play someplace else if you don't raise the limit. One owner, a few years back, had a player beat out of $80,000. The player wanted to raise the limit and was very persistent. The owner, knowing that he would get paid, said to the player, "You can make four bets in the field at $20,000 a bet. But only 4 bets. Of course the owner figured that he should win 2 of the bets—maybe more. The player knew that he was going into it with the worst of it, but said O.K. He won all four bets and finished even.

As most of us know a player will do anything just to gamble. I had a player call me from New York a few years ago. I had charge of the day shift at a strip hotel. He wanted to impress a couple of girls of the evening—he also was drinking.

He was a high player and bet wrong most of the time. He started to bet over the phone $500 they lose, and lay the full odds against the number. I held the phone so that he could hear the calls of the stickman. We were on the phone for 45 minutes. He lost $29,000 just to impress the girls. He also paid for the phone call.

Another player, a big oil man from Texas, played at a strip hotel, lost quite a bit of money and went back home. He was on a binge and a few days later called the club and said, "I am betting $5,000 in the field." He liked to play the field. The shift boss called one of the bosses over and the boss said O.K. It didn't take long—the player lost $80,000 all in the field. He also paid for the phone call.

Quite a few years ago, this incident happened in Saratoga, N.Y., a resort and racing town. A millionaire sportsman playing the roulette wheel at a big club lost $92,000, made out a check for $100,000 and said give the $8,000 change to the wheel dealers. All this is to tell the small player that you don't have to have a lot of money to be a good gambler.

Sometimes the more money you have the more trouble you get into when gambling. You probably have heard people say, "the more money you have the easier it is to win." Don't you believe it. I can recite many a story of players with plenty of money getting hooked and not getting out. Their money didn't help them. One incicent is of a big gambler that would come into town, had unlimited credit, gave him anything he wanted.

We use the expression "open card." Where he got the name of being a gambler, I don't know. He was under the impression that if you have enough money you can overcome many a bad hand. Many a time he would stop at a crap game, walk into a little hand, win a couple of thousand and run. A few times he would stop and the dice didn't make a few passes. So he would stay and wait for the hand to show to get him even. Sometimes he would be $25,000, sometimes $50,000 and three or four times over a hundred thousand loser. He would get out—very pleased with himself. He would say, "The power of money does it." If you have plenty of money the hand must show. Well a couple of times the hand didn't show, because he was so much loser and when the dice did pass they didn't pass long enough. He was in too deep. We in the business knew that it would happen that way. This so-called gamble was a soft touch. He couldn't win much but could go for a lung or package. Which means quite a bit of money. This gambler, and I use the expression lightly, lost a quarter of a million dollars in two plays. He would play for 10 to 25 hours when he was loser, trying to get out. He didn't run these two times.

So remember if you read an article telling you that somebody saw a player betting thousands of dollars on one number, or one 21 hand, or one number or color of the wheel, do not believe them. It is not true. Today in Vegas it is very rare that you will see a player bet $1,000 on a number. The clubs don't need that business. There are plenty of small players around where the club doesn't have to worry or sweat about them winning too much. Most all clubs have a limit and stick to it. The grind is good enough for them.

Inflation has hit the country, and so therefore it has hit the casinos. Some casinos today have a $1,000 limit on even bets. It used to be that $500 was the top amount that would be allowed.

Of course, on 35 to 1 shots, like the roulette table, in most clubs $100 is the limit.

14

SYSTEMS

God have mercy on the system players. Only idiots play systems, so if the shoe fits, wear it. First let me explain to the thousands of deluded fools that come to Nevada to try a system that they have figured out or that somebody has told them about, that if they think systems could beat a gambling house that the owners have spent millions to build, they are nuts.

Usually a system player has a pencil and paper with him to jot down the figures with when he plays so that he can keep track of what he is doing. We have a saying, "All that the system player winds up with is his system, pencil and paper—but no money." Owners of gambling clubs don't spend millions of dollars to build a club so that a system player can come in and win whenever he wants to. If systems were any good do you think a gambling house would tolerate system players and let them grind them out of their money? Don't be silly—which you would be if you thought so.

I can't understand why people think they can outsmart some of the smartest people in the gambling business because somebody told them that they have a way to beat a gambling game with a system. Especially when they have only been to a club a few times and they think that makes them an authority on what they are playing. I have found out that the public goes for anything and will listen to anybody when it comes to gambling or how to beat a gambling club.

Do you know what we call a system player—an unpaid shill. A shill is a person that is hired by the club to sit or stand at a fame that is empty or short of players.

At a crap game they shoot the dice and in 21 or roulette they sit at the table to fill it up. It seems that some people don't like to sit at an empty table or at an empty crap game—they like other people around. So the club hires people to fill up a game. When the game fills up the shill leaves the game and waits until he is needed at another game. These shills are working people like anyone else and to them it is a job like any other job. But a system player will come to a game, sit there for hours and take up space. He fills up the game, loses his money, and the best part of it is the club doesn't have to pay him for it. That is why he is called an unpaid shill. I hope that this penetrates through some thick skulls. Of course we will always have some non-believers I guess. I could fill this book with some of the systems and what people have told me about how they could beat a game.

Here are a few important facts about systems. A good player does not waste his time playing a system because he can't win much. Most systems are based on winning a little at a time—we call it "trying to grind out a few dollars." But all the money can be lost in a couple of minutes if the system goes bad—which happens quite often. I want some of you system players to be honest with yourself and think of the times you have won 20 or 30 dollars for a couple of days and then your system goes bad and you chase it until you lose hundreds of dollars—common occurrence.

One of the most important factors against the system (and it is a pretty big factor) is that all gambling clubs have a LIMIT on their games. By a limit we mean that you can only bet a certain amount on any single bet you make. People seem to forget this important factor, because if a club did not have a limit on their games anybody can beat a game if he has enough money. As I've said, a club isn't stupid enough to let players bet anything they want to. I will explain the limit further for any prospective system players, so they will know what they are in for. All legitimate gambling clubs have a limit on their games, so if you should ever walk into a club and there is no limit—pass don't play. You are in the wrong club.

If you walk up to a crap table and their limit is $200 that is the most you can bet on any one number—in other words if you were betting on the pass line you could bet from one dollar to $200—no more. If you are playing 21 and the limit is $200 you can bet from one dollar to $200 on one hand. This is what stops most of the system players. Some of them don't even know that there is a limit on a game until they have to bet over the limit to follow the system—that is when they wake up to the fact that whatever they are doing doesn't seem to work out right.

A young lady sat down one day in the club and took out a pencil and paper—put $40 on the table, asked for silver and checks and started to play betting small. I asked her what system she was playing as I like to ask players that come in with a system what method they use (so I can get their silly answer). Her reply was, "The 1-2-3-4-5 system. You cross off the one and five when you lose, then bet the three and four." I didn't know what she was talking about and neither did she. I watched for a while and she was winning and losing so I walked away. I returned about 5 minutes later and she was betting $26. During all this time she was playing I noticed she never hit her hand. She stood with two cards every hand. As it so happened she had fair hands. Finally the dealer called me over and said, "This lady is stopping on 8 and 10. Just staying good all the time."

I asked her, "Who gave you this system?" She said that some friend of hers gave it to her. So I asked, "Why do you stop on 8, 10, and 11?" "My friend told me when I get a bad hand to stop" she answered, "As I don't know what a good hand is or a bad hand is I decided to stop on 2 cards on all hands." By this time she was losing all her money so I made her quit and told her not to play any game until she at least knew the basic facts. There are hundreds of examples like this where people hear of some system or read about it in some paper or publication then come to Nevada with the idea of trying to grind out a few dollars.

When a system player comes into a club, sits down, takes out his paper and pencil, the employees laugh and usually say to themselves, "Here is another sucker that is going to show this gambling club a thing or two." Did you ever watch a system player trying to do 4 or 5 things at once? It is very funny to us, because they are trying to get their next bet ready in case they lose the bet they are making. Very few can handle chips and silver. It is difficult if you aren't experienced. They also are jotting down what happened in the previous bet they had made, trying to light a cigarette or take a sip of their drink all at the same time. Believe me this is very hard to do. It is also very funny if you are paying attention to this pantomime show because there isn't any talking involved and it would put some of the greatest pantomime artists to shame. I don't know why some comedian doesn't use it in one of his numbers, because this goes on continuously during the time they are playing. They are usually wiping their brow after they lose a few bets regardless of how comfortable it is in the club. The final analysis is that they are nervous wrecks after they are through playing—win, lose or draw.

There are ads in papers and magazines that tell you

about systems that can beat the clubs in Nevada. There is one that tells you that they guarantee you to win if there is no limit on the game. Now doesn't that sound silly? As I told you there isn't a legitimate gambling club in the world that doesn't have a limit on their games. Another ad reads, "Positive system of beating dice game." *One that casinos fear.* Another reads, "How to beat 21 or roulette. Send $2 Box—." Now does that make sense to you? Only an idiot would answer ads like that and there are plenty that do.

If the systems were that good why would they have to wait for your one or two dollars? All they would have to do is go to Las Vegas and win all of the money they would ever need. A system player will tell you about how much they lost. I have seen system players come in that win a few dollars at a time.

They may be sixty or seventy dollars winner after a few times they have played, and all of a sudden the system turns and they are few hundred loser before they know what happened. That is the way systems work. You aren't supposed to win too much but once you chase the system you lose hundreds of dollars. As I said there are hundreds of systems and people are always concocting ways and combinations to beat a game, but I am going to use one of the common ones, as they all amount to the same thing in the end—a loser. I will use the progressive or double-up system as an example.

You walk into a club that has a $200 limit and are going to play a system. Not all clubs in Nevada have the same limit. You start with $5, which is called a unit. In this "double up" system you keep doubling your bets until you win a bet. As soon as you win a bet you revert back to five dollars, so after every winning bet your bet is five dollars. But on the other hand after every losing bet you must double your bet. Let me give you an example. After you lose your first five dollar bet, your next bet is 10 dollars, and if you lose that, your next bet is $20. Now let's say you lose the next three bets consecutively. Your last bet was $160 and now you are supposed to bet $320 because your system calls for it. But as the house limit is only $200 that is all you can bet—$200. That is the end of the system. Thus if you should win this bet you have invested $515 and are still $115 loser. Naturally if there was no limit on the game you would have kept doubling your bet until you won one—and wound up a winner. So what stopped you? The house limit.

Pretty good percentage for the club, which remained cool and calm during all this procedure knowing that all they could lose at one time would be five dollars. Does that sound like a good investment for your money? All you system players that read this think of all the times you played a system and this happened to you. Remember how you felt when you had to bet a large amount of money to try to win a small amount of money. Try to be honest with yourselves and think what you went through and how many times you cursed the system and the one that gave it to you. Isn't it nice and sweet and calm when the system is working in your favor and you are sitting back relaxed winning that one little bet at a time, telling jokes, having a ball until all of a sudden everything is going wrong. Now you are serious and every little thing bothers you.

The dealer is unlucky, the people next to you annoy you. You just changed from a Jekyle to a Hyde. Many a time I wished I had a camera to take some of the expressions on their faces when they are going through this change. Did you ever see how some system players look when they have lost the big bet and are out of money? Their expression is like a little child who is saying, "Who am I and where am I?" It happens so fast that they're not aware of what is happening to them. The system player is indoctrined with the idea that according to the law of averages they are supposed to win one bet out of so many bets they make, but they forget to remember that the law of averages doesn't always act that way. After losing 3 or 4 bets they think they are supposed to win the next one. It doesn't have to happen. You can lose the next 20 bets. Remember, there is nobody that can tell you what is going to happen on the next bet. They may guess what will happen but cannot guarantee that it will. I am sure nobody will bet their life that they will win the next bet. I was standing next to a fellow that was just watching the rolls of the dice and he was guessing whether they would make a pass or miss a pass.

He guessed the first 3 in a row. He said, "See, I can guess them pretty good can't I?" I said, "If you can guess them so good, why don't you play? It would be a soft game for you." He said, "I can't—I just got broke shooting crap." Remember this, if systems were too tough for the gambling houses they wouldn't allow you to play them. Everytime a bet is made, the club earns something, so the longer you play a system the harder it is for the player. A system player is what we call a soft play. By that we mean they can't win much, but can be beat out of whatever they have.

We are liable to get 20 or 30 system players a week in the club. Let us say that 5 or 6 win an average of $50 a piece, but the rest of them lost their money. This is a pretty good investment for the club. They lose about $300 and win thousands of dollars. The few that won go home happy. Now they have a way of winning their expense money everytime they come to Nevada. What a rude awakening they are in for? There was a time when three college students came in with a machine that they had perfected in college. I think they had brought their professor with them. They went to the club owner and said that they had a way to beat the 21 game and they would like to try the machine out on one of the tables. The boss agreed. On this machine were knobs and 2 instrument gages that told you when to hit and stop. The owner only limited them to one bet of $5 which was alright with them as they were only experimenting with the gadget. The one that was manipulating the knobs had everything he could do to keep up with the game. He could not take his eyes off of the cards as he had to register every card in the machine.

They played for hours and you should have seen the one that worked the machine—he was bleary-eyed. I'll bet if anybody asked him where he was he couldn't have answered correctly. They played four or five times in a couple of days and then left a small winner. But I had their "hole card" as we say around the business. I knew what they were up to. They were trying something that is pretty old in playing 21. They didn't have to go to college to try to figure that out. I can't divulge what it is as quite a few people would try it and it would make it much more difficult for the help in the casinos. Not that it is illegal in that sense of the word it is not cheating. These students came back about 6 months later and started to play without the machine, but used silver to keep track of what was going on.

I politely told them they were wasting their time playing here. I also told them that they didn't have to waste their time in school trying to devise something that was twice as old as they were. I stopped them from playing for that is what I get my small salary for, amongst other things protecting the club from things like that.

Did you ever see a system player that makes his bets but doesn't know how to play? All they know is that you are supposed to bet so much at a time. They forget that you also have to know what to do and how to play. At least if you are going to play a system, please learn the game first.

I have seen system players go against a $25 and $50 limit and that is like taking candy away from a baby. The smaller the limit, the tougher it is for the system player to win. Also the bigger the limit the more money you need. Either way you are in trouble. Also the smaller the limit the harder it is to get even once you are loser. Most system players don't even know what a limit is until they try to bet over it—then they are in for a rude awakening.

I've been thinking of opening a club for system players only. I would never have to worry about money the rest of my life. That's how easy it would be.

We had a player that would buy in $2,000 worth of chips, start betting one dollar and never betting over $5. People standing around would see all the chips and say, "This fellow must have a pretty good system. Look at all the chips he has." He would play for an hour or so, lose a little or win a little. Then he would quit and come back a little later and go through the same ritual. All I can think of is that he was trying to impress everybody that he had money.

Oh yes, I forgot to tell you. There has been only one person that could beat a game with a system. A Cuban woman—won all the time. But she died and took the system with her. (HA! HA! HA!)

15

CHEATING

I am not going to waste a couple of chapters on ways to protect yourself against the pitfalls of gambling. It is impossible for the ordinary layman to see and know what is going on while playing at a game for money. I am referring to being cheated in card games or dice games. As some of you know this has been put into publications or books, so the public can protect themselves against the men or women that are trying to make an easy living at the public's expense.

Where anybody ever got the idea that a shoe salesman, drug clerk, businessman, white collar worker, or industrial worker could ever catch anybody cheating them by reading an article or book, I don't for the life of me understand. Do you know that cheaters get cheated by smarter cheaters than they are? I knew of one cheater that took a job in a factory, actually went to work for a living. Why? So that every payday he could shoot craps with his fellow workers. After all he was one of them. He lasted quite awhile, until it got a little "hot" for him. He never lost.

Do you know it takes years of practice to be a good cheater? There are some cheaters around that would make a magician's eyes blink—they are so adept in handling cards and dice. Even many an experienced eye in the gambling business have trouble seeing the moves that takes years of know how. Also, how do you, the poor gullible player that is having enough trouble watching his money and bets, expect to see an expert do a few tricks with a deck of cards or dice. It can't be done.

Years ago the cheaters had a much softer time of it than today. Not as much "heat" on the cheater. All they had to be was a fast runner or good fighter, because when they were caught they had to pay the consequences. Years ago cheaters or hustlers would work clambakes, club picnics, stags, smokers, outings and anywhere there was a crowd. One outfit that worked clambakes would place five or sic pair of dice around the area—always. Somebody would pick one up to start a crap game. The cheater's asset—somebody else would start the game.

We have a saying that the average player wouldn't even see a white elephant cross the table they were playing at. They are too engrossed in what they are doing.

I worked in a big club in Florida quite a few years ago. One of the bosses, who had been in the business a long, long time and was one of the smartest men in the game, said to me and a couple of other fellows, "I am going to show you how easy it is to beat the public—especially at a gambling game where the player is so busy watching his money and bets." He walked over to a very busy crap game where the dice were passing. We were using red dice and after the shooter had made another pass he moved in a pair of green dice. Not one of the players paid any attention to it. Even the shooter picked up the green dice and kept right on shooting. He made another pass and missed out.

The boss then moved in the red dice and the game went on. Not one player out of the 20 around the crap table noticed that there were two different kind of dice used by one shooter. I'll bet many of you don't think it's possible. Well, I'll bet this has happened to quite a few of you, only with the same color dice, which makes it much easier for the cheater. He wasn't trying to just prove a point—he was only trying to win your money, and succeeded many a time.

Years ago I was working in a small club in the East. In came two gentlemen that had probably received their lessons out of a book. We call them "half the rear end of a donkey hustler." If you follow me. They were crimping the cards—that is bending them so that they could tell the high cards from low cards. It is very obvious if you are not an expert at it. I told the dealer to let them continue to crimp the deck—it takes a few minutes to mark the deck. Meanwhile, while they were marking the deck, I had called a friend of mine who was very adept at handling a deck of cards. I put him into the game and he broke these so-called donkeys. I didn't waste my time to try and smarten up these wise-guys. I let them learn the hard way—not to fool around in somebody else's backyard.

Many a time a cheater will beat a club, but it does not pay in the long run. It is not worth the price they have to pay.

In Nevada today anybody caught cheating a game can go to jail. Years ago you had to fight or run, but now with a jail sentence over a cheater's head they are a little more careful. But some keep on trying—they have an affliction against working for an honest living.

For ever gambling game in existence there is a way to beat it illegally, but there is also a way to cope with this. Most of the men that hold important jobs in the casinos (outside of relatives) are trained through long experience in the business, to detect most of the so-called tricks by the so-called hustlers. You don't learn how to outmaneauver these sharpies by reading a book or having somebody try to show you—you have to learn by experience alone.

Let me tell you about the card magician that came into a club, showed everybody card trick s and he was very good at it. He would sit in at the poker game every week-end. The players would tell him that they are watching him and no funny stuff as they are playing for money. This made him feel good and his ego jumped one hundred percent. The funny thing about this is that this card magician never won. He would go home broke at the end of the play.

This went on for a couple of years. He would go on the road and when he came back he would have another card trick to show at the poker table, but he never won.

He was playing with some professionals that could really show him some card tricks, but after all he was the magician—not them. Besides he was their annuity. This magician was lucky that the club closed and to this day he still thinks he is an unlucky poker player.

When he reads this article, which I am sure he will, he will know that he was given "cards and spades" as we say in the business, but still no can win. The moral of this story is "Don't show somebody how smart you are." There is always somebody a little smarter than you are at the game you are playing, besides you might fall into the trap this magician fell into. My advice to you players that are green at gambling is don't play with strangers and even be careful of some of your friends.

Sometimes friendship ceases where money is involved. Only play in legitimate clubs—you won't have any trouble finding them—there aren't many left. If you are playing in a game and are a little doubtful about it, don't be afraid to quit loser. Write it off as experience, you have learned something, but don't let it cost you too much as it will if you wait until you are out of money before you have decided there is something wrong. They say you have to pay to learn. It is true, but the less you have to give up to learn the better off you are—don't wait until disaster strikes.

Above all don't be one of those obstinate players who

can't understand why they can't win because they are such good players, but keep on playing because they are hardheaded and stubborn. In gin-rummy they say "When in doubt discard an ace." Well, when you are in doubt about a game that doesn't look right, quit, pass the deck.

A few years back I was in a resort town in the midwest. It is a town where people go for the baths and also to gamble. Some of the smartest players in the country congregate here to match wits against each other and anyone else that has the nerve to play with them—they bar nobody. One of the top gamblers in a club who was drinking challenged anybody to a $10,000 stud poker freezeout, which means you play until one or the other player wins all of the money. The challenge was accepted by a fellow who was sort of a newcomer. He had only been coming to this resort town a couple of years, and was much younger than this top gambler. He had pooled his money with four of his friends. The top gambler sat himself against the wall so nobody could look at his hand, was ordering glasses of whiskey and saying, "I am the best player in the world."

The other fellow was drinking milk and saying, "Yes, you are the best player in the world—after me." They played for hours, seesawed up and back. Then the roof caved in for the top gambler—he was tapped out in one hand.

He took the cards and had some sharp men look at them but they couldn't find anything wrong with the cards. But this gambler knew that he wasn't beat on the square, although he couldn't put his finger on it. He confronted the young fellow the next day and said to him, "You did something to me last night, what was it? I paid for the information." The young gambler replied, "Did you think I was going to sit down and play with you without having an edge? (Which means a little the best of it) You old time gamblers forget that new tricks of the trade keep coming up. You have to keep up with the times—it costs money to fall behind." With that he walked away. It wasn't until a couple of years later that this gambler found out how he was taken for his money. I will tell you what it was, because even knowing what it is I am sure that it will be very difficult to find if you don't know what you are looking for. It takes weeks of practice and card studying to accomplish this art. It is called white on white, and is put on the cards by hand, by an expert at this profession. I am sure it is used today in a few spots without even the knowledge of the owners.

Never underestimate who you are playing with. Give them some credit for knowing something, so if anything happens to you it won't come as a big surprise. I have seen and heard through the years of many a "know-it-all" being taken by a new gimmick that had just come out, and they didn't find out until it was too late. You are never too old to learn, especially where it benefits you. Above all where money is concerned.

You know the old story. A salesman came to a town, asked a cab driver if there was a crap game going on any place. The cab driver replied, "There is only one game in town, but it is crooked." The salesman's retort was, "What's the difference? It's the only game in town. Let's go."

It is very difficult to distinguish a cheater. They could look like anybody, and do. They have no trademark like a fighter. Some look like school teachers or doctors. I am going to tell you a couple of incidents about one of the greatest cheaters that ever lived. He is dead now, so I can use his name, which was "Little Abe." He was about 5'2, had small hands, wore glasses, and looked exactly like a college professor. That's what he was called—Professor, when he went in the many jobs he was called to. Little Abe was a genius in the art of beating a gambling game—you name it and he had a way to beat it. I could relate many a story about the Professor or Little Abe, but here are two of my favorites.

I am going back about thirty years ago. There was a clambake at a little resort town that I was working in. There was a very big bettor in this town, who also was a very tough character—carried a gun all the time. A couple of town gamblers that didn't care too much for this tough character, sent for the Professor, through an outside source. The Professor wasn't known at all in this town. His greatest asset was that he would do the work and leave—never hang around.

There was a crap game on one side of the room and a 21 game on the other. The Professor was dealing at the 21 game, as it was known that this tough character liked to show off at playing 21. The Professor was the originator of the "back peek" at 21, which is taking a look at the top card from the back of the deck. He went to work on this "live one" as soon as he sat down. The Professor's policy was to get them hooked as soon as possible so the "sucker" can't quit if he should get a little winner.

These gamblers that banked the dice and 21 games had a $100 limit. Well, the Professor (who was a very smart fellow), knew that he was in tough company and took plenty of time—no hurry. After playing for 3 hours he had this tough guy in for $10,000. Then this tough guy pulled out his gun, put it on the table and said, "I know you are doing something to me and when I find out I am going to blow your brains out." The Professor kept right on dealing and replied, "If you find anything on these cards you can blow my brains out." The Professor knew that he had nothing to worry about as he never used marked cards in a 21 game—too easy to catch him. Also, he didn't have to, as he was one of the best "two man" or "second dealers" in the business. That is exactly what happened. A few minutes later the tough guy said, "Give me those cards." The Professor answered, "Certainly, just a minute."

He then asked for a knife and cut the deck of cards about one-half inch down the middle—sideways. The tough guy said, "What's that for?" The Professor replied, "So when you bring them back I want to have them match the half I have here—just in case you might try to do something to them." The Professor didn't miss a trick—he was always wide awake. The tough guy lost $12,000 and paid off the next day. That's when Little Abe left, after he received his commission. The Professor was what we call an all around mechanic. Jack of all Trades. Two-handed dice man, dealt cards with both hands, tops at poker, 6 and 7 card rummy (a big game years ago) You name the game—he played it. The Professor must have made a million dollars in his day.

Another time the Professor or Little Abe was hanging around a town between jobs. He was playing horses in a horsebook, which up to a few years ago were wide open. This was one of the Professor's two vices. He would bet pretty high when made a good score. One of the bosses of the horsebook liked to play single-handed pinochle and was pretty good at it. Seeing that Abe had a bankroll, he asked Abe if he played.

This boss (who didn't know who Abe was) put his foot right into the lion's mouth. Abe said, "I play at it." For a few days they would play between races, and Abe lost about $1,000 to the boss, who was taking a little edge— meaning he wasn't playing honestly with the Professor.

Of course, this was O.K. with the Professor, who knew what was going on all the time, but he was also one step in front of the boss all the time. This is to show how hard it is to beat someone at their own game. What the Professor did to beat this boss is one of the smartest gimmicks I had ever heard of at that time.

The Professor knew that they buy their cards at the corner drug store, which was two doors away. So the Professor decided it was about time to teach this boss a lesson in the art of playing pinochle. He went into the drug store and bought 6 decks of pinochle cards, left and came back a couple of minutes later. He told the clerk that he had made a mistake, he meant playing cards, not pinochle cards. The clerk put the 6 decks of pinochle cards back in the box and gave him the playing cards, but the Professor had now switched his own cards which he had some work on the night before, and resealed the decks. The trap was now baited and open.

The Professor walked into the horsebook, made a couple of bets, and the boss said, "Well, are you ready for your lesson?" The Professor smiled, "I am always ready to learn, but I have to leave town tomorrow. How about raising the limit. Maybe I can get out before I leave." The boss said, "Sure, how about $500 a game. You might get out in two games." He said to one of his clerks, "Herky, get 4 decks of pinochle cards at the drug store." That's all—the trap was sprung. Now all the Professor hoped for was that at least 2 of the decks were his. That's why he put 6 decks in the box—in case some were sold. He didn't miss a trick. All he had left in his pocket was $1,100 and if the first deck opened wasn't his he was going to quit and try him some other time. Sure enough, the first deck the boss opened was the Professor's. They played for a few hours and used all 4 decks. All of them were Little Abe's. After winning $5,000 the Professor said, "I think I have enough—see you on the next trip." This boss never knew what hit him. He was a little out of his class, but didn't know it. I am sure he never did find out what happened to him. After all, he got the cards at the drug store.

Pretty smart fellow that Professor, yes? But let me tell you about his other vice, which was the worst of all. He was a junkie toward the end, and that was his downfall. He died in a rooming house, broke.

Today in Las Vegas, gambling is as clean as it can possibly be. Of course now and then you might find someone that is trying to cheat the player or the club—without the owner's knowledge. The penalty is very severe when they are caught because they are barred for life from ever working in the state of Nevada As you must have a working permit to work in one of the casinos, once you are caught doing anything detrimental to the policy of the state you are through.

We have a State Gaming Board. They have men that police the entire state. Their job is to see that all games are run honestly—beyond a doubt. These men know what to look for and are schooled to find the slightest infraction. We have a clean slate and intend to keep it that way. Do not be afraid to gamble in Nevada. If you lose your money you can rest assured you weren't cheated out of it.

A friend of mine showed me an article recently by a reporter out of New York who had interviewed a so-called professional card sharp on how to protect yourself against being cheated. Quote from the article "Never take your eyes off the deck, the dealer's hands, each player's cards, the discards, the pot, the score pad, or if it's a catered game, the waiter." What kind of a mumble jumble is that? How is anybody going to play at the game if you have to do all of these things at once.

A person would be a nervous wreck after a few minutes of playing. Also he might accuse an innocent person and get shot on top of it. Here is another "quote" in the same article. "Never play cards with a dealer who tells jokes, whistles, sits, stands, or puts a mirror on the table before dealing." How does he expect the dealer to deal—sideways. You would also need eight pair of eyes to make sure the dealer isn't doing any of these gestures.

Years ago I knew a cheater that was an ace at dealing 21 and poker. He won plenty of money at these games and never spoke at all. He was a mute and his nickname was the "Dummy." He didn't have to talk to win the money. He was very successful in his field without having to whistle, tell jokes, or talk to distract the players.

I worked in a big club in Florida a few years ago. The boss of the club, who was in the gambling business for many and many a year, was known for his honesty in running a square club whenever and wherever he would open. He had a big following of customers that knew they would always receive a square shake for their money. Every time he opened he did plenty of business. This one season there was a so-called authority on gambling visiting in Florida. He was what we call a "J.C.L." in the business, which means "Johnny Come Lately"—a newcomer. He had written a few articles on dice so now he was an authority. He walked into this club, watched awhile and left.

The owner knew who he was but paid no attention to him. The next day there was a blast in the newspaper saying that the club was using crooked dice. He also said that the dice the club was using were six-ace flats. This is dice that is shaved off or cut down on the sides of the six and the ace—factory bought. When this is done to a pair of dice it will bring up the sixes and aces more often like seven with six-ace or two or twelve with two sixes. This does not help the players who are betting that they are going to win. Well, to put it mildly, this boss was fit to be tied.

Three days later this J.C.L. authority walked into the club, and lucky for him that two of the guards saw him first and threw him out bodily, because if this owner had seen him he would have killed him as he was a pretty tough man. Also his reputation as a square gambler was beyond reproach. I am sure that this J.C.L. couldn't tell the difference between six-ace flats and square dice unless they are picked up and examined. It is very difficult, even for an expert on dice, to watch a dice game and tell the difference between a light pair of six-ace flats and square dice. Even then he probably would be guessing. Besides if a gambling club wanted to win the money, there are many easier and safer ways than six-ace flats.

Another time I was working for a big time gambler who also had a very high reputation as a square gambler. We had opened a club about forty miles from New York City. All our customers came out in limousines that were furnished by the club. We were open a couple of weeks and doing plenty of business. One fine morning there was a piece in one of the city's newspapers, written by one of the top columnists, to the effect that there was a crap game going in this town in upstate New York, named the town, and also said that it was a bustout joint, run by crooked gamblers. This owner of the club who knew the columnist very well, blew his top. He went to see him and explained to him that he was running this club and asked him if he was trying to ruin his reputation. The columnist admitted that he had received the wrong information, because in the next day's paper was a retraction saying that this club was a square club run by a square gambler. Two days later we were raided. Too much publicity—after all we didn't have a license.

I suppose many of you have read articles on how to win at 21 or blackjack by counting the pictures or tens and aces. Also to bet small until there are a few cards left in the deck and if there are two or three aces and a few pictures left in the deck to bet a large amount of money because the odds are in the player's favor. What do these writers that write trash like this think we in the gambling business are? Idiots, I guess.

Why do they think owners of clubs pay men like us for. You don't think we walk up and down a 21 pit (which the inside of the 21 games is called) for our health, or to take exercise. We are there to see that the club gets an honest shake for their money, to protect them against such small and trivial ways of trying to beat a club out of some money, which this is one of them. We have more important gimmicks to look out for than a greenhorn that has read an article, which to them looks good on paper but is a little more difficult when playing.

I had a player come in with the three large white cards, sit himself down at a 21 game, spread the cards out, ask for change for a hundred dollar bill and was ready for action. On these cards were all kinds of figures. so I watched him as I was curious as to what he was trying to do. His first bet was one dollar, he lost. His next bet was one dollar, he won. His next bet was one dollar. By that time I had glanced over his shoulder and read the cards he had spread out in front of him. On one card was how to hit the hand and how to double down. On another was what to do with the soft hands. On the third card was how to figure out what to do after so many cards were dealt and how big a bet to make. i.e. If 30 cards were dealt out and three aces and six pictures or tens were still in the deck, to bet $60, or if forty cards were dealt out and four aces and four tens were still in the deck to bet as much as you could. This player was really something to watch, trying to figure whether to hit the hand, trying to count the tens and aces, saying to the dealer, "Hold it a second while I see what I have to do." He was in dire straits.

I said to him, "You have this game figured out pretty good." He answered, "Pretty good!"—like the cat that had swallowed the mouse. I stood right with him, waiting for him to make his big bet during his state of confusion. After a few deals he finally made a bet of $12 and lost it. I told him that he could also lose playing this way and he answered, I'm beginning to believe you." He started to bet his dollar. Towards the end of the deal he bet fifty dollars. The dealer looked at me and I said one word—"Shuffle". The dealer broke the deck down and shuffled the cards. The player asked the dealer, "How come you don't deal out the rest of the cards?" I said, "We have a policy here that when a player bets a fair amount of money, we like to give him a better chance to win, so we use the full deck of cards." Then I told him that if he played the hands natural he won't have to be a nervous wreck while playing the game of 21. I neglected to tell him that most dealers in most of the clubs are instructed to automatically break a deck down or make a new deal which means reshuffle the cards, or call a pit boss over to see the play as there are experts at doing what he was trying to do. We call them "countdown experts." They don't need any cards in front of them. Everything is by memory. You don't just learn all this by reading it in a book. It takes a long time to perfect this method of playing—also they know how to play the game of 21. There aren't too many around—that is experts I mean. There are plenty of novices that are trying to learn, but I am afraid most of them won't ever make the grade. These few count-down experts (I am one) will beat any 21 game in the world. So if anybody thinks it can't be done, just put your money up and start dealing, and before you know it you will have a full table.

There were a few clubs in the state that didn't think it could be done, but have found differently and have changed their style of dealing the deck to the bottom—too expensive. This gimmick was O.K. a few years ago, but now it is what we call "played out."

All the clubs know about it. I think, of course, every now and then one of these count-down sharpies will catch a dealer or pitboss asleep and make a winner before the club wakes up to the fact that instead of having the best of it the club is the player and the player is the banker with the club's money. Here is the punch line to this whole gimmick

CHEATING

The club can't do anything at all to the player. It is not called cheating in a sense. The player does nothing to the cards, doesn't even have to touch them. You can deal them open which he would like even better as he can see what is going on more clearly. So you can't accuse the count-down expert of what he is thinking about in his mind.

So when clubs that have men in their employ that know how to protect themselves against this gimmick, all they have to do is tell the dealer to reshuffle the cards when they see this operation. That is the end of the "count-down."

Let me straighten out the readers on a few facts about cheating at a 21 or blackjack game. A very good cheater NEVER uses a marked deck—that is the surest way for him to let the sucker catch him. He doesn't have to. He has surer ways of protecting himself against any accusations made by the sucker who thinks he is getting cheated. One is taking a peek, which is exactly what the word means—to look at the card on top of the deck without the player seeing him doing. This is simple for him. The other is to give the player not the top card of the deck, but the second card. This is easy for him to do without the player's knowledge. We call that pulling a second or two. I will simplify that. Let us say the dealer's face or up card is a ten. He looks at his hole card and it is a six—hard sixteen (bad hand for the dealer). Now he takes a peek at the top card and it is a five. That five is a lovely card for him as it will make him 21. Now if any of the players should ask for a hit, he pulls what we call a "second or two" and the five remains on top of the deck until it is his turn to hit then he nonchalantly turns over the top card and lo and behold it is a lovely five which makes the dealer 21. Isn't that pretty?

Best of all, if you have any doubt or think that you saw this dealer doing something to you, you can't prove it. By the time you open your mouth to accuse him, the move is over with. What proof do you have, even if he had done something. His word is as good as yours. Besides there is nothing wrong with the cards—no marks on them and they are all there. Also, you might get arrested for accusing the dealer of cheating and can't prove it.

Remember, a real top all around card cheater, as I have said, could give any card magician cards and spades, and beat them. Also a card magician does card tricks to amuse the public. A card sharp knows when and how to do the card tricks, but does it for money.

I am going to tell you of one sure way to protect yourself against anybody that you think is doing something to you in a 21 game. This is a trade secret I learned over 30 years ago by one of the smartest cheaters that ever lived—"Little Abe." Many a good and high player will benefit from this and will be able to leave the trap he fell into before it is too late. Don't watch the dealer's hands and cards. You won't see a thing—especially if the dealer is a top mechanic (very good at his trade). WATCH HIS EYES! That is the give way. A dealer has no reason at all to keep looking at the deck in his hand. He deals the cards, hits the players and does this automatically. Try it yourself and see if you have any reason to look at the deck. You will find out you don't. In order for a cheater to see if he needs the top card of the deck he must find a way to look and see.

The two most popular ways to peek, as it is called, are the front peek and the back peek. Even if the dealer is foolish enough to use marked cards there is one thing he must do—that is lower his eyes to look at the deck. So, if you find a dealer that has a tendency to look at the deck quite often, fold your bankroll and take it on the duffy. Run.

There is one thing you must understand. Never be afraid to play in the state of Nevada. I can't speak for any gambling club in the world, but I know this much: You will get an honest shake for your money in the state of Nevada. We don't want anybody to cheat us, but you can rest assured we will never cheat you. Most of the information I have given you is just to help you when you are playing at clubs, affairs, smokers, stags, Bar Mitzvahs, weddings, brists, and even when you go into the men's room and see a card or crap game. Don't laugh, the men's room in hotels and clubs were a favorite spot to spread a game. I am sure many of you male readers of this book have had the experience of playing in one of these games—where no women are allowed.

Nobody is immune to getting beat at a game, anytime and anyplace. Most everybody loves to let themselves go and take a chance. Know who and where you are playing. You must give yourself a chance or you will never have a chance. The only advice I can give the cheaters to be is: keep your nose clean, stay out of Nevada—you can go to jail.

Don't let the larceny come out in you. In other words, don't be greedy and listen to any proposition made to you by someone that tells you he can get you some help at a game. If this so-called friend of yours could get some help he wouldn't need you.

I am going to relate one incident that was very commonly used a few years ago and still might be used in some spots around the country. This is to show how some players let greed overcome common sense and fall into their own trap. Don't let this happen to you. This trap could be applied to any game, not only about a crap game, of which this story is about.

Years ago, as well as today, around most resort cities there usually was a crap game going someplace in the town. Sometimes these games are not on the level. The ones that aren't so "kosher" have men or women that patronize the best hotels and make acquaintances with good players that are known to them. These men and women are called "steerers" in our vernacular. They steer the suckers to the club by conversation. Sometimes the sucker is a little careful about going so the steerer will use one of their pet larceny gimmicks. They tell them that they have a dealer who will give him a little help when he buys his chips. For instance, if he buys a stack of $25 chips, which are twenty in a stack ($500 worth), the dealer instead will give him two stacks of $25 chips ($1,000 worth), and charge him $500.

As the game is always full and busy, the dealers aren't watched too closely. Now the greed or larceny comes out on the sucker. His ears become large as an elephant's, and his eyes as large as saucers. This deal is for him! "Let's go," he says and go he does. When they arrive at the club there is a full game going. It is even hard to get to the table, but he manages. He doesn't know of course, that everybody playing at the game works for the club and it is called "shilling up the game" so it will look busy. This player gives the dealer $500 and the dealer gives him two stacks of $25 chips. Now the sucker says to himself, "That's the way to gamble." How could he not miss beating this crap game. So he starts to play and before you can say, "I am a sucker" he has lost the chips. His dear friend the "steerer" tells him to buy another stack and the dealer will do the same thing— two for the price of one. Just like some drug stores used to do—buy one and get two. The "steerer" and the dealer tell him, "It's just a bad break—the dice are cold, but must warm up eventually." So the sucker continues to buy two for one until he has run out of money. He, at least, had a chance. He got what we call "drugstore odds." Two for one.

It is very difficult to give you the lesson to this story, because there are thousands of gimmicks like this camouflage to look like a legitimate deal—but have the same ending as this story did.

All I can tell you is don't listen to any "get rich" scheme in gambling as a player against the house—there isn't any. If there were, we would be out of business. So the "get rich" scheme hasn't been invented yet.

In closing this chapter on cheating, I have a few words for the dupes that have any idea of making cheating at cards or dice their future. It is a very tough life, and don't for one minute think that it is easy to be a good cheater. Besides having to be very adept at handling cards and dice, you have to have plenty of guts. It is very simple to cheat at a friendly card or dice game but when you are doing this where money is concerned it becomes a difficult situation. I have seen cheaters go to work (which means start cheating) against the toughest men in the country where with one slip of the dice or cards you become a weighted down mummy.

CHEATING

I knew of one cheater that hung around a little store in Brownsville, N.Y. that was the hangout for a few of the boys from Murder Inc. That's who he made a living from until the gang was disposed of. That takes guts. So if any of you have any silly notion of trying to make an easy living off the fat of the land, you had better have plenty of guts.

16

HORSE RACING

Well we've had all this time inside, let's go outside to the great outdoors and horse racing, a noble sport that takes anywhere from 15% upwards out of every bet you make. Remember you must compare this with the 1.4% the casino takes from your bet on the dice table. So unless you like the fresh air and want to contribute to the continuation of the sport of kings don't count on winning too often at the track. That is unless you want to read, study carefully, painstakingly all that follows.

If you have intentions of winning money at the track, you should know the history of every horse, jockey, trainer and owner. Plus that you should have a good mathematical mind. It's not easy, is it?

I do like the Daily Double if you know what you're doing and have taken note of the above paragraph.

Non-horse fans will probably think the Daily Double has something to do with Farrah Fawcett-Majors. Not so. The Daily Double is an attractive mathematical presentation designed by race tracks to relieve the fan of more money by its sheer munificence. The impressive pay-offs compared to the normal mutual win on one horse is magnetic indeed. It takes a gambler with iron will-power to resist the Daily Double. And normally iron will-power and gamblers go together like romance and onions. They don't. It follows then like the night and day that if you must bet the Daily Double you might as well be armed for it. So take the following ammunition to wrap up in an old Racing Form.

On October 5, 1960, *Shapter Rebel* won the first race by a half length at Hollywood Park and paid $3.20. *Town Byrd* won the second race by a length and paid $10.40. Had you parlayed the two winners you would have won $16.60, but had you played those same two horses in the Daily Double your payoff would have been $38.00. That's why the Daily Double (called "sweet deedee" by some) is so popular.

Ninety percent of the time the Daily Double gives you a better payoff than a straight parlay. That's why any method of play that concentrates on beating the Daily Double is very valuable. For example, the best handicappers among the regulars at Del Mar buy a $2 ticket on the favorite in the first race with every horse in the second race. If there are ten horses entered in the second it costs them $20. Average payoff is $50. As you know favorites score in a little less than half of all races, so the boys cash in about 1 in every two days using this system. It negates the gambler's lament "Daily Double, Full of Trouble."

Starting from that basis I have several refinements on the above that ease the tension somewhat and also add pennies to the piggy bank.

First I'd rather play the favorite in the second race because the first race usually consists of untried horses and the form is poor. That means I play all the horses in the first ract to the favorite in the second. If a good long-shot wins in the first race I'm really riding high. But I refine even further. In a first race there are always a couple or more long shots who couldn't even come in on an answered prayer. They are just running for the exercise. You need only look at the form and the odds to know this is true. By skipping them, you have less of an investment and just as good a chance of collecting.

Statistics and form though are quite deceptive and you must make allowances for that. Many automobile clubs will tell you that there are more pedestrians killed crossing with the green light than on the red light. But they don't tell you that there are hundreds more times people crossing with the lights so your percentage is better crossing with the light.

So it is with favorites. Sometimes the most heavily bet horse isn't the favorite. I like the second favorites very often because the overlay is greater—they have overnight odds of 8-5 and end up 3 or 4 to 1. All this because an eccentric crowd bets too much on a favorite because of the jockey, handicappers or maybe the color of the horse. When figuring the Daily Double it is always wise to examine the second favorite before plunging on the favorite.

Many of the gamblers who migrate with the stables from track to track look upon Daily Doubles as bread and butter money even though the Internal Revenue Department recently put a cramp in their operations by ruling that "pool" winners of over $600 must give their name and address to track officials. With Uncle Sam ready to share in their big winnings but disinterested in their losings, gamblers are reluctant to bet a lot on the Daily Double unless they can "spread" their bets among syndicate members. In fact that $600 ruling aimed at the Daily Double winner is an indication of how popular this bet is and that the take is considerable. How badly the Internal Revenue Department ruling will hurt the "sweet deedee" take, I can't say, but my guess is the professional will find a way around it.

Before we go into another popular system for shaking loose profits from the Daily Double tree, we feel it only fair to mention that every once in a while a fellow will come along with a big D.D. win and a system as solid as Arpege vapor. Yet he has the profits to prove his success. Take a 76 year-old man who on October 6 won $6,280.00 at Hazel Park Race Track. He said he had a dream. The program numbers of the winning horse would be 10 and 3. He has these dreams often. All I ever dream about is walking around Times Square in my pajamas.

Sig Shore of Valiant Films in New York won a huge Daily Double at Del Mar when he arrived too late to figure the horses. He looked at his watch. It was ten of two. So he played positions 10 and 2. The two horses both won. However I don't suppose Sig has any consistent wins with this system.

Up to now I have been conservative in my suggestions. I have given you just one system at which you would be hard pressed to lose $20 on a Daily Double plunge. With that $20 and including one favorite you could still snag a $400 or $500 winning day. A few of those and you could retire to the gambler's paradise, a Horse Room in Las Vegas where you can play all the tracks at once all day, every day.

But lets throw caution to the winds—especially since we're talking about paper money and not hard cash at the moment. There's a Daily Double system that a friend of mine loves and I wish I could afford to play it. I've checked it many times on paper and the results have been astonishingly good. With a $3,000 investment during a season he showed a $12,000 profit. Don't take my word for it—play it on paper for a while. If you get results, take your bank-roll to the track. But be sure you have stretch pockets because you're very liable to come back with quite a bit more than you started with. I'll tell you why that warning: About three years ago, my friend outlined this system as a gesture of friendship to a stockbroker, whose name shall be secret because of the story. He gave him the usual warning that no system is foolproof but over a period of time will give you the breaks. The stockbroker hit the double for $5,500, stopped at the bank on the way home right after the second race to exchange his win for 5,500 one-dollar bills. He burst into my friend's office, stood on a desk and tossed his bundle of money, without rubber band, into the air so that it scattered and floated down over the entire office and amazed employees. The storm of dollar bills, believe me, was memorable. It's a better story when I tell you he won $2,000 more than he should have because he made a mistake in his figures.

Here's my friend's favorite Daily Double betting system, the exact system he outlined but with a unique increase in betting so that you can really cash in when you win.

Here's an example of how it works where the win was more modest, then we'll go further into it. For a perfect example we go back to Fair Grounds, New Orleans in February 1958. The first race lined up like this:

Blue Mountain	10 to 1
Driscoll	5 to 1
Why So	2½ to 1
Homespun	8 to 1
Mighty Blow	27 to 1
Denver Fox	42 to 1
Desert Battle	67 to 1
Snappy Verse	2 to 1
Darby Dedre	22 to 1
Macwill	10 to 1

First cross off *Denver Fox* and *Desert Battle* as being out of it. Then using $20 as the basic win needed, he played $2 on *Blue Mountain* (at 10 to 1, $2 would give him the $20 basic win) to *Regal Maid,* the favorite in the second race. Then $4 on *Driscoll* (4 x 5 is $20), $5 on *Why So,* $4 on *Homespun,* $2 on *Mighty Blow,* $10 on *Snappy Verse,* $2 on *Darby Dedre* and $2 on *Macwill.* All these to *Regal Maid* in the second. Total money bet was $32. *Why So* won the first race and paid $7. *Regal Maid* won by a neck and paid $10.20. The $2 Daily Double paid $40. Total win in the $32 bet with your $6 from *Why So* to *Regal Maid* was $120. Total profit in the kick $88. Not so bad.

But sometimes if you open all car doors for your wife

and wink at an ugly girl once in a while, you can bet real lucky with this system. At Hialeah in the same year, 1958, this was the line-up in the first race:

Hygrow's Flyer	2 to 1	10
Miss Columbus	90 to 1	—
Ben DeHaven	9 to 1	4
Maudeaux	7 to 1	4
Deby	70 to 1	—
Pretty Girl	60 to 1	—
Grand Jam	70 to 1	—
Danna Like	13 to 1	2
Sun Carrier	6 to 1	4
Miss Galbuc	4 to 1	5
Lady Reanelle	4 to 1	5
Tenacity	8 to 1	4
		——
		$38

His betting was (after eliminating *Miss Columbus, Deby, Pretty Girl,* and *Grand Jam* as being out of it) $10 on *Hygrow's Flyer,* $4 on *Ben DeHaven,* $4 on *Maudeaux,* $2 on *Danna Like,* $4 on *Sun Carrier,* $5 on *Miss Glabuc,* $5 on *Lady Reanelle* and $4 on *Tenacity.* All these tickets were linked with favorite *Air Power'* #8 in the second race.

Tenacity won it by 2 lengths and paid $9. The Daily Double paid $108 which gave me a $216 win and $38 investment. Total profit: $178, a nice Daily Double win. Incidentally the totals on the pool for Daily Double that day was $87,622 which will give you an idea of how popular that play is.

This doesn't look difficult, does it? Yet, I'm afraid I'm going to complicate it out of necessity so you can get your maximum benefit from it. Just this summer, my friend took a solid hour explaining this Daily Double play to a lovely young motion picture actress, Nora Hayden and as is customary when you have the pleasure of good company at the Turf Club, promised her one-half his winnings if he connected. Winner of the first race was *Wedding Call* at a good price. But in the second race, favorite *Free Copy* didn't make it by three lengths. In fact, *Blue Moon* won it and he was third favorite. Nora was defected especially since the Daily Double paid $315.20. But she needn't have been. He had *Blue Moon* because his price, post position, jockey, trainer, last work-out time and the way some newspaper selectors were backing him, were just too good.

I'll give you a specific: At the Fair Grounds in New Orleans he covered all the horses in the first race as usual like this:

Flying Miss	12 to 1	$2
Champagne Cal	Even	20
Little Stick	6 to 1	4
W. A. Moore	10 to 1	2
Leap Year Lass	7 to 1	4
War Chance	4 to 1	5
Better Pay	10 to 1	2

There were three more horses that didn't warrant a bet so his total betting was $39.

In the second race the favorite was *Tony Leo* and he was a heavy favorite bet down to less than even. But there were two other horses he liked very much, *Son's Style* and *Driscoll*. Two popular newspaper handicappers liked *Driscoll* too and his last workout was blazing. Yet he was a 13 to 1 bet. My friend was puzzled especially since he was a product of a good stable—Detroit Stables. *Son's Style* had won some good previous races and was best at the distance of ¾ mile. On the strength that *Tony Leo* was not a good mudder (and it was drizzling) and that *Driscoll* was a fast finisher and liked dirty weather, he put his money on him. He won by four lengths and paid $28. The Daily Double payoff was $249.60. *Flying Miss* won the first race so he only had a $2 ticket riding but it was a sweet win and his total profit was $200.60. *Tony Leo*, by the way, finished third and *Son's Style* was far back.

So you're going to have to start reading the Racing Form and going to the races more often to get some of that horse sense drummed into you. I can give you some short cuts. To wit: I know of no newspaper selector who shows a profit at the end of a racing season. But there's always one in each city who does better than others. Keep your eye on him and notice too if he does better at certain distances and at different purses. Follow him for picks in some races. Also its a good idea not to play horses who haven't won or placed in their last two races even though they are favorites or are being picked by a good handicapper. Also I like to stay away from a horse that hasn't run in a while. It always creates a worry within me and I don't enjoy my day when a shadow is hanging over my bets. Remember a man's best friend is supposed to be his dog but its really his horse if he picks his horse wisely.

If you do pick wrong don't blame it on anyone but yourself. Even I assume no responsibility. I only offer this system as a recommendation for you to use or laugh off. I hope you don't behave as a trainer friend of mine did one fine Saturday at Santa Anita when Johnny Longden failed to bring the favorite home by at least ten lengths. In fact the horse, an in-and-outer finished seventh. The trainer who also had a sizable bet riding on his horse, accosted Longden agrily. He screamed, "You had your chance on the stretch turn, why didn't you come through?" Said Johnny coolly, "What, and leave the horse behind!"

There is big revenue in the popularity of the Exacta, so that at some tracks, there are as many as five Exactas, also quinellas, with big payoffs.

What is also interesting is that states and government have taxed their people to the utmost at race tracks and now have to find other ways of revenue. What better than the painless way of casino gambling? I think you will probably see the whole fifty states go in for legalized gambling to get their governments more revenue, many states of which don't even have racing.

It's a painless way because there will always be gamblers. For example, recently in Los Angeles, Bingo was made legal if some of the money is given to charity. That too is springing up all over.

Country by country they somewhere along the line are legalizing gambling. The numbers rackets still go on, which is illegal, but legal lotteries are big in New York and New Jersey and popping up in other states. Things like "purely luck" games, if you're lucky you win and if you're unlucky you lose. As for Exacta, it has been a blessing to newspaper handicappers, who in the history of newspapers have never shown a plus mark in a season. No handicappers on any paper in any city or state in the world has shown a plus at the end of a season. But with Exacta betting and their not having to invest their own money, but purely doing it on paper, they are wheeling the favorite in Exacta races and occasionally catching a long shot in the 2nd spot. This has been in quite a few handicappers a plus for the season.

Take notice and imitate them. If you'll wheel your favorite in Exacta races, you'll win money at the end of the meet. The reason is that the average gambler can't afford to bet the favorite with more than two or three horses, and if you've got a bankroll you can catch those long ones and they're the ones that set you up for the season.

Where the Action Is

Not only are there horse books all over Vegas, many more than there used to be, but you can go to the MGM Grand and bet on Jai Alai which is relatively new, although it has always been an action game in Tijuana. And don't forget the growing profits of off-track betting in New York.

Dog racing has sprung up in a couple of spots too, and of course, there are constant arrests for betting on cock fights, especially in the east, in New York, Pennsylvania, Virginia, New Jersey, etc. But this is illegal. It is our prediction that every gambling game will eventually be legal, and the state or government will dip its hands in the till and take its share.

Another change that will affect few gamblers, because the game isn't that popular, is in baccarat. Several of the clubs now instead of using bills — money — as they always have, are using different color and different shape chips. In fact, you could hardly call them chips. Some of them are three or four inches long, and somehow they capture the imagination of the players — they like it.

17

MORE HORSES

Here's a good method of play which a friend of mine sent me. Study it carefully. He says:

"On February 1, 1947, with a press pass I borrowed from Louella Parsons, I went to the Turf Club at Santa Anita Race Track. I took along the only money I had in the world — $2,000 — and a sheef of figures, prepared to play a horse racing system I had worked out.

"I was no amateur gambler. I had written many articles and three books on odds and gambling. But this was the first time I was willing to put my money — real money — where my mouth was. In other words, I was confident that a racing system I had played on paper for over a year would work at the track.

"It was a beautiful day and the track was fast. I was a little nervous but not flustered. I was alone, no friends to rattle me. I needed a clear head for the mass of figures that would be sprouting from my pencil.

"First I'll give you a race by race report of how I did and then I'll tell you how. If you are the usual doubter, I refer you to back newspapers or the 1947 Racing Form Chart Book.

"In the first race at 1 P.M. sharp I won $14. I had drawn first blood. I won $14 on the second race too when *Pluck Chat* placed. He placed by six lengths so there was no strain. I lost $28 in the third race when my horses faded away.

"Now I was even. I lost $16 in the fourth race and won $11.50 the fifth. I was delighted in the sixth when I won $32 as a result of a place win by *Cum Laude.* He was just nosed out by *Danada Red* or I would have been richer. In the seventh, despite a place win, I lost $14, and in the eight I was clobbered—but really clobbered. I lost $60. My horses were far out at the finish. Well, eight races is all you get and I counted my money. I lost $46.50. Some genius!

"That weekend and Monday (no racing Monday) I pored over forms, charts and my own record. I wasn't disheartened at all. In all the time I had worked this system on paper I never had a losing week. In fact, I was rather smug about it.

"Tuesday was another beautiful day. With my bankroll of $1953.50 I was on the firing line early, had a nice lunch in the track restaurant and started working my figures.

"To get fast over the bad news, I lost $90 on the first race. Jackie Westrope rode a terrible race on *Shirvani.* But no excuses. I lost $81 on the second race and $70 on the third. (The system actually required a safe $5,000 to start but I didn't have that much. I was beginning to sweat.) I was now $284.50 behind including my first day's losses.

"In my own defense and without conceit I must add that this is where a system player needs guts. I was very young then and had the guts. The fourth race required a bet of $84. It was a big thrill when *Yuca Loma* came in three lengths in front. He paid $43.50 to win and $15.60 to place. I had $14.00 on each spot. I won $413.70 which put me $129.20 in front. I lost $4 on the fifth race. And then not being able to get out of the habit, I dropped $32, $12 and $36, respectively, on the next three races.

"So for the two days I was $47.20 in the black. No fortune, it is true, but things were looking up. That night I slept well.

"My third day at the track was exceptionally good—so now, I suppose for the skeptics and those who are bound to check up on me, I will have to outline my method and the explanations of why I play this way. I must also add that I use the two-dollar bet as a base figure, try for $750 a week winnings and recommend no less than a $5,000 bankroll (several players can form a syndicate for this amount).

"*Here's the play:* You put $2 on all horses paying 9 to 1 or better to both win and place. If you lose you increase the bet $4 in the second race and if you lose again to $5 then $6 then $7, etc. (I play with a $7 top but you may have more guts.) When you win you revert to a $2 bet again. If you have winning horses but lose on the race anyway, (sometimes it is sad but true that you can win a small amount which is less than your total bet) you drop your bets a notch, i.e., you bet $5 to win and $5 to place on your horses. You have a winning horse but show a loss on that race so the next race you bet $4 to win and $4 to place on your horses.

"No caution: You must mix a little common sense with this system. For instance, I don't like to play a race where I have to play too many horses. What's too many? Well, five in an eight horse race, for example, is too many. Also, when I'm getting into the higher bets like $7 a horse, I like to cover horses that pay as low as 8 to 1. Also, I do not like to play the trotters.

"Why do I play (and win) with this system? First, favorites are always overplayed by the crowd, which means that long shots are neglected. The axiom is that playing a long shot is a sure way to the poor hourse. But no one ever gave us an axiom for playing every long shot in a race. In the win and place spot you'll get your share of winners each day like clockwork. If you don't the progression of betting is not rapid enough to destroy you. I have never seen a combination of losses big enough to dent a good bankroll when this system is used.

"Well, to get back to February 5th at Santa Anita. With my $47.20 winnings, I relaxed and put my bets down for the first race. I lost $92. There went my winning bankroll out the window. I dropped $192 in the second race. No excuses, but I almost played a $7 horse who came in second because there were few long shots in the race.

"However, for the big one: With $54 bet in the third race, a lovely sorrel named *Pilot Sis* came in and paid $67.80 and $20.90. I had $18.00 on it to win and place. It gave me a sweet $798.30 total. I lost $36 on the other two horses in the race so my profit was $762.30. Profit for the three days to post time in the fourth race: $615.50. Not bad, thanks greatly to *Pilot Sis*. But in the 4th race I had another good win. *Vicksburg*, with Jackie Westrope up, came in by a head and paid $46.50 and $15.70. Total winnings for the 4th race after deductions of losing horses: $108.60. In the fifth race I lost $24. Then I lost $16 in the sixth. In the seventh there were no horses for me to cover, so I just enjoyed watching.

"*Meltonian* gave me a win in the eight with a $135 profit. At the end of three days my total profit was $819.10, a tidy sum.

"It was weather clear, track fast on Thursday. My day went like this: First race: Win $42.20. Second: Lost $20. Third: Won $57.40. Sixth: Won $62.40. Seventh: No play. eight : Lost $5.20. Winnings on the day: $142.80. Total winnings for four days: $961.90.

"The fifth day, Friday, closed out one full week of racing. I lost $94 on the day. My first week gave me a profit of $867.90. And—Imight add—I knew it would.

"I won't bore you with statistics. The second week I won $433. The third week I won $520. The last week of my vacation I won $945. The total for four weeks was

153

$2,765.90.

"Now you might say: "That was 15 years ago. How do I know the payoff average is still the same?" I have tried this method on and off, on paper and at various tracks for 15 years and the winnings varied little.

"Now let me caution you. Do not, I repeat, do not take my word for this. Don't believe figures. Buy a newspaper each day. Don't go near the track. Play the horses on paper. Don't bet your cash. That is, until you are satisfied. BUT IF YOU PLAY, STICK TO THIS SYSTEM WITHOUT ADDING YOUR OWN GIMMICKS.

"But as I pointed out, you must use common sense. You may find after you've played it a while that you don't like to play a race with more than 10 horses in it. Or you might not like big purse races (I like them best of all because Saturday or holiday crowds always bet the favorite, giving you lush odds on the longer shots.) Use this system as a base. AND DON'T ADD A POST POSITION GIMMICK, A JOCKEY GIMMICK OR A TRACK CONDITION GIMMICK. It won't help."

Off Track Betting

The OTB stores in New York have a huge success. It was thought that if people could bet without going to the track, they wouldn't go to the track, but attendance is still up and the city and state and tracks are getting added revenue through OTB.

There is much talk of OTB betting in California, probably the day will come soon where we will have it. There's also talk of OTB in New Jersey and Illinois. Of course, London has had it for years, and in Paris you can make bets by telephone, with code numbers. So when you sum it up, gambling will be akin to your corner grocery. It won't be like the old days where you had to call your friends to find a bookie. It will all be legal and you'll makeyour bet and perhaps someday watch it on television. As for betting on sporting events, the public broadcasting system has a program now from the Mint, downtown Las Vegas, which gives you the odds on football games and the like. That would never have been permitted years ago. Now it's taken in stride.

You watch—soon it will be on commercial television, so that on Friday nights you'll know what the college odds are on Saturday and what professional football is on Sunday , and of course the OTB places will take your football bets just like the horse bets and just like in Las Vegas.

18

HORSE STORIES

There are certain tips that horse players who have winning averages, will pass on to you. You best heed them because if you don't in the beginning, you will in the end, and it will cost you a lot of money.

For example, don't play horses that haven't run for a while. Yes, they'll occasionally win but their average is bad.

Eliminate all maiden or 2 year old races. They are too uncertain.

If a horse has not finished 1-2-3 in his previous races and he's up against horses who have, beware!

I don't like to play races when track conditions have changed suddenly.

Stay away from Show bets as much as possible. They just don't pay enough in the aggregate.

When a good horse has a big overlay (much bigger odds than the morning line or what you think it should have) take a gamble.

Let me quote an interview I had with Johnny Longden. (Keep in mind that *Flutterbye* had never run at this time. He won three of the four races Longden talked about and was second in the fourth.)

"*Flutterbye,* he's the one," said Johnny Longden in his high, one-note voice. "I'll be riding him in four big races this year and I have a hunch he'll win them all."

The scene was the world's winningest jockey's (5500 wins) brood-mare stables in Arcadia, California. The time: sun-up.

"Can you tell a winner by looking at him, Johnny?"

"You feel them. You look at the horse's conformation. But you gotta ride them to tell if they're champion blood. Take *Count Fleet.* The greatest horse I ever rode. We won in the Preakness, the Belmont and the Kentucky Derby. Yet in the beginning he couldn't get out of the chute."

He held up his hands—big for a 5-footer at 115 lbs. "You feel a horse through these as you ride. I knew the *Fleet* was a winner no matter how he fought the chute in the beginning."

Johnny is fifty-four years old. He gets uncomfortable when you talk about his age and retirement.

"I'm in good health. I chew each day away. There's no thought of retiring." He patted a colt on the rump. "I'll ride as long as I can help the horses."

The champ jockey believes a jock is forty percent responsible for a horse winning. He credits sixty percent to the nag.

"Sure jockeys make mistakes. I make them too. You take them out too fast, fight a jam instead of riding with it at the wrong time. There's lots of riding room for error. But when a jockey rides a perfect mare, he can push a middling horse a long way."

As the glare of the white early morning sun deepened

the shadows in the crags and crannies of Johnny's face, he did not look like the movie version of a champion jockey.

Resembling a heavily-muscled pixie, Grandpa Longden daily fights the battle of weight. He eats one meal a day and sips Metrecal (chocolate) the rest of the time. He is the victim of scores of falls and of many cracked, chipped and broken bones. His wife, Hazel, says Johnny's skeleton would resemble a Christmas tree two months after the holidays.

Despite thirty-four years of hard riding, the jockey still loves the daily routine. "I get up at six A.M. to look over some of my mounts. I don't ride every race like I used to. I like the longer races because it gives me a chance to get everything I can from a horse."

"Do you bet, Johnny?"

"Never. I usually get a percentage of the winning purse so I'm gambling to win out on the track."

"After all these years around horses, would you have any advice for the day-to-day bettor?"

Johnny scratched his head, seemingly puzzled and reluctant to go out on a limb. But he responded bravely. *"If I were betting, I'd stick to a good horse and wait for him to be set down in class. That's when he'll win. If you keep your eyes on several horses who have good workouts and run up there with the leaders, you'll catch them down in class sooner or later. That's when you step in."*

There's no need for Johnny Longden to scramble around at the betting windows. His in-the-money mounts over a lifetime have earned $20,000,000 for their owners. Johnny's take is about 10% or $2,000,000. He has won many stake races of $100,000 or over. His rewards are a beautiful home in Arcadia (near Santa Anita Race Track), a stable, ranch at Riverside and money in the bank.

What was the jockey's biggest race—the one which gave him the biggest thrill?

His eyes shone and there was a fondly reminiscent look on his face. "Back in 1950 for the San Juan Capistrano, I raced *Noor* against *Citation* for $100,000 stake. Though I felt like a winner when we got off, there was reason to worry at the half-mile post. *Noor* wasn't responding. Then a kind of electricity seemed to charge through both of us and we came on to win against a fine horse. That day I'll never forget."

Longden thinks the ingredient most necessary for a winning jockey is courage. He takes it for granted a good jockey has skill and also style. But courage is distributed unequally. Longden feels that without huge helpings of courage a jockey won't move in tight spots where a brave gamble may pay off.

We might add that courage reaps rewards but also results in spills, injury and in some infrequent cases, death, for a jockey on the track.

At Jamaica, Longden rode in a mile race for a nominal purse with no greater incentive to win than in any other routine race. Making the ¾ mile turn and in fourth place but moving up, he saw an opening along the fence and tried to push his mount through. There wasn't enough riding room. Longden's horse veered in instead of out and crashed through the fence, impaling his rider's foot on a jagged length of two-by-four. Pale, in terrible pain and bleeding, he was carried from the track.

Next day he rode in an important race and won it. Then he collapsed. "Broken foot and spine injury," was the medical verdict. Johnny was out of action for eight months, his longest period away from racing in his career.

"Yeah, that was pretty bad," recalls Johnny. "But what about Lady Jinx nabbing me twice in one season, both times with broken legs? The first time my horse was acting up in the starting gate. He reared, hit a post and fell back on me. Broke my leg in two places. Then my bones knit pretty good and I started working my horses mornings at Del Mar. I was up on one filly and getting around the oval pretty good when the horse drops dead in her tracks. I went flying over her head and ended with another broken leg."

"Didn't these accidents put any fear in you? Weren't you superstitious?"

"Jockeys are humans," Longden smiled. "So we are fearful at times. I don't think it is superstition. I'm often

159

nervous—especially before and during a big race. Accidents are part of the sport. They didn't make me any the more or less afraid."

A stablehand who stopped to take a horse from Longden put in his two cents. "Eyes open. That's what the boss says. If you're always alert, keyed-up. Keep your eyes open, you can cut down on spills and trouble."

"You can't eliminate them," argued Johnny. "In Canada I was racing alone, a horse comes from behind, trips my mount. There's a spill and I have a broken collar bone. Almost the same kind of an accident in Chicago. A horse veers in on me, I get twisted up in a spill and another broken leg."

The stablehand walked away shaking his head, almost convinced of the inevitability of broken bones.

We asked Johnny if the crowd ever disturbed him. Longden has always been colorful and therefore a target for both cheers and boos. "Unless the wind is right, you can't hear the crowd. Most of the time you're concentrating on your ride. Crowds are usually sympathetic. There have been rare times when the sound of the crowd has upset me."

Actually, though Longden is a money-runner, doing his best in the big stakes, he likes races with fewer horses and a quiet track. He gets his mounts from an agent, but has the privilege of turning down horses he doesn't want. He turns down many mounts. Mostly he refuses a horse because he believes it is over-matched. He has faith in his own selections and he must be right because about 20% of all his mounts come in the money.

Says Johnny about his wins: "I try hard in every race. I use the same style of riding today as I did thirty years ago.

"I think the most important part of a jockey's equipment outside of his brains are his hands. I've had my hands torn several times in a race and my winning percentage fell way off while they were healing. I feel through my hands. I can tell how my horse is running and how its responding. There's a magic in good hands and a sensitive horse can hear and work through its jockey's fingers."

Johnny often walks with hands still by his side. Perhaps

a subconscious protective instinct. Like a concert violinist he indulges in no exercise that could endanger his hands. He likes golf and big-game hunting, which he explains off: "I'm very careful. I go to Canada every year after elk and bear. It's a big thrill for me. It's a way of getting off with my friends."

Most of Longden's friends are away from the track. He doesn't mix much in the jockey's room or in their horse-play. Most of the younger jockeys can always borrow a few bucks from grandpa and pay it back when they please. He never brings it up.

At home his two sons, wife and daughter have learned long ago not to re-run the wins and losses of that day. Johnny doesn't ever look back. He's philosophical: "Some days are good. Some are bad. The future has something the past doesn't have—hope. So I concentrate on what's ahead and seldom look back."

His three-word recipe for success is: "I keep trying.

"I've changed some," says Johnny. "I used to have a temper. If another jock would give a horse a dirty ride, I'd be in there punching. I was a pigeon for the track stewards. I was always getting a $100 or $200 fine. But I got smart.

"It was tougher in the early days. First I had a repu-tation for riding losers. That didn't help. I was sensitive. I didn't have any money either. So I was always on edge."

Though the jockey got his start on Canadian tracks, it was oddly enough a Mexican track that sent him on his winning ways. "They started to call me 'The Pumper' down there because I developed a lean-forward style of riding. When you get a nickname, it helps. It gives you colour. But not only that, my style helped me win. Sports writers called it 'pogo stick' riding. Whatever it was, I won like crazy.

"Then when I got to the States, I found some tricks to get my horse out of the gate in a hurry. It all added up to wins. In among the losses, that is."

19

BEATING THE RACES

Stories about the horses and the track are legion and many of them have either happened to me or I was part of the action. You'd be surprised how illustrative and helpful the yarns of the track can be to the gambler.

For instance a heavy gambler named Jim Robin on a New York track was set into action when a 90-1 long shot won the first half of the daily double. He went around buying $2 tickets for anywhere from $60 to $500 depending on the combination on the ticket. Many wouldn't sell but many did. He figured the pay off had to be very big yet many bettors would like a bird on the hand and cash beforehand.

The second horse was also a long shot and the daily double paid $1,700 for $2. Jim bought $4,000 worth of payoffs and his take was eight winning tickets at $13,700.

The story probably apocryphal, is often told that a timid husband took his wife's two dollars and sent down to play *War Man* but a tout switched him to *Hindmost. War Man* won. In the next race the timid soul went to bet *Saw Saw* and the tout switched him to *Banter Boy. Saw Saw* won. The man's wife was furious. This time she sent him down to buy two hot dogs. He came back with two hamburgers. "I met that fellow again," he said abashedly.

Las Vegas money built a race track a few years ago but it was a flop. The reason given was that for much of the summer (the only time the track could get horses to come in) the weather was unbearably hot, keeping the crowds away. But in reality the more cogent reason was explained clearly by a gambler, "I could win or lose a fortune in the half hour between races. A gambler wants action. The track wagering is too slow."

An owner once told me seriously, "When *Materak* (his horse) sweeps his tail back and forth before a race, he's ready and anxious to run. Bet him." I went through four of his races before he stood in his stall before his race and swept his tail back and forth violently. I and my friends bet him heavily. He came in fifth on a poor race. Later I asked his owner what happened. He replied seriously, "You didn't watch him carefully. When he's ready he flicks his tail. He was swishing his tail." That's the owners for you.

I used to go to Hollywood Park with a dyed-in-the-wool gambler who bet consistently on *Olden Times*. He won five times in a row and made a small fortune for my friend. On the sixth time he came in second. "It's a plug," screamed my friend. "A dog that can't run!" That's the gambler for you.

This happens often but a bettor named Old Sam carried it off best. There was a 3-way dead heat one day and Sam with a big cigar tilted at an up-angle showed three win tickets. He had all three of them. Everybody congratulated him. Later he confessed it was one of the few races he had every horse but one (a dismal longshot) in the race.

Time and again I've seen gamblers who couldn't stand prosperity. One fellow who had been winning and losing at the track for years, had eight winners out of eight races on one day. He had what the doctors called a nervous breakdown and didn't get out of a sanitorium for 6 months. Another fellow won $11,000 one day at the races when $200 had been his biggest win before that. He went on a two-week tear that ended in a year jail sentence for burning a block of slum houses. And still one more bettor, and he was just a young fellow still in his twenties with $20 on a hundred-to-one-shot. He married the first girl he saw during a drink that night and it cost him and his parents a fortune to get rid of her.

One gambler figured that you had to win $100 everyday to break even. He worked it out this way: You bet $100 on the first race and the track takes 15% or $15. That leaves $85 for the second race. Fifteen percent of that is $12.75 so now you have $72.25. And so forth through eight races. Then there's admission price, parking, food, program and racing form. If you don't lose a cent on the horses you still lose $100.

Odd wins are rampant at the track. I took a girl relative engaged the night before. She played *Wedding Ball* and it won at big odds. A lieutenant friend won a bundle by playing *GI Joe*. It's a well-known story that Jimmy Durante played all horses wearing red in their colors and hit seven winners.

Of course you don't hear of the thousands of losers who play wrong hunches that go all the way from betting on all grey horses to that insanity of betting on bald-headed jockeys and horses whose names begin with "S" when they have the outside position.

Dreams are the inspiration for many bets. I've had normally, serious people call me with a suggestion, (which did happen) "Play any horse wherever he runs that has a white right foreleg."

I was awakened from a pleasant dream myself one night by a friend who just had to call. He had a dream just like life (they always are). In it he saw TV Lark winning a big race. It did too. But it was a favorite.

BEATING THE RACES

Lord pity a gambler who sees a horse's name on a moving van or in an advertising sign on the way to the track. He'll bet his wad on the hunch. And usually lose. But that won't stop him from doing the same thing again.

There have been match races for $100,000 to fire the imagination of racing fans and "Bet-A-Million" Gates won $250,000 on a horse race later said to have been fixed (never proven though).

Don't for a minute doubt that it takes lots of guts and iron nerves to bet big money on a horse race. Many gamblers can only get a thrill at the races if they bet more than they can afford. They also maintain when they bet big money, they are more careful and have a better chance of winning.

Big bettors have to be very careful how they bet because big money will depress the odds so they have one more dimension to worry about than the average bettor. These days too if you win more than $600 in a race, Uncle Sam wants to know about it for income tax purposes.

Everything has happned around a race track even the kidnapping of a horse. Three gamblers once kidnapped a Vanderbilt horse before a big handicap race. They got their ransom money and returned the horse. It was brought back on time for the big race but lost. The strange quirk about it all is that there is no law that covers the kidnapping of horses unless you call it burglary. Recently the TV show "Untouchables" wanted to dramatize this kidnapping but finally decided to drop the idea since the public would probably not believe an outrageous story.

But the horses are the prime reason for the greatest army of non-quitters in the world. What I mean by that is that the races inspire more people to quit gambling (and then start again) than any other game. A bad day at the races and I don't know how many times I've heard the loser say, "That's it. No more for me." And actually they mean it and sometimes swear off for a week or even a month but it takes strong men to stop forever which is a long time.

The ladies love the horses and the girls have come up with some beauts when it comes to betting.

The ladies constantly ask the men at the pari-mutuel windows for the wrong horses and then after the race insist on collecting anyway. Women are not practical gamblers but they are more discreet with their winnings. Men have a penchant for blowing their gains but the girls are much more conservative.

A girl I know has for ten years followed an ace handicapper of a Los Angeles newspaper. Like every other handicapper he has never had a winning season. None of them ever had. Last year she was ecstatic because betting $2 on every race, every day, she only lost $90. It makes no difference that she hasn't won, she just follows her hero.

I know a married couple who have each played the races for years, each going his and her own way. He knows a lot about the horses and is even friends with some jockeys but she has a better win average than he does every year and she just trust to instinct. He'd give anything to beat her one year but so far it isn't in the cards.

It is the mark of amateur gamblers that they never trust their decisions but always trust everyone else's no matter who it is. When George Raft was hitting it big some years ago many gamblers would watch him between races and follow him the the windows betting whatever he did.

After a while George realized what was happening and that the bets of gamblers imitating him were affecting the odds. So he hired a man to do the betting for him. But the gamblers got wise and followed his employee. George was too smart for them after that. He'd have his man make some token bets, while he'd sneak away and make the big bets.

I remember another time one of Chicago's big gamblers was hitting the races pretty good. He'd sit in his box and his wife would make the bets for him. She was a heavy plunger too. Well, the amateurs followed her to the windows and bet along with her thinking her bets were his. She had a bad streak and dragged them down with her. You see, her husband only made one or two bets a day and he usually won.

Perhaps you've been exposed to the horse-racing games

aboard ship. Six large wooden horses in multicolors usually with pretty girls aboard as jockeys are moved ahead by the throw of dice. If two three's turn up, the three horse is moved ahead two spaces. If one's the one horse is moved, etc. Obviously the odds are the same against each horse or 5 to 1.

One crossing a continually inebriated fellow was winning most of the races and he was betting big money. The dice were examined carefully but they were found to be fine. No evidence was found of any fixing. The man kept winning and the end of the trip a ship's officer couldn't help but asked him what he accounted for his surprising winning streak. Still drunk he yelped, "Sally." What came out was that on whichever horse a pretty girl named Sally rode he bet on. She was just lucky and it followed so was he.

I must tell another ship crossing story even though it doesn't concern horse-racing. One of our better known columnists crossed to Europe with his wife. He loved to play poker but was warned that many card sharks ran the ship's course and he was told to be careful. One night three men asked him to play. He told his wife, "I've been asked to play and they might be sharks but I just got to play— even if I am taken it'll be worth it." HIs wife took one look at the three men and screamed, "You could tell from 10 feet away they're crooks." Nevertheless the colomnists played. The first night out he won a little. He and his wife had a big laugh about it. They agreed the sharks were feeding him bait for the kill.

Well he won a little more in the second, third and fourth night and on the last night he brought along the amount of money he expected to lose. They played all night and to the surprise of the columnist he won a large amount on the last night out.

As they were preparing to leave the ship, the columnist's wife overheard two of the wives of the other players talking and one said pointing to the columnist, "There's the card shark that fleeced our husbands."

20

HORSE SYSTEMS

If you want a gander at what kind of advice is being passed out by "experts" on how to beat the races. Here's a recommendation from one "expert" whose name we'll leave out in deference to a fellow writer.

The System
Patience and Pyramiding

Patience—here is the system. Let us say we arrive at the track at the beginning of a thirty day meet and have planned to attend every other day. So we begin. We watch the totalizer on the Win Pool only until it is certain that, for instance, Number Three will be the favorite. We slip down to the two dollar window and bet $2.00 on Number 3 to win. He runs out. So does our favorite in the second on whom we have bet $4.00. So we go on the sure favorite in the third race and bet $8.00. He comes in and pays $4.20 for $2.00. That means we collect $16.80. Now we begin the fourth race with a $2.00 win bet on the number again on the totalizer, which has the largest sum after it. We don't win again until the seventh when the favorite pays us $5.00 to $2.00—by then we have pyramided to a $16.00 bet. We go back again to the $2.00 bet and lose the eight race. When we come to the track next day, we must begin where we left off, i.e., our eight race ran out, so we must bet $4.00 on the first race favorite the next day.

Where should we stop pyramiding? To my mind after a day of loses—a day that occurs so seldom that it could be made up if we had courage and enough money left to begin the next day with $2.00. Is it hard to keep books on this system at the track? Absolutely not. Just mark your next bet on the top of your program page for the next race, watch the totalizer record the one chosen as best by the entire attendance; then bet, and return to a $2.00 ticket after doubling up until you have won on a favorite. Go back to a $2.00 bet any time you win.

HORSES—ONE SYSTEM THAT WORKS
"PYRAMID"
(explained for horses)

2
4
8
16
32
64
128
256

This is a pyramid in the sense used here. In other words, you must build wider each step, once you decide what the size of the top will be. Build down so that you can support that top $2.00 bet.

Here is an idea for your bridge club. Why not save until the races come to town and make a run of it for a few weeks on ladies day. Save sixty five dollars apiece and then pool your money. Play the system as long as your money lasts. Maybe it will last all Summer and gain sufficient profit to begin the Fall Bridge Season with a tidy melon to split. At least there will be many happy memories and funny incidents to recall. As soon as your pool is all spent, you can sit and moan about this fellow and his crazy ideas! That's all right. Go ahead and rave! I have my own ideas about some of the hats you gals will pay $20.00 for. At least, the system will give you four hours of thrills, whereas a peculiar hat may be worn but once and discarded because it can be so easily remembered.

When you win a race, your pyramid is finished, and you start a new one. Always go back to $2.00 except when you do not get at least even money. The idea of the pyramid is to put a foundation underneath the two dollars, until you have won it back. When you have lost five hundred and ten dollars, your pyramid must cease as a total loss. Then shoot me, and start over again with a new day! No matter how often you win, always return to a two dollar bet after visiting the cashier's window.

Let me warn you about one thing: If you make a big kill and have to sign income tax papers and show your Social Security card, don't—I repeat, *don't*—hire someone to collect for you. It's done all the time, constantly. A man in a high income tax bracket doesn't want to lose 75 percent of his winnings, so he finds someone that is in a much lower bracket, gives him $100, and lets him collect under his name, so that that person may not have to pay any income tax at all or very little. It's easy to get away, but brother if you're caught, the penalties are stiff . . . both for the person collecting and the person winning. It isn't worth the caper, so take heed.

21

HORSES, HORSES

We hope during the previous chapters we didn't give the impression at any time that the bookmaker, the casino, the gambling bosses need some financial help or charity. To the best of our knowledge they are doing very well and will continue to do so. Where gambling is legal the men behind the cash have the front of a chain store operator or dress shopowner. They are respectable, pay their taxes and make a nice piece of everything gambled in their casinos which is usually considerable.

A gambling casino in the overall is not much different than a pari-mutuel machine at the track. The public puts all its money into a pool, the gambling casino takes its cut,

Uncle Sam takes some and the public divides up what's left. The casino does this at quicker intervals than the track (in dice about once a minute) but the action is the same. The casino, like the track doesn't care how the money is divided up among the players as long as they get their cut.

A bookie who is actively taking bets on the races has a policy, when one horse is played much heavier than another. He tries to lay off such money so that no matter what horse wins, he'll win a little. So it is in the gambling casino. The bosses would much rather have 500 people betting $10 each during a day than a $50,000 bettor betting the limits. With the latter, they could get hurt if things didn't break properly.

A small-time bookmaker suddenly found himself with a lot of money on a 30-1 longshot and found it impossible to lay off some of the money. The horse, *Whereabouts* was a nag who had never won but nevertheless the bookie was worried. But when his jockey was pulled off and Shoemaker was substituted the bookie really got worried.

He went to the track and watched the race. *Whereabouts* took the lead, lengthened it to 4 lengths and down the home stretch the favorite *Minute Man* started to creep up.

The bookie, moaning, kept his eyes closed at the finish. It was a photo finish and as the crowd waited for the result, the bookie, pale, eyes closed, sat waiting for the verdict. He was sure *Whereabouts* had won. The announcement was made. "Number 2", *Minute Man* is the winner, *Whereabouts,* Number 6 is second. The bookie couldn't believe it. He screamed and yelled and pounded people on the back. He was raving lunatic, he was so happy. When he was through hollering, the man in front of him asked "How much did you have on *Minute Man*"—expecting him to say, "Hundreds!" "Nothing," grinned the bookie and walked off leaving the crowd around him completely bewildered.

One old friend of mine played the horses for years. He was on the inside, knew when certain horses were trying and therefore made a few dollars here and there. But he got ambitious and wanted to run his own horses. So he bought a couple of nags at auction and now had the nucleus of a stable. He began to prosper and hired a trainer and put a jockey under contract. He had faith in one of his horses, "Black Spur" and entered him in a big money stakes race. The horse was on perfect condition, his workout times were marvelous, the jockey was a good one and my friend was sending him out to win against horses that weren't up to his class. My friend then bet a bundle on him to win. "Black Spur" came in dead last. There was no reason for it. The horse just didn't run. My friend sold his stable and is back to making a few dollars every day betting the races.

There are a lot of pretty smart horse players who say the tracks are pricing themselves out of the business. Admission prices have gone all the way up from a dollar to five dollars, valet parking and other parking has doubled. Food has tripled. The price of the Racing Form has gone up, prices of programs have gone way up.

If a man takes a girl to the track for lunch, he can figure it's $50 for the day before he starts gambling.

22

DICE STORIES

I first must impress the crap shooter that the only luck to shooting craps is to be at the right table at the right time.

If you should walk into a club and stop at a table where the dice are passing you are lucky, or if playing at a table for awhile and the dice start to pass before you leave, you are lucky. That is the only luck to shooting craps.

Now, what type of player are you? Do you know how to take advantage of lady luck? No? There are very, very few players that know how to take advantage of dice when they are passing, and that, believe me, that is the strength of a gambling club. This has been proven a thousand times, by the players themselves that run into a big hand, which means dice are making a lot of passes and numbers, which happens quite often contrary to what players hear that it is hard for dice to pass. Dice are passing sometime and every minute of the day some where in Nevada, but you the player have to be at the right table at the right time; before I started this Chapter on dice, a player won $93,000 at a club downtown. The dice passed for hours, by that I mean each shooter would make quite a few passes before he missed out, and it continued for quite awhile. This player was also a good gambler with his money.

During this same play another player who had $5,000 credit at this same club went broke, and he also was betting that the dice hit, the same way the big winner was. His only mistake was, he didn't know how to gamble. He liked to bet on eleven and all the hard ways. He would bet a $100 on eleven every roll of the dice and a $100 on the hard 4-6 8 and 10, so even when the dice were passing it could not make up for the amount of money he had bet on eleven and hard ways. This player plays that way all the time and loses all the time. Incidentally, this big player wasn't satisfied with his winnings, went to the Strip and lost the $93,000 at two hotels; the money was burning a hole in his pocket.

I was having coffee with George Burns one afternoon at our club where he was performing, and we were telling gambling stories. I had just started to tell him about a crap dealer working in the club who was $60,000 winner shooting craps and only started with $7.80. Just then this crap dealer walked by and I asked him to tell George the story. He told George that he came to town a few years ago and went to work as a shill in a downtown club and his take-home pay was $7.80, so every now and then he would shoot craps with it. One day, he walked into a club downtown and won $1,200; went to another club and won $5,000; went into a bigger club that had a $500 limit, as all clubs do not have the same limit, he wanted a bigger limit so he could now win some money. He played for 16 hours and was $60,000 winner and the end of 20 hours, he was broke. George asked him how much he wanted to win, wasn't $60,000 pretty good, after starting with $7.80. The dealer said I wanted to win $100,000 but couldn't quite make it. His parting words were, "I am still trying." He might get there yet, as he is a fast player with a short bankroll, tough player.

It is a funny thing, but it is very seldom that you will find two crapshooters that play and bet alike, they all have their own peculiar quirks and that makes the bosses of the clubs very happy. They like it the way crapshooters devise their own way of losing their money. As I have said, there are very few tough crapshooters and even if the dice should pass the club doesn't lose one eighth of what it should as not many players know how to take full advantage of passing dice.

Had a player come up to me one New Year's day after he made 24 passes and said, "I almost got even, that broke me up." I said, if you had only made 18 passes you would have quit loser to the hand. As it was, the club lost $100,000 to the hand. Three good players took advantage of the dice passing. When dice are "spitting" or "burning up" (which means they are passing and making a lot of numbers), the player now becomes the wise guy, not the bosses of the clubs, providing they know how to play. I remember years ago in a club I worked in, the dice started to pass and every player around the table was a tough player, up came a big hand and the boss said that's all, the game's over, right in the middle of the hand, had everybody cash out and said, "We open at nine tomrrow." The boss didn't want to get broke on one hand. This has happened in many a small club around the country.

Here in Vegas a player can shoot all day and the bosses can't do anything about it, just look at the shooter making numbers, smile at him and wish they could cut his arm off, or wish he would order a drink so they could put a mickey in it. Once the dice are passing the player who knows the game has the bosses at his mercy, he is betting the money and all the bosses can do is pray for a seven. I have said praying doesn't help. Dice are made out of celluloid, they can't see, hear or smell and above all have no feelings.

Nobody can fortell what is going to happen on the next roll, law of averages be damned.

I have seen dice miss for hours, also have seen dice pass for hours. In one club back a few years ago, the dice were passing week after week, big hands were showing quite often the bosses were going out of their head, they used every possible dice imaginable. After six weeks, they called in one of the top dice men in the country for advice. He stayed around the club for a week. Told the bosses that they had two alternatives; either close for awhile or if the club can stand it stay open and let the dice shoot themselves out and nobody can foresee when this will happen. The bosses who had been in business a long time decided to stay open and wait it out as long as they could. This dice sizz lasted another week and finally started to act normal again, the bosses started to eat again.

This happened just recently. A player was staying at a club, very friendly with everybody, played craps, one and two dollars at a time, nice upper and good all around fellow. One day he walked up to one of the bosses and said; "do me a favor, when you see me talking to your partner and I look at you, just wave, I am going to kid with him." The boss said O.K. Anything to kid his partner. This fellow walked over to the other partner who was standing next to the cashier cage and said to him, "Your partner said for you to give me $1,000"; at that moment he looked across the room at the other boss on the other side of the casino and the boss waved his hand like he was okaying it. He got the $1,000 and left. Nobody knew who he was, he was just a friendly guy.

A friend of mine suggested I name the book "Don't be Chicken." He is so right when it comes to gambling. Most players are afraid to bet, the dice could be passing and the poor crapshooter is now starting to bet less and less; everytime a pass or number is made, they lose heart and feel sorry for the club, so it seems to me, but the fact is that the average crapshooter is under the impression that dice can't make too many passes and the dice must miss sometime, they are now authorities on the game. These people are the type that tell their children it is very bad to gamble as all you do is lose your money. When a young adult asks their parents how they did in Vegas, there is a standard answer, Don't ever gamble. If a son or daughter asks a parent a question pertaining to 21 or craps they are hushed as if they were saying a vulgar word. Why a parent won't answer a question, I don't know, of course they can go out and gamble all they want to, but not their children. If parents today would use a little common sense they could understand that the young adults are going to gamble like their parents do when they are older. I am glad that some parents don't tell their offspring anything about gambling. How can you teach anybody something you know nothing about. Even if some parents did teach their children what they know, which could be put in an eyedropper, their children would have at least a fighting chance instead of walking into a club making bets that a six year old child would hesitate to make and lose their money because they weren't taught anything when younger.

When you bet you must give up some kind of percentage on every bet you make, that is how they earn their money.

In describing the game of craps, I must first explain what everything on the layout means, so that a player may have a better understanding of the game. But I want you readers to understand that by explaining the different bets does not mean that you have to play that way. It is only to give you a better conception of what has been happening to the players that wonder why they lose their money and in order to have a better chance for their money. They will have to change their style of playing to the right way.

In looking at a picture of a crap table you will notice that the numbers on both sides of the table are identical, so that a player can bet from any position he is in, as a table will hold from 15 to 25 players. There is a dealer on each end of the table to handle the bets made by the players. There is also a dealer in the center of the table to handle the dice. He is called the stickman as he uses a long bamboo stick or pole that is bent on the end to rake the dice in. Directly in front of the stickman is a long square box, in his box are what we call the propositions. The box is about 23" x 18". On top of the box is the word seven 5 for 1 which means anytime a player thinks a seven will show on the next roll, he throws or gives his money to the stickman and says seven, the stickman will place the bet in the box where it says seven, on this number the player only receives one roll. If a seven shows the player receives $5.00 for every dollar he bets, if the seven does not show the stickman takes the bet and locks it up.

Underneath the seven are what are called hardway bets, these are drawings of a pair of threes, fives, fours, and deuces. They are called the hard six, hard ten, hard eight, and hard four. If a player thinks the dice will make any one of these hardways they give their money to the stickman and specify what hardway they want and the stickman will place the bet for them. The hardway must be made the exact way it is shown on the layout. Example, say a player wants to bet on the hard six which are two treys, he gives the bet to the stickman who places the bet in the square where the treys or hard six are. That is exactly how the numbers must show on the dice when thrown, two threes. If the six is made another way, like a four and a two or a five and an Ace, also if a seven is rolled before the two treys are made, you lose the bet. This applies to all the hardways and you receive as many rolls of the dice as are needed to reach a decision, either the number is made the way it states on layout, or it is made the easy way, or a seven shows. The hard 6 - 8 pays 10 for 1, the hard 4 - 10 pays 8 for 1.

Underneath the hardways, are three, two Aces, which are two, two sixes, which are twelve, these are called crap numbers and are one roll numbers, quite a few players bet on these crap numbers when they have a good sized bet. It is called taking insurance on their money because if one of these crap numbers should show on the first roll the player betting that he wins, loses his money; when betting on any one of these craps you must specify which one you want as they are individual bets.

On the Strip, when betting on Ace-deuce, 3, the payoff

is 15 for one, on two Aces, the payoff is 30 for 1, on two
6's, twelve, 30 for one. Underneath the crap boxes are the
drawn numbers of a six-five which are eleven, there are two
boxes and you receive one roll when you wager on eleven
showing. You receive 15 for 1. Downtown or in other parts
of the state you will receive 15 to 1 on 11 and 3, and 30 to
1 on the 2 and 12.

Underneath the eleven boxes are the words any craps, 8
for 1, which means that if a player wants to bet on any one
of the 3 craps to show he gives his money to the stickman
and says any craps, meaning he is betting on any one of the
3 craps to show and receives 8 for 1 for every dollar he
bets. A player can bet on any one of these propositions
anytime he wants to, just give the bet to the stickman and
call out what you want to bet on. Remember one thing,
when you bet on one of these numbers and if you should
win you are always left on the numbers unless you tell the
dealer all off or all down. Example: Say you bet a dollar on
hard eight, two fours and it shows, the dealer will give you
nine dollars and you are still up on the hard eight, but if
you say all off or all down you receive $10.00. Many a
player has left the table after winning one of these bets
thinking they have all their money, and if their number hits
again the player is gone. You can't blame the club, they
don't know the player has left until they want to pay him
for the bet, and as we do not take the name and address of
every player, we can't send them the bet they have won.

Let me tell you about the big gambler who was considered a good crap shooter by himself. He always protected
his bet against craps, so he would bet a chip on two sixes, a
chip on two Aces and two chips on Ace-deuce, when I say
chips I mean $25.00 chips. This gambler has been playing
this way for years, sounds okay doesn't it, but there is a
slight catch to the bet in favor of the club. By betting this
way this so-called smart gambler loses fifty dollars every
time he makes a bet, and he has made thousands of them in
the years he has been playing around here. When he bets on
the 3 craps individually and one of them hits, he receives
650 and he is still left up; let us say two sixes show, he
180

receives a total of 750, thirty $25.00 chips; now he must put up a total of a 100 to cover the 3 bets again, that leaves him with a total of 650 left, but if he had put a 100 on any craps that pays 8 for 1 and one of the craps show, he would receive a total of 32 $25.00 chips, $800, and when taking the same bet he would put up another 100, leaving him with 700. He is making the same exact bet, getting full coverage and earning $50.00 more a bet, instead of losing 50. He just forgot to read the fine words in this insurance policy. As that is what these bets are called—insurance bets—when betting on craps, a player does that to protect his bet so if a crap is thrown he will receive part of his money back. That's very good, for the club. One of the biggest money makers for a gambling house is when a player bets on the propositions. We call it paying the overhead. In one club I worked in a while back, there was a big lawyer who we called crap-eleven Bill. He bet on craps and eleven every roll of the dice; he had plenty of money and he needed it. He was a one-man crap game, money and chips were flying all the time he was playing, but only one way, to the club; this player had lost one-half million, all on craps and eleven.

Just like the player that came into the club one day and asked me what the limit on the game was. I told his $500. He walked away and came back an hour later, started to bet on seven, bet one-two-four-eight, won a few bets, now he had a way to beat a crap game. He had won about $15, left and came back one half hour later, did the same thing, his chest expanded about 30 inches, looked at his wife like he just stole the goose that laid the golden egg. He left and came back 4 minutes later, he couldn't wait, as he was losing money by staying away too long. But this time he had a rude awakening. The seven didn't show, he bet 1-2-4-8-16-32-64, wanted to bet 128 but I told him the limit on seven was 100. You can bet $500 on the line. That was the end of him, he lost $1,400 beside having made one of the worst bets on the crap layout.

It is not necessary to further describe everything on a dice layout. It's too confusing for the ordinary player. By just referring to the dice layout when reading the chapters on the field, big 6 and 8, pass line, come, don't pass and don't come. You will understand more thoroughly the game of craps.

There is one thing I must impress the players to be is that there isn't a gambling club in the world that doesn't have a percentage on their games. They have the best of it at all times, regardless of what game you play. If they didn't, they could not stay in business. The player actually decides how much percentage the club earns by the way he plays and bets, so the most important factor about gambling for the player is to know how to make the right bets and keep the percentage of the house at a minimum, so you wouldn't be eaten up by the grind or "pc" as we call it.

In speaking about a dice or crap game, all players have their own way of playing or betting. That is what makes the world go round, also makes millions of dollars for the clubs.

A player walks up to a crap game for the first time and sees all the beautiful colors, white, red and green and says to himself, "Isn't that beautiful, just like Christmas colors" but finds out after playing awhile that he gave the party, not the club. Everything on this dice layout as we call the cloth the numbers are on, is not put on for decorations. Every number means something and is played by someone at one time or another. Some of the bets made by the player, the percentage is very high against him and he doesn't have a chance for his money, but not knowing he keeps on playing and can not figure out why he loses his money. He was beat by what we call, "hidden percentage", the player feel the percentage reaching into his pocket and milking him dry, because he doesn't see it happening. But everytime a player made a foolish bet and had to take the money out of his pocket and pay for every bet in hard cold cash, he would soon wake up to the fact that something is amiss. Example: If you walk into a clothing store to buy a suit, you know that the store must make a profit on the suit or they can't stay in business. That is fine, but you just bought *one* suit. In a gambling club the player makes more than one bet, some players make hundreds of bets during the course of the play and give up a percentage on every bet they make. Let us say you are the player that likes to bet on big 6 or big 8 which is a very lovely bet for the club, as you only receive even money, and give up a fraction over 9 cents on every dollar you bet, so if you were to bet $5.00 and had to reach into your pocket and pay .45 everytime you made the bet, you would soon realize how stupid a bet it was, also, if you like to bet on the seven and had to take over 16 cents out of your pocket for every dollar you bet, as that is what it amounts to, 16-2;3 percent against you. You would soon be out of money and out of your head. There are plenty of bets like this on the dice layout that the average player makes, thinking they have a good bet. Why, I don't know.

The most popular, exciting and fascinating game in a gambling club to play is the crap game or dice game. It gets the most action and that is where the big money is won or lost. It also is the best gamble for your money, if you know how to bet and manage your money. I will tell you readers this, that a crap game is much easier to play than 21; believe it or not, I have seen many a person look at a crap game in fright, they walk up to the table and see all the colors on the layout, money and chips flying all over and it scares the hell out of them. To be truthful, I don't blame them one bit, it is pretty frightening, especially if you don't know anything about the game. The game is much simpler and not as hard as it looks. All you need is a little common sense and money which nobody comes to Vegas without. They may leave without it, but never come without it. There was only one person that I knew that would come to Vegas broke and leave with money. He was called the Titzer, he would stand next to a big player and when the player would lose a bet he would shake his head in sympathy and go tsk-tsk. If the player won he would give the Titzer something. If he lost the Titzer would look for another live one. He has not left town without money yet, a lucky Titzer.

A gambling club is only interested in the player making a bet. Any kind in any game, and doesn't care which or how you make it as long as you bet some place.

Quite a few years ago the game of craps or dice was beneath the dignity of the higher ups. To them it was only played by the riffraff and wasn't cricket for high society to indulge in such a vulgar game. For a woman to participate in such a game was a rare sight to see, as a crap game was supposed to be a man's game, for men only; but seeing that most women wear the pants in the family, they now are trying to learn how to shoot craps and so far are not doing such a good job of it. I will say this for the better halfs, they are at least trying and willing to learn. A woman will walk up to a crap game and admitting they do not know and will ask a question once in awhile. The smart men will just play and wouldn't dare ask a question—it hurts his ego, after all isn't craps a man's game. But I will say this for a woman player, they have plenty of guts as I have yet to see a woman player that knew what she was doing around a crap table.

They will holler and whoop it up everytime the dice are thrown and then will say to the dealer, what happened, did I win or lose, after all if it is good enough for the weaker sex it is good enough for them. The American public likes to move fast and that is what you get in a crap game. Speed, all kinds of bets anytime you want to, you don't have to wait one second to bet. There are many ways for the player to lose his money, which he does. I have seen players make so many bets that they didn't know which ones were theirs, many a time a dealer would tell a player to pick up their money or call a player back to tell them they still have a bet on the layout.

23

DICE ODDS

There is only one bet in any gambling club that a player receives free. It doesn't cost him a cent to make and there isn't anything the club can do about it. I have mentioned it before as I must do again. If a club could find a way to do away with it, they would. This bet is called the ODDS in a crap game. You will never see any dice layout in the world that has the word "odds" on it and the less a player knows about the odds the better the club likes it. Out of the millions of crapshooters there are a very small percentage that take the odds and out of this small percentage very few know that the odds are free. It is what we call a "dead even bet." Nobody has the best of it. Neither the club nor the player. It is the only bet made in a gambling club that a player doesn't give up some kind of percentage.

Before explaining what the odds are, and why it doesn't cost anything to make, I must first talk about the pass line so that you will follow my explanation on the odds much easier. The pass line, as I have explained, means that a player is betting to win. He is betting against the house or club. The player places his money on the pass line and the dice are rolled. Let us say he threw a 4. That is his point. He must make the four before the seven. Now four is a hard point to make. Why? Because there are six ways to make a seven and only three ways to make a 4.

So the odds are 2 to 1 against the shooter making the four. Come hell or high water, you cannot change the odds. Let us say you are betting five dollars on the pass line. You can put any amount up to five dollars behind your bet on the pass line. That means you are taking the odds on the point four, and if the shooter makes the four you are paid even money for the bet you have on the pass line and are paid 2 to 1 for the bet behind. That bet you made behind the pass line is free. That is called taking the odds on the point, and anytime you get something for nothing in a gambling club you had better take it.

The only time your odds are free is when you have a bet on the pass line or come. You have already paid your percentage by making the bet on the pass line and as soon as one of these points are made, 4-10-4-9-6-8, you are allowed to take odds free, no charge and a dead even bet. The odds on a 5 or a 9 are 3 to 2 as there are six ways to make a seven and 4 ways to make a 5 or 9—so the odds are 3 to 2. The odds on the 6 or 8 are 6 to 5. There are 6 ways to make a seven and 5 ways to make a 6. So the odds are 6 to 5. The 4 and 10 are the same, 2 to 1.

As you see, the odds on these numbers are different, because a 4 is harder to make than a 5 and a 5 is harder to make than a six. Each point has an opposite. Like the 4—if you looked at a pair of dice with the numbers 3 and 1 face up, underneath would be the numbers 4 and 6—a total of ten, the opposite of 4, and pays the same odds, 2 to 1. If you looked at the numbers 5 and 1 face up, underneath would be the numbers 4 and 5, a total of 9, the opposite of 5 and pays the same odds, 3 to 2. So when I am referring to a number I am also including the opposite—which pays the same amount.

Every number on the dice has an opposite, outside of the seven which will show the same numbers up—seven on top and seven on the bottom. If at any time you should happen to pick up a pair of dice and the top and bottom are not opposite of each other, or a seven is on top and no seven on the bottom, get lost. You are in the wrong game. Only if you are a big strong fellow and have a few friends with you, you might get your money back.

In taking odds on the 5 and 9, which are 3 to 2—that is for every dollar bet, you would receive $1.50, for every two dollar bet you would receive three dollars, so you must bet even money when taking the odds on 5 and 9. Some clubs in Nevada, especially on the strip in Vegas, do not deal in half dollars and the smallest bet on strip is one dollar, so if you were taking $5 odds on a five or nine, you would only receive seven dollars in return, instead of $7.50 which is the right payoff. The club does not have half dollars on the crap table and would be silly to give you a dollar. They give the player $7.

This happens quite often to many a player, and I don't care how much he bets as long as the money comes out odd, the player must lose a half dollar. Believe me, those halves mount up pretty fast during a course of a play. To a player that plays long enough, it amounts to paying for his expenses and room.

I will give you another example. Say you are betting $25 on the pass line and the point is nine. You take $25 odds, half of $25 is $12.50 and 3 times $12.50 are $37.50, which you should receive if the nine is made before a seven. But no halves so you only receive $37—lost another half dollar. The player doesn't pay much attention and doesn't care. After all the point was made and he got paid. That's all he is interested in.

But you take the small player that bets one and two

dollars and loses 50 cents every time he takes the odds on 5 or 9 and bets odd money like 1, 3 or 5 dollars. At the end of the evening instead of being 30 to 40 dollars loser, he would be even instead of loser, if he had taken the right odds.

On the points 5 and 9 a player is entitled to take even odds and the club gives the player a little leeway. Say you have $3 bet on the pass line. You are allowed to take $4 odds in back. If you have $5 bet you can take $6 odds, and so on. Take all the odds the club will allow you to take on any number. It is to your advantage. We call it taking full odds. As much as the club will allow you. Remember, you don't have to take full odds on any point or number. You can take odds up to the amount you have bet on the pass line. Say you have $6 bet on the pass line and the point is 5, you can take $2 odds, $4 odds, or $6 odds, or you don't have to take any odds at all—which the club would like very much.

As I have said, the odds on the 6 and 8 are 6 to 5 so pay attention to what I have to say. This applies mostly to the small players, as they are the ones that suffer most with this bet. And there are thousands more small players than big players. This bet does not affect the players that bet chips all the time. Just the poor small $1 and $2 and $5 players who lose millions of dollars a year by taking the odds on 6 and 8 and not knowing the right odds.

I will start at the bottom so a player will understand what I am talking about. I do not use graphs, diagrams or a lot of figures to confuse you. Instead of using the word money, I will use the word "unit". It will be much simpler to understand. For every five units you bet as odds on the 6 or 8 you are supposed to receive 6 units in return. If you were playing in a small game and were to take 50¢ odds on the 6 you would receive 60¢ in return. If you were playing for pennies and took 5¢ odds on the 8 you would receive 6¢ in return. That is the correct odds.

Even if you were betting 5 potatoes as odds you would receive 6 potatoes if the six or eight were made. For every 25¢ bet you would receive 30¢ in return. Every nickel you bet you are supposed to receive 6 cents in return. As you notice, 5 is the key figure in taking odds on the 6 or 8. If you bet $1 you should receive $1.20 in return—$2—$2.40 in return; $3—$3.60 in return; $4—$4.80 in return; $5—$6 in return.

Now most of the clubs do not deal in dimes or quarters and the clubs on the strip in Vegas the smallest bet is $1. The player that takes $1, $2, $3 and $4 odds on 6 or 8 will receive even money in return. In betting $1 you should receive $1.20, no dimes—you lost 20¢; on a $2 bet you should receive $2.40—no dimes or quarters, you lost 40¢; on a $3 bet you should receive $3.60—no dimes or halfs, you lost 60¢. On a bet of $4 you should receive $4.80—no dimes, quarters or halfs, you lose 80¢. On a bet of $5, you receive $6 in return. That's fine and the correct odds.

The club does have dollars so they must pay you. Now to some players this doesn't sound like much money, but when a player gives up 9 cents on each dollar bet he makes on the 6 or 8 at the end of the trip, it runs into a little money for the small player and many a time it is the difference between a sinner and a loser. It is not what you lose when you gamble but it is what you save during a play by not making foolish bets. By saving, you may not realize it, but you are lasting longer—and that might be just the time for the hand to show. By taking the odds on a number, the player is giving himself a chance to win more money with a little more investment.

He will also win 8 times more money when a hand should show. You will never hear a stickman or dealer telling the player to take the odds. If they did they wouldn't last a shift out. If you are in doubt about how much odds you can take on a number, ask the dealer. He will tell you. That's his job. Don't be bashful. It's your money. A smart fellow once said, "Show me a happy loser and I'll show you an idiot."

24

WINNING DICE

There is only one way to gamble for your money at a crap game. That is betting on the pass line and come, taking odds on every bet you make. If you don't take odds you cannot win any money, and you are not taking advantage of a hand if it should show. Now if you are the player that is just learning the game or have been playing at the game, don't try to make as many bets as you can. It will confuse you and you won't know where your money or bets are. I advise the beginner to just bet on the pass line, take the odds and then make one come bet. Also take the odds. Remember, betting on the "come" is just like betting on the pass line, only you are looking for another point. So now you have 2 bets and that is enough for the ordinary player to make as he will know where his money is and won't be confused.

A "good" player will make a total of 3 bets. The pass line and 2 come bets and take the odds. He will now wait to see what happens. If the dice are making his numbers he will now take another come bet and if the dice are still making his numbers he will take another come bet until he has all the numbers filled. As you notice when making new come bets it is not your money. It is money you have earned from the previous bet you have won.

You never make a new bet until you have won a bet. Example: Say you are a $10 bettor. You bet $10 on the pass line, the point is 4. You take $10 odds. Now you bet $10 on the "come" and the shooter makes a 5. The dealer will place your bet on the five. You give him $10 and say "odds". He will place your $10 bet on top of your original bet which is called a "flat" bet but he will not completely cover the chips. He will what we call "cap" the bet which means he will place your chips half on and half off your original or "flat" bet. That signifies that the bet on top is "odds." You now have 2 bets, so you take another "come" bet and the shooter makes a 6. You give the dealer $10 for "odds." Now you have 3 bets and 3 numbers. You wait to see what happens. Your points are 4-5-and 6. The shooter must make any or all of these numbers before he makes a 7.

A very important part of a crap game that the reader must know is that all "odds" are automatically off on the "come boxes" when the pass line number is made. Many a player will leave the table not knowing that he has not lost his money. Let us say the shooter has make the line number 4. He now is shooting for another point or coming out for a point. He also has 2 bets on the come 5 and 6 and has odds on these points. The shooter throws a seven and is paid off immediatley on his line bet. Now the dealer will give you your odds back from the 5 and 6—ten dollars on each, but will lock up your "flat" bet or original bet of $10 on the 5 and 6.

Now if the shooter should throw a 5 or 6 on the come

out roll, you won't be paid the odds as they are automatically off, but you will be paid $10 on the original bet you have made as a seven wasn't thrown on the first roll. A player can call his odds off anytime he wants to. That is his privilege. The club wants a player to do that as they can't earn anything when he takes the odds. The less odds a player takes on a number the better the club likes it. I have seen players taking less odds and bet less as the dice keep on making passes and numbers. I have even seen some idiots quit in the middle of a hand saying, "I've got mine." How stupid can you be. Why quit when the dice are passing. I have seen players so superstitious that if a die would go over the table they would take their odds off and stop betting or if the dice should hit somebody's hand they would off all their odds saying. "A seven must show." Dummies! As I have said, dice play no favorites and are made of celluloid. Don't be one of these type players. Play the game the way it is supposed to be played. Don't be a guesser. If you guess you are gone. Take the guess work out of shooting craps and you have a chance for your money. Take advantage of dice passing. It doesn't happen too often to you.

By betting on the pass line and come bets, you the player are getting the best gamble for your money in a gambling club. You are giving up the least amount of percentage possible for a right bettor and still have a chance to win whatever you are beig enough to, if you should be lucky enough to be at the right table at the right time. This is the simplest and best way to play—not confusing to anybody. Actually the game of craps is much easier to play than 21—believe it or not. I am sure that many a woman will play dice after learning the couple of basic facts like how to take odds and how to bet on the pass line and come—which isn't very difficult to learn. Just practice at home first with a pair of dice or sugar cubes. Take the sugar cubes and put sevens on both cubes—like a 4 on top and 1 on bottom.

Do the same thing to the other cube and you have a pair of dice. Now practice until you know what you are doing.

I, CAESAR, INVITE YOU...

BACCARAT

• How The Game Is Played •

This ancient game is played with 8 decks of cards. The cards are shuffled and placed in a box called a *"shoe"* to be dealt.

Those participating in the game place a wager on either **Banker** or **Player.** Two hands, of two cards each, are dealt from the shoe. Later, a third card may be required for either hand. The first hand represents those betting on **Player**, the other those betting on **Banker**. The winning hand is the one which totals the closest to **9**. Tens, cards totaling ten and picture cards count nothing. Ace is counted as one, deuce as two, etc. If the cards total a two digit number, only the last number counts *(i.e.: 7 + 8 = 15; 15 counts as 5)*.

The cards are dealt from the shoe by those wagering on the game. The shoe is passed one person to the right each time **Player** wins or if the person dealing elects to pass it.

The hand representing **Player** is given face down to the person with the largest wager on **Player**. He then exposes those cards for all to see and passes them to the house dealer who calls out their total value. In the event there is no wager on **Player**, the cards representing that hand are turned up by the house dealer who calls out their total value. If no further cards are required, the house dealer will declare a winner. If a third card is required for either or both hands, the house dealer calls for it, face up, and declares a winner. Again, only the last digit of the total counts. In case of a tie, the hand is replayed.

Bets are paid even money but a 5% commission is charged on winning **Banker** bets. A bet on a tie hand may be made which pays 9 for 1.

BACCARAT
• RULES FOR DRAWING CARDS •

1. If:

Banker and/or Player has 8 or 9 on first two cards, no further cards are drawn.

2. If not, then:

Player having 0 — 5 must draw one card.
Player having 6 — 7 must stand.

3. Then:

Banker stands or draws one card as indicated by the chart.

BANKER'S HAND FOR TWO CARDS TOTALS:

PLAYER'S HAND	0	1	2	3	4	5	6	7
0	DRAW	DRAW	DRAW	D	S	S	S	STAND
1	DRAW	DRAW	DRAW	D	S	S	S	STAND
2	DRAW	DRAW	DRAW	D	D	S	S	STAND
3	DRAW	DRAW	DRAW	D	D	S	S	STAND
4	DRAW	DRAW	DRAW	D	D	D	S	STAND
5	DRAW	DRAW	DRAW	D	D	D	S	STAND
6	DRAW	DRAW	DRAW	D	D	D	D/S*	STAND
7	DRAW	DRAW	DRAW	D	D	D	D/S*	STAND
8	DRAW	DRAW	DRAW	S	S	S	S	STAND
9	DRAW	DRAW	DRAW	D	S	S	S	STAND

PLAYER'S HAND FOR TWO OR THREE CARDS TOTALS: (rows 0–7)

PLAYER'S HAND FOR THREE CARDS TOTALS: (rows 8–9)

* - IF PLAYER TAKES NO CARD BANKER STANDS ON 6

WINNING DICE

Don't just read about a crap game and decide that you are now a veteran player. Correct your mistakes while playing for fun because when playing for money and you make a mistake you must pay for it. You can't say, "I didn't mean to do that." Once a bet is make you have to wait for a decision as the game of craps moves very fast. Before you can open your mouth to say, "I didn't mean to make that bet" you have lost your money. So study and practice before you decide to play. It will be to your advantage and you won't have to pay while learning. That is what is happening to the most of the players that are gambling today. They are learning the hard way—with money.

What good does it do a poor player if the dice are passing at a crap game. He walked into the right table at the right time. He was lucky but it doesn't make any difference to him as he hasn't the slightest idea of what he is doing. It does make a difference to the club. They save money by the ignorance of the player. I have seen 15 passes made by a shooter and the table would be packed with players, but the club would only lose a couple of hundred dollars. Pretty sweet for the club. They breathe a sigh of relief when the hand is over because there wasn't a good player at the table to take advantage of that 15 pass hand. This happens every minute of the day in the state of Nevada. As I have said, the club doesn't beat the player, the player beats himself by the way he plays—lousy.

Here is a good example of what happens at a crap game. The table is loaded with 20 players. Everybody is playing their own style or doing the best they can. The dice start to pass but do any of these players know it. No, they just play the same way. Some might bet a little faster as they have more money. Others will start betting on everything is sight. Maybe 2 out of the 20 players might have a knowledge of the game and take advantage of the dice passing and bet more as they are winning. The other 18 players will win a few dollars and are very happy about the whole deal, but after the dice stop passing will continue to play and are in for a sight shock after they have lost their money.

Some players will even lose money during the time the

dice are passing by making foolish bets that they make all the time regardless if the dice pass or not. They are pleasure players. Just want to play at the game. This is what club owners like—players that can't stand to win or don't know too much about the game. The player will leave the crap game after a big hand, only winning one tenth of what they should, come back a while later, go broke and wonder what happened. How come they lost their money so fast? Most players at one time or another have an opportunity to take advantage of dice passing, but it reverts back to the old saying, "how can you beat a game you know nothing about?" A gambling club likes it when a big hand shows and the 1 and 2 dollar bettors are whooping it up. It is good advertisement but let us say that out of 20 players at a crap game 10 good players. Now if the dice should pass, God help the owners. They are in trouble and there is nothing they can do about it. This kind of advertisement they don't care for. They would rather these players were at some other club giving them the advertisement. Don't think for one minute that bosses of clubs don't sweat when dice pass and there are some good players at the table. They are human too—they don't like to lose either.

Some club owners are very superstitious. They will change stickmen, dice, dealers, boxmen, even floormen to try and change the dice from passing. One time a girl shill in one of the clubs shot up a big hand—made a lot of passes. The boss saw that she was wearing a blue dress. He issued a notice that no girl shills wear any clothes with blue or any part of them. Well the dice were working perfect and the shills weren't making any passes. The boss was very proud of himself. He told everbody that by eliminating blue it stopped the dice from passing. That is what the girl shills were waiting for. Another owner had them buy blue panties and knowing the boss would start to brag how he stopped the dice from passing. It was the right opportunity. Three of the girl shills walked up to the boss and showed him their blue panties. Even he had to laugh.

We had a player that would come into the club for lunch a couple of times a week. He would buy in $40 worth of silver and bet $2 on the line and $2 odds. He would bet $2 on the "come" and $2 odds every roll of the dice. He would progress as he won. If he lost the $40 he would go to lunch. He did this about 10 times and never won. A few of the employees would laugh at him and say. "pretty expensive lunch." But I told them one of these days they will laugh out of the wrong side of their mouth, as I had a little experience with this same player in another club. A couple of weeks later this $40 player came in and bought his usual amount of silver—$40, but this time the dice caught hold and started to pass. Nobody was laughing now. He cased out $2,400. He was a "tough" player as he would only lose $40 and leave, but he knew that when the hand ever showed and he was on it he would get even for many a $40 he had lost previously. He has done this many a time. The club has to grind that money out at $40 a time, but during this time he might walk into another hand. The only praying a good player does at a crap game is that the dice stay out a long time when passing. Many a time you will hear a player say out loud, "Please God just a few minutes longer" but not even knowing they had said it. Good church members at heart.

As I have said the "toughest" player is not the big bettor that comes into a gambling club and bets the limit of the club right off the shoulder, the biggest bet he can make. A club is not afraid of these type of players, knowing that the player can lose a lot of money and if he should win it doesn't bother them too much. But when a small player that comes in with 3 or 4 hundred dollars who knows how to shoot crap and take advantage of the dice passing, then the club doesn't like that one bit. They can only win a few hundred but lose thousands. That bothers them very much. The small player with a short bankroll who knows the game is the tough player. He is the one we worry about. So study and practice up and you too will be known as ta "tough" player. When the bosses see you coming they will say, "I hope the dice don't start to pass with this shortstop playing." "Shortstop" means a player with a small bankroll. If you play the right way instead of you having the club right

where they want you the club will have you right where
you want them.

Just because you see a big bettor with a lot of chips in
front of him doesn't mean he is a smart player. "You can
go to college a dummy and come out a dummy." He just
has more money to play with. There are many a big player
that comes to Vegas to gamble. They call it gambling—we
call it making a deposit, but can't withdraw. An investment
with no interest or dividends. That is what happens to most
big players who are very successful in their own line of
work but as soon as they start to gamble their cleverness
eludes them and they become run of the mill players like
everybody else. Many a time we in the gambling business
would say to each other, "How did this dope acquire his
money? He plays so bad." You would think that he would
at least try and find out why he keeps on losing and
throwing his money away.

One club I worked in Florida we had a president of a
Union playing. He would only bet the field, $500 at a time.
A very smart man in his own profession. He kept on losing
and said to the owner, "Why don't you raise the limit to
$1,000. How am I going to get even at a $500 limit?" The
owner said, "I will raise the limit—just for you, but
suppose you know you also can get in deeper." This top
man said very intellignetly, "Money doesn't mean anything
to me. I just want to show my friends that they can't win
with such a small limit." He was only $50,000 loser at that
time. He lost $50,000 more at $1,000 limit and paid it.

We had another player that would only bet on the pass
line. He owned a chain of jewelry stores on the east coast.
He would bet $500 and wait for the dice to pass. After
being hooked a few thousand he would ask to raise the
limit to $1,000. The owner would very graciously say
"Just for you as we never do this for anybody else." After
$25,000 later the jewelry man would quit. Now this hap-
pened every time he came to the club. He never won
because the limit would never be raised until he was at least
$10,000 loser. Many of you wonder why a club will raise a
limit for certain players. It is simple if a little common

sense is used.

Very seldom will a club raise a limit unless it is for their benefit. First a player must be hooked enough, second the play must be "soft" enough. These two combinations are strong enough to even make an owner of a gambling club walk the plank to get it. The above "field" player was only giving up over 11 percent of his money every time he made a bet in the field as every bet was even money. No double or triple on aces or sixes. The Jeweler betting on the pass line was a very "soft" player also. He never took odds so the club could afford to let him bet more on the pass line All he had to do was wait for a point and take $500 odds on the 4 and it was made. He would win $1,500 instead of $1,000 as he would receive 2 to 1 for his $500 odds. He also wouldn't have to give up a percentage for taking the odds.

Many a player will play this way and wonder why they lose their money. I can understand a player doing this a couple of times and then wake up to the fact that they are doing something wrong. But I see the same players come to a club and start right in betting the same way as they always do—like it was their first time in a gambling club. This is something I can't understand and probably never will. How dumb can the public be? How long will it take them to learn to play the right way.

Quite a few years back when I was working in a club, there was a top lawyer in that city that hated all gamblers as he was cheated out of a lot of money in a crap game when he was much younger. He would come to our club about once a week and only when he was drinking would he shoot crap. He would stand next to the stickman and nobody could touch the dice when he was shooting. He would drop them right in front of him—about 6 inches from the table. That was his style of playing.

We never stopped him because we knew him. He incidentally lost a couple of hundred thousand playing this way. The reason I am telling this story is that today if a player doesn't throw the dice clear across the table and hit the back rails they are reprimanded and sometimes aren't allowed to shoot anymore. If some of the clubs would have a little more consideration for the short player that has enough trouble making a bet on the line let alone shooting the dice across the table, they would have happier players. It is very difficult for even a tall player to hit the back rails sometimes as dice are not round—they are square and nobody knows how they are going to bounce.

Knowing the customer, it is very easy to distinguish a cheater from a poor player trying to reach the end rails. It is a fallacy that dice must get the "roll" as we say, in order for them to work according to the law of averages. As long as they bounce and roll dice cannot be controlled by anybody and it doesn't matter how far they are thrown. Even from a height of 6 inches as our "smart" lawyer friend found out.

A friend of mine has his own system on how to play craps. He has the patience of Job. He goes from club to club, walks around the crap tables and if he see a table that dice are passing he stops and plays until the dice cool off. He doesn't just play because playing the field or the proposition and they might be showing, but that isn't for him. He is looking for the chips on the pass line and the "come." Sees how loaded the boxes are, then he will step into the game. He is the only player I can safely say has the game of craps beat. But he has one other vice—he likes to bet on the horses, so he has to keep looking for hot dice to feed the horses. This friend of mind hasn't worked in years, lives like a King. His advantage is that he doesn't have to wait for the dice to get hot—they are hot when he steps into a game or he doesn't play. Many a time he would play and the hand would just be over, so he would quit. But many a time he would step in and the hand would stay out (by hand I mean the dice are passing).

So contrary to what people say that you can't win at craps, just try to follow this style of playing, if you have the patience, control and know what to look for. Many a player will say to me, "Why do I have to fight to get even? Can't I ever start off winner?" I will tell you what I tell them. Most players that come to Vegas to gamble will stay

2 or 3 days. In the course of this time they will play at a game or games 20 times. They might quit a game and come back and hour or so later and start all over again, and as most of you don't know that the more times you play the more percentage is against you. Also many a player will be winner the first hour or so they are in town, but how can they quit—after all they are here for a couple of days and won't have anything to do. That is why they continue to gamble and now are loser. They forget that they were a few hundred winner a little earlier. There is a player from Texas that comes in about once a month. He will bring on the average of $3,000 with him. He also has a credit of $1,000 in a few clubs. He is a "tough" player. He will start off slowly and if he should lost 5 or 6 hundred in a club will leave and go to another club. He came to our club one evening and had about $700, lost it and had a $20 bill left in his pocket, bought 20 silvers and started to bet 2 dollars at a time. The dice started to pass and after the hand was over he had $8,000 but he continued to play and at 6 in the morning he was $60,000 winner.

He quit a while later, winning $48,000. The owner of the club took him to the airport to catch the first plane out. He didn't care where it was going—he wound up in Los Angeles. Another time he came into our club with about $800 and won $18,000, made the rounds of 5 other clubs and won $100,000 and sent the money home and started all over again. He lost $5,000 and left town. He is a tough player. He can win the club if the dice pass long enough, but can't beat him out of too much money.

He is not afraid to quit winner, knowing that the more he plays the tougher it is for him to win. He only continues to shoot craps when he is a winner at a club, but once he is winner he never quits loser. He will put so much away and gamble with the rest of his winning. He knows that he is coming back again, so what's his hurry. I knew a crap-dealer, took his paycheck and walked into a Strip hotel and started to play small—5 and 10 dollars. The dice started to pass and a few hours later he was $46,000 winner, but didn't quit. He played a couple of hours more and after I had kicked him in the shins he quit winning $18,000. I had just walked into the club and knowing this dealer well, I knew he needed the money but he like to show off and I knew he would go broke. He told me that he was $46,000 winner but wanted to win $50,000. I said, "What's the difference? You just like to play," which was the truth. He has done this a few times. He would be 20 or 30 thousand winner with a short bankroll of 2 or 3 hundred but would never quit. He is a very good manager of his money UNTIL he is a few thousand winner. Then he tries to win the club. Now when he gambles and "gets off" a few thousand winner, somebody that knows him calls his wife and she comes out and takes some of the money away from him. He is afraid of her, which is very lucky for him. Out of the $18,000 I made him quit with, he bought a car and 2 days later he was broke and back working again as if nothing had happened. His biggest mistake when gambling was that he would drink too much and didn't know when to quit. But drunk or not he still knew how to take advantage of the dice passing. That is what I am trying to bring out to you readers. If once you know that right way to gamble, you will play that way regardless of how much you have to drink. All you have to have is the will power to quit when you are winner. Also you can win with short money. I have seen it happen thousands of times. All you need is a little common sense and management of your money.

25

MONEY MANAGEMENT AT CRAPS

As I have said and will always say, if you don't know how to manage your money at anything you do you cannot be successful. This applies more so to the game of craps. A good manager of his money will play and last longer even if he doesn't know how to play well, but a good player and a good manager of his money is a tough combination to beat, even if the dice are going against the player as he will not get excited and bide his time. Knowing that you must take odds on every bet you make, do not be like a player we had in a club I worked in in Washington D.C. He would guess when to take odds on the number. He was putting his brain against a pair of celluloid dice and the dice would 𝑑 usually outwit him. Every time he didn't take odds and the point was made he would shake his head and say, "No odds." So that became his nickname—"No Odds." He comes out here to gamble and does the same thing—guesses when to take odds and still shakes his head when the point is made and says, "no odds." When Palm Springs was open there was a big shoe man that would gamble quite a bit in one club. They had a $100 limit but this wasn't high enough for him, so they told him he could bet more but he must pay 5 per cent and if he wanted more odds that would be 5 per cent also. The shoe magnet said that that was fine. This poor sucker was paying even to breathe but didn't know it. It is a good thing that they closed or the gamblers would have been in the shoe business. There are many incidents like this that tend to make the bosses of gambling clubs breathe easy when dice are passing, knowing that the idiosyncrasies of the players will prevent them from winning at least half of what they should. I guess it is human nature for a player to hoard their meager little winnings and bet less as the dice are passing, but in business won't even hesitate to break themselves if the right deal comes along. If a player stopped to think that when dice are passing it's just like a sure investment as everything is in their favor. They are now playing with the club's money and if knowing anything at all about the game will take advantage of their good fortune. But I know that most of the time these players of the other side of the table don't understand or know our business as well as we don't know theirs. So I am going to try and even things up a little for the weaker side, as I am tired and disgusted of seeing the American public making asses out of themselves when playing in a gambling club. Besides it makes us look bad to our foreign friends, especially when you go over and fall into their gambling traps that are open to American tourists as they all love the "Yankee dolla."

Please let me refresh your memory as to letting your bets ride until you have reached the limit of the game. Just read the chapter on limits and you will understand why it is not for the ordinary player to do so. We know that the best bet for a right bettor to make is the pass line and "come". So the next problem is how to bet and when. I am going to take the guess work out of betting for all types of players, as every player will come with a different size bankroll. Just let me tell you that if walking up to a crap table and the shooter has a point, don't wait for the shooter to make or miss his point before you bet. I have seen many a number show in the "come box" and the shooter will never make the line number. Some players will wait not knowing they could bet on the "come" and will miss out on a lot of numbers. If the shooter has a point just bet on the come. It is another point. You don't have to wait for a decision on the line.

Here is how you manage your money and progress as you win. Remember, you must progress as you win. If you don't you will be ground out of your money. It is called a slow progression—leave a little and take a little. A $2 bettor must be careful when taking odds on the six and 8 as he must have a $3 minimum bet on the pass line to receive full odds, which are 6 to 5. That is if you are playing on the strip in Las Vegas. You must put $5 behind your bet on the pass line. That way you will receive full odds if you take less than $5 odds you will receive even money. (See chapter on odds.)

A $2 bettor must play this way—$2 on the line and $2 odds. If you lose the first bet, stay at the $2 level even if you lose the next 10 bets don't change your bet. Never bet more when losing. If you should win the first bet you now bet $4 and $4. $4 on the line—$4 odds. The next is $6 and $6, the next is $10 and $10—the next is $10 and $10—that is to give you a little more money to play with. After you win the second $10 and $10 bet, you now bet $15 and $15. That is a high enough limit for a $2 player to arrive at. Of course, if you the $2 bettor has a little more "guts" than most $2 bettors (which incidentally the game of craps is—how much nerve does the players have when winning— NOT WHEN LOSING) you can bet more as the dice are passing.

You will notice that after winning the second bet you

are now winner and cannot lose, regardless of what happens after that. Example: Say you are betting $2 on the pass line and the point is 5. You take $2 odds and the shooter makes the 5. You now have a total of $9. You now bet $4, the shooter makes a 6, you now take $5 odds and he makes the 6. You now have a total of $20. $19 from the second bet and a dollar left over from the first bet. You now bet $6 and take $6 odds. Even if the shooter should miss the next point you still have $8 left and still $4 winner to the hand. When winning, never decrease your bets. The only time you bet less is when you have lost the bet. Then you revert to your original bet of $2. This applies to all types of *bettors*. Example: You make a bet on the line and lose it. You still make the same bet until you win. Now you progress until you lose a bet then revert to your original bet and continue to do so all the time. Don't get mad or disgusted and bet more when the dice are missing. If you do, quit before it is too late—that will be your downfall.

Now after making a bet on the line and taking the odds, you take a come bet which is exactly as betting on the pass line and works the same way. You progress on your come bet the same way you do on the pass line—slow progression. If you have a fair knowledge of the game and can watch and make your bets without any hesitation or fear. You can take another come bet and progress the same way. Three bets are enough for the above average player, and he can win quite a bit of money at this rate and not be confused as to where his bets are. If at any time a crap shows while betting on the pass or come, make the same bet and continue the same way. Do not let the "crap" upset you. They are on the dice and must show just like any other number. A good player doesn't worry about "craps", all he wants is numbers.

A $5 bettor starts at $5-5, $10-10, $15-15, $25-25, $40-40, $40-40, $50-50. By $5-5 means $5 on the pass line and $5 behind or odds. A $50 limit is sufficient for a $5 bettor and it is applied the same way when betting on the come.

A $10 bettor starts at $10-10, $20-20, $30-30, $50-50,

MONEY MANAGEMENT AT CRAPS

$75-75, $75-75, $100-100. Plays the same way when betting on the "come."

A $25 players starts at $25-25, $50-50, $75-75, $125-125, $125-125, $200-200. Plays the same way when betting on the "come."

A $50 players starts at $50-50, $100-100, $150-150, $150-150, $250-250, and can either stop at $300 limit or if he has the guts continue up to the limit of $500. Plays the same way when betting on the "come."

A $100 player shouldn't waste too much time in arriving at a $500 limit. $100-100, $200-200, $300-300, $300-300, $500-500. He can afford to reach the limit as fast as he can, but he must still give himself a chance to save on the way up. Plays the same way when betting on the "come."

Here is a little warning for you high players. There are quite a few clubs in the state of Nevada that do not have a $500 limit on their games and many a player will get "hooked" in a small limit and even if a hand should show it is impossible to get even because they are in too deep and the limit will stop them. It doesn't hurt to ask what the limit is before playing. Many a time a big player will be a few thousand loser in a small game and say, "How am I going to get out of this mess?" We have a saying for players like that—"get out the way you got in." So be careful high players that this doesn't happen to you.

In playing this way you are now managing your money and saving while playing. You are now a "tough" customer and many a time instead of being broke and standing on the side lines watching the hand show or dice pass, you might be right in there betting it up with the rest of the players. Gambling is a very funny game—you cannot play without money. Instead of many a player standing and berating themselves saying, "If I only had a little more money I would have been on this hand." They forgot how they unconsciously threw their money all over the layout not knowing and caring of the outcome. By playing this way— the right way—you are FORCED to take advantage of dice passing and after a shooter makes the second pass you cannot be loser regardless of what happens after that. If the dice are "cold" and not making any numbers you are betting your minimum bet and the best part of it all is that you the player are relaxed and are not chasing your money. The only time you will be a "steamer" or "chaser" is when the dice start to pass, with the club's money and they won't like it one bit.

When playing, and the dice are sort of "staying out" (that is making a few passes and numbers—then missing out), you are now gaining in money value as the dice are making 3 to 4 passes and a few numbers. Do not be afraid to raise your original bet. You are now at the higher limit. That way you are taking advantage of the dice passing and are getting full value out of the club's money. If the dice should catch on and really start to pass, you are in the driver's seat. If they start to "cool" off, just revert back to your regular style of playing. Do not let the amount of chips you are betting scare you. They are in action and don't belong to anybody until a decision is reached. Remember this, in order for you the player to be betting any amount of chips, you had to win them first. You didn't wish them in—you won them by betting the right way. This is the downfall of most players—afraid to bet when winning. Don't play the Greek way—backwards. Don't bet more when losing. This is the ruination of most players. Remember in playing the right way, after the second pass you cannot lose to the hand. So take advantage of it and show some guts—bet when the dice are passing and believe me there is no sweeter music to the ears than when the stickman says,"Winner pay the line" and he looks at you with some respect as you are betting it up when the dice are passing.

I have seen many a player walk right into a hand and only need to pull out a $20 bill and win thousands of dollars. Just by betting it up and not worrying themselves in the process. You can win 3 to 4 thousand by starting to bet $10 and 10 if you should be lucky enough to walk into the right table and 10 passes are made. I am not even counting the "come" numbers. It has been done thousands of times by good crap shooters and will continue to be done, but only by players that know how to manage their money and above all by knowing how to play the game of craps where they make the best bet for their money and take advantage of the dice passing.

Above all don't give up. As long as you have money in your pocket you have a chance. They say anything could happen in a gambling club—it does. I have seen many a player down to his last bet and the bosses are now smiling and kidding with each other. Then lo and behold the dice turn for the bettor and before the bosses can say, "fire that unlucky stickman" the player is out and winner. Nobody is going to say what will happen on the next roll of the dice. They can guess—that's all. Let the guessing to the bosses, you are not guessing by playing this way. You are biding your time making the right bets and hoping the dice catch on. Many a time you will leave loser, but the time you do walk into a hand, I assure you if you follow this style of playing you will recoup many a previous loser. That is the strength of management and knowledge of a crap game. Play this way—don't go back to your old style of playing where you don't have a chance for your money. Learn how to manage your money and stick to it. Give yourself a chance to enjoy playing at a crap game instead of suffering after every play. Best of all when walking into a gambling club you will be known as a "tough" player and even some of the bosses might play your way. Amen.

ALWAYS TAKE ODDS. They are free—the only thing you receive for nothing in a gambling club.

26

WRONG BETTORS

Betting wrong or against the shooter or with the house as some players like to call it, is not in the players favor as some wrong bettors find out when playing in a gambling club. The "wrong" bettor has practically the same disadvantage as the right bettor when betting on the "don't pass" or "don't come." If a club didn't have some advantage on a bet made by a wrong bettor every smart player would be betting "wrong" all the time.

All clubs in any part of the world that has a crap game will either bar the two aces or sixes and will state so on their layout. That is the only edge the club has against the "don't" or "wrong" bettor. Here in Nevada they bar the 2 sixes. By barring the sixes means that you, the wrong bettor, will get a standoff if the shooter should throw 2 sixes-twelve on his first roll of the dice. You don't win or lose—a standoff. The bet stays there until the shooter rolls again. But if the shooter rolls any other craps like one and a two or two aces, you will win your bet. That is the clubs percentage against a "wrong" bettor and the club is entitled to it. If playing a friendly game at a club or at home the wrong bettor has the best of it because if any craps should show he will win the bet. But the moment the shooter makes a point, you the wrong bettor have the best of the deal.

If the shooter throws a five or nine the odds are 3 to 2 that he doesn't make it. If he throws a 4 or 10 the odds are 2 to 1 that he doesn't make it. If he throws a 6 or 8 the odds are 6 to 5 that he doesn't make it. So once a point is made, the wrong bettor has the best of it. The club will gladly allow you to take or call your bet off anytime you want to when betting wrong and many a player will do so if they think the number will be made. But a player betting right can't take his bet off as he has the worst of it once the point is made. When betting wrong, you must lay the odds on a number. A right bettor takes the odds, a wrong bettor lays the odds. Example: Say the shooter makes a 4 for a point and you have $10 bet on the "don't pass." If you don't think he will make the 4 you can lay $20 to 10 he won't make the 4. That is the right odds, two to one as you are betting the shooter loses you have to lay two to one against him. A right bettor would take the odds of two to one. He would only have to put up $10 to win $20 as he has two to one the worst of it. Neither the wrong bettor or the club has an advantage on the odds. It is a dead even proposition—it favors no one. It is up to the player whether he wants to gamble and try to win a little more money by laying the odds.

"Nick the Greek" is a staunch wrong bettor and will play for hours or days if necessary if he is going good and the dice are missing. All clubs welcome his business as he is an attraction and a famous character, but still dice have to be going his way. If not he goes broke for the time being, like any other player. I have seen him lose thousands of dollars, pulling money out of all pockets and never bat an eyelash—just chew on his cigar. I have seen him win thousands of dollars and his reactions are the same way—never batting an eyelash. Anybody watching him could never tell whether he is loser or winner. A remarkable man, his "well" never runs dry. He is always in action, but you can rest assured he is more loser than winner at a crap game.

There are many a died in the wool "wrong" bettor like Nick the Greek that doesn't think dice could pass. I worked around New York some years ago and there were quite a few fading games going on. That is where players bet amongst themselves on the points only. A dead even bet for either side. We had a fellow called "Sam the Carpenter" out of Brooklyn who had been coming to these games for years. He would lay $6 to $4 on a five or nine. He was a small player and most of the time he couldn't even get in the game and would have to bet on the outside of the table with the other small players. They would have to listen to the calls of the stickman to find out if they won or lost. This carpenter, who during the years would lose his $40 to $50 everytime he came to these games started to win and won $8,000 the first night. Now he found plenty of room at the table. The next night he won $20,000. He won every time he made a play at one of these games—even the bosses of the club were taking a "shot" at him trying to break him. At the end of three months he was a half million winner in cash, but that didn't stop him. He just liked to play and everything he did was right. Many a time as soon as he would quit the dice would start to pass. He got to believing that he could guess when it was going to happen, but like anything else all good things must come to an end. He forgot to guess when the dice would pass and was broke in a week. He never bought a pair of shoelaces with any of his winnings. After going broke, the next time he came to a game his first bet was $6 to $4 on the 5 from the outside of the game. He couldn't get to the table.

Another time a small gambler stopped at a Strip hotel a

couple of years ago and started to bet small on the outside, betting wrong. He would make two bets and lay the odds on both numbers. The dice were a little "cold" and he won a couple of thousand. He left and came back a couple of hours later and won $5,000. This continued on for 3 weeks. He would now bet $500 and lay the odds on two numbers and was winning 10 to 15 thousand dollars every time he would make a "laydown". He also would play at another strip hotel and was beating them. The bosses at the first hotel used every method they knew to check the dice, but nothing was wrong. This player was $250,000 winner—more money than he ever saw in his life. Did he quit? Of course not. He told a friend of his after he went broke in 4 days, "What was I going to do with the money? I couldn't show it as Uncle Sam would be after me." That was a fine answer, but he did leave in a fifty thousand dollar car—a Greyhound bus.

I once worked in a little club outside of Baltimore, Maryland whose owner was a bookmaker who had a couple of crap games in his horseroom for the players. Just in case they should win at the horses he would get them at the crap tables. He had the aces barred against the wrong bettors. Why, because he said that the aces showed more than the sixes. I asked him why he thought so. He said by percentages the aces show more than sixes and he being strictly a wrong bettor, he should know by experience. I know by experience that the boss is never wrong, and if a boss told me that a rooster could pull a freight train, I would hitch up the rooster. But aces and sixes are a dead even bet. I worked in a big club in Maryland that allowed a wrong bettor to either bar aces or sixes—whichever suited his fancy. We had red and black checkers for that purpose. If a player wanted to bar sixes, he put a red checker on his bet and a black checker to bar aces. Both bets are 35 to 1—there is only one way to make either one.

There are many players when betting wrong, will take their bet down if the shooter throws a 6 or 8 for a point. They say it is too easy a point to make so will try for a harder point. That is the height of stupidity—how dumb can people be. It is tough enough for a wrong bettor to get a point—any point, let alone take his money down after a 6 or 8 is made. Remember, you "don't" bettors, once you are on a point you have the best of it. Don't do the club any favors by taking your money down if a 6 or 8 is made. You are giving up nine cents of every dollar you bet, when taking your bet off the 6 or 8 and you, the player, can't afford to keep on doing that time after time. Those nine cents mount up to quite a few dollars after a few bets like that.

There is nothing wrong to betting against the dice. Plenty of money is lost as well as won betting "wrong." The downfall of the average wrong better is they chase their money after losing a couple of bets thinking the dice must miss. Sure they will miss—but when. A "wrong" bettor must bet a slow progression while winning and if he wants to lay the odds—fine, if he doesn't that's fine too. That is up to the bettor himself how much can he afford to gamble with. As a "don't" bettor must lay the odds he must have a little more money to bet with as he must win more bets than he loses when laying the odds. If a "wrong" bettor won a bet and lost the next bet he would be loser to the two bets.

Doesn't sound right to some people who can't understand why they shouldn't be even after winning one and losing one. Example: The odds are what makes the difference in laying or taking the number. Say you bet $10—they lose, the point is 4. You now lay $20 to $10, the shooter make the 4. You lose $30. You bet $10 again, the shooter makes a 5—you lay 15 to 10 and you win the bet. You are still $10 loser. A "right" bettor is taking the odds—just the reverse of a wrong bettor, on the 4 he is $30 winner at making the same bet of $10 and 10 odds and on losing the next bet at $10—10 would still be $10 winner, so there is a difference to betting "right" or "wrong." You use the same method of managing your money betting "wrong" as a "right" bettor does. The only difference is that in betting wrong you must lay the odds.

Dice are supposed to miss more than they pass and they

do. So if you are a dyed in the wool wrong better you too can catch many a miss out in a row which I have seen happen many and many a time and quit winner to the play. If you manage your money and bets the right way and just be lucky enough to be at the right table at the right time. But I must tell you this. A "right" bettor will win much more than a "wrong" bettor as the right bettor is getting more for his money and doesn't have to put up as much as a "wrong" bettor. I know, I have played both ways. Read the rules on management of money on craps and apply it the same way when betting "wrong." BET MORE WHEN THE DICE MISS AND LESS WHEN THE DICE PASS.

27

FIELD BETS

To settle a few arguments and controversies on how bad it is to make a bet in the Field. I am going to show and prove to the players and some smart gamblers who are percentage conscious that the Field is a much better bet than most bets on the dice layout.

When you hear a player say, "Me bet on the field? Do you think I am crazy? It's the worst bet you can make." He will then turn around and make worse bets than on the field. He will bet on craps or eleven, hard ways, seven, or Big Six and Eight. He doesn't know it but on some bets he gave up as much as 5 times more than a Field bet would be.

Years ago the field was a bad bet for a player to make as

THE FIELD BET

the clubs around the country made the crap layouts to suit themselves, but today gambling is a little different. It is concentrated in the state of Nevada where the clubs are very competitive and also want volume. So they have made it more lucrative for the player. Years ago clubs had the 2-3-4-9-10-11-12 in the field, and when a player made a bet he gave up 11 cents of every dollar he bet. Why? Because if any one of these numbers were made a player was paid even money. Today clubs on the strip in Las Vegas have the same numbers in the field but if the aces or sixes are thrown the player is paid 2 to 1 for every dollar bet. That dropped the percentage to a little over 5 cents on every dollar bet.

In playing the field in most any other part of the state of Nevada, like downtown Las Vegas or Reno, the player is paid 2 to 1 on aces and 3 to 1 on sixes. That drops the percentage to less than 3 cents on every dollar bet. Not a bad bet for a player to make—especially when they don't know much about the game of craps.

There are 29 ways to make a bet on a crap layout, but in any club where it states in the field, "aces 2 to 1 and sixes 3 to 1", there are only 6 bets that have a lower percentage than the field. They are the "pass line," "come," "don't pass," "don't come," and "placing the 6 and 8" which average from 1.5 percent on the place bets of 6 and 8 to 1.4 percent on the "pass" and "don't pass" bets. These are the best bets for a player to make in any crap game. There are 22 bets in the layout that average from 4 percent to 16 2/3 percent against the bettor and where the percentage is less than 3 percent in the field where it states 2 to 1 on aces and 3 to 1 on sixes. A player would be better off percentage wise playing the field.

The field actually is a much better bet than the big 6 or 8 where the player gives up 9 cents on every dollar he bets, the seven where he gives up 16 2/3 cents on every dollar bet and all the hard ways and craps and eleven where he gives up from 9 cents to 14 cents on every dollar bet.

It is about time that the "smart" players that place the 4-5-9-10 or buy the 4 and 10 are smartened up to the fact

215

that they aren't making such good bets as they are told or believe. They would be better off playing the field where the payoff is 2 to 1 on aces and 3 to 1 on sixes. There are hundreds of layouts like this in the state of Nevada.

There are 12 clubs on the strip in Las Vegas at the present time and they have 2 to 1 on aces and 2 to 1 on sixes in the field. There are 11 bets that the ordinary player will make and take the worst of it all the time. The big 6 and 8, all the hard ways, craps, eleven and seven. If a player that makes these bets would play the field instead he would have a better chance for his money—percentage-wise. That is how a gambling club is run—by percentage and the more percentage a player gives up while playing the less chance he has in winning. Consequently, the field is not such a bad bet for the players that are betting all over the layout and don't know where their money is or where it is going.

I don't want anyone to think that I advise players to play the field—I don't. I am just trying to settle many an argument that comes up when a player plays the field and somebody calls him crazy or an idiot.

There are only 4 bets to be made on a crap layout where the player will get the best for his money. The pass line, come, don't pass, don't come—whichever way the player likes to bet. We have a saying that goes like this—"Double up and sleep in the park." Which means, double up when losing and you will go broke. Don't let this happen to you.

Simple rules on craps:
Don't—bet any propositions
Don't—bet on big 6 and 8
Don't—bet on the field
Do—bet on pass line
Do—bet on the come
Do—bet on the Don't pass
Do—bet on the Don't come
ALWAYS—take ODDS on your numbers
Don't listen to anybody telling you how to play your money or how to bet.

Play this way and continue to do so. In the long run you will benefit by it.

28

FADING GAMES

I was working in a big club in Florida right after the war—a banking crap game. A few miles down the highway was a club on Biscayne Blvd. in Miami. It was the biggest fading game in the history of craps. I will explain the meaning of a fading crap game. It is a crap game where players bet amongst themselves on the points only. Some players will bet on the pass line or "don't pass", but the good players won't. They wait until a shooter makes a point then they start betting each other. Some bettors will take the odds on the point. Some bettors will "lay" the odds on the point. It is called "laying the point" when betting wrong and "taking the point" when betting "right".

It is up to the player whichever way he likes to bet. The "right" bettor will say, "I'll take it" for whatever amount he wants to bet.

The "wrong" bettor will say, "I'll lay it" for whatever amount he wants to bet. Sometimes a player will bet another player on the opposite end of the table. They just put the bet down in front of them and whoever wins will have the bet relayed to them. The table is much larger than an ordinary crap table. There are two stickmen to handle the dice, one for each half of the table. In betting amongst themselves the players have what we call a "dead even bet". There is no percentage against betting right or wrong. Why? Because nobody has to make a bet on the "pass" or "don't pass" line (where the club will earn a percentage on the bet) in a fading game. But directly in the middle of this large crap table the club will have 3 to 4 dealers with 2 to 3 hundred thousand dollars in front of them—all in cash. That is how a fading game is played—in money not chips. These dealers are there to cover any bet up to the house limit, any player wants to make. In this one game it was a $2,000 limit. This is done for the players that can't get down on a bet or want to bet more money so they go into the "book" which means they will bet the house and pay 5 percent to make the bet. Quite a few players like to bet the opposite of a point like the point is 5—they like to bet on the opposite—9. Some like to bet on all the points or the 4-5-9-10. All these bets must be made into the "book" or "house". Players can only bet amongst themselves on the point the shooter throws. The house doesn't care which way you bet as long as they get thier 5 percent on the bet. But the most you could bet was $2,000 on any one number. That was their limit. That was much larger than you will see around a crap game today, but the size of this fading game made it so. This fading game didn't just last a couple of days. It went on for weeks and millions of dollars changed hands. The top gamblers in the world were playing at one time or another. It was nothing to see a gambler lay $30,000 to $15,000 on a 4 or 10 or $60,000 to $40,000 on a 5 or 9. They didn't count the big money. It was a waste of time. They used packages of money. $5,000 and $10,000 in a package, and would just throw the packages to each other. Many a time 2 or 3 gamblers would combine their bankrolls and bet 4 or 5 players at one time. Some would have a man next to them just to watch their bets as they could bet all over the table.

A dealer who worked in the club at the small game (which got the overflow of the smaller players that couldn't get to the big game) would, on his break and when he could borrow money, take a "shot" on the outside of the big game. He was called the "Spanish Count" and was a desperado player. One day he got a little lucky with $200 and before you knew it he was laying $21,000 to $14,000 on a 5. The shooter made the 5 and he went back to work at the small game like it was all in the day's work. A gambler I knew from New York was also playing. He was called Ice—a very smart player. He never lost his head shooting craps. He was what we call a "hit and run" player. Win or lose a little and run. He had very good control and never was afraid to quit loser. He had ice water in his veins—hence the nickname Ice. He would play and grind out a few thousand and quit for the day. He was strictly a "wrong" bettor and if a shooter would make 2 or 3 passes he would lay off the rest of the hand or shoot. He would wait for the next shooter. If the dice still were making numbers he would quit—take a walk, get something to eat, or call it an evening. He also never drank when he gambled. One night he lost a few bets, and as we say, he got caught in the wringer and started to run a hand down. That was one thing he had never done. It was against his policy to chase the dice when passing. He had lost his strongest asset—the will power to quit loser. He lost $125,000 in one hand. He had accumulated this money in three weeks of playing by hitting and running. He lost it in one hour of playing. I saw him the next day and asked him what made him change his style of playing. He said, "Greed! I saw all that money and couldn't quit. If I had the nerve I would kill myself."

FADING GAMES

There are still some fading games going on around certain parts of the country, but they will never come close to this high-rolling game of the forties and there probably never will be another game this size again. The smartest one of the whole lot was a parking attendant. One of the gamblers, after winning quite a few thousand, quit and the attendant brought his car up. The gambler gave him a folded bill and said, "Here, buy yourself a Cadillac." The attendant put the bill in his pocket knowing it was a joke as the gambler gave him a dollar every time he came. Later on, however, he unfolded the bill to put with the rest of his paper money. It was a $1,000 bill. He knew it was a mistake but he said to himself, "I guess I might as well try to win the Cadillac." He walked into the club and up to the big fading game. The point was 4—he took 2 thousand to 1 thousand. The shooter made the 4. He came out with a 10. He said, "I'll take $6,000." The shooter made the 10. The attendant picked up the $9,000—walked out, got into his car and left. Incidentally, the shooter made 4 more passes.

29

ROULETTE

Albert Einstein, a pretty good man with figures, once said you cannot beat the roulette wheel without stealing money from the table. His contention was that no arrangement or rearrangement of betting would change the original 5 5/19% the house has against the player. Albert had one exception—if there were no limit on the table—and if you were fabulously rich—you could double a starting bet of a dollar until you won.

Considering twenty-eight blacks have been known to come up in a row, you can see where you might have to bet several million in order to win a dollar.

Enough of that.

ROULETTE

The point is, if we all would take Mr. Einstein's facts at face value, there'd be no reason to write such a book as this. Las Vegas entrepreneurs figure one out of every five players leaves the roulette table with more money than he started with. Let's say they're being too optimistic in their efforts to lure other players.

Let's say one of every ten players wins. We still must take this winner into consideration. How did he win? Was he just plain lucky? Does he win consistently?

We can't just disregard him. We now have found it is too pat to accept Mr. Einstein's theory that no one can win on the roulette table. Someone can win, even if he can't win often. But how?

How? First rule—in order to win, you must play.

This is one gambling game that praying will help the wheel player. Playing the roulette wheel is strictly luck and nothing else. There is no skill or thinking attached to this game. You bet on a number, sit there while the dealer spins the ball and wait until it falls into the slot with a number on it. If you have any chips on the number you are paid, if not the dealer sweeps the layout and you start all over again. One time a player in a club picked up a young lady and asked her to join him at a roulette wheel. She obliged him and they started to play. He was giving her money to bet on numbers and she wasn't hitting any. Finally he gave her a 25 dollar chip and told her to bet it on her birthday and told her that if she hit it she would receive $875.00. So she daintily put the 25 dollar chip on number 26 and up came 36 and she fainted.

Years ago the elite or the four hundred as exclusive society is known, never indulged in any other game but roulette. It was beneath their dignity to play such vulgar games as twenty-one or craps. One of the most famous roulette clubs was Bradleys in Palm Beach, Florida. They dealt mostly to the society people, if you were not known you could not get in. The wheel is very popular in Europe and the Latin American countries and has been the favorite game for many a year. Many a player has lost hundreds of thousands of dollars playing the wheel over a period of years and there are still many a big player around today that loses $25,000 and more everytime they come to Vegas. One incident happened a short while back.

A big player in a club in Vegas was "stuck" $50,000 playing the wheel. They would raise the limit for him as they could beat him out of a lot of money. He had to go to the men's room so one of the owners said that he would play for him. By the time he got back he was even and winner $10,000.

I have noticed that most of the big wheel players are old timers that have been playing for years as that is the only game they know. Of course we get quite a few system players at the wheel as they think they have a better chance at betting the simple bets that look like an even bet, i.e. Betting on the red and black or odd or even numbers to show or one to eighteen to show, or nineteen to thirty-six. All even money bets are simple to make, but they soon find out that they aren't even money bets—like betting on the red and the black shows up; they lose their money.

But there are also a couple of other numbers on the layout with which they lose their money if either one shows. They are the single 0 and double 00. If either of these show, all the even money bets lose. A rude awakening. There are 38 numbers on a roulette wheel—the numbers 1 to 36 and the single 0 and double 00. A woman bought a stack of chips but hadn't made a bet. The dealer said to her, "Lady, you have to make a bet." She replied, "I am looking to play my birthday number. Where is number 38?" That is par for the course. We are asked all kinds of silly questions by first time players that want to sit down and play the wheel because it looks fascinating. Money doesn't count as long as they play. One woman asked a dealer, "How do you play?" He told her to just pick some numbers out and put her chips on them. So she bought a stack of chips and as the dealer spun the ball she threw the whole stack of chips in the wheel as it was spinning.

We have players that will try a system on red and black. They will bet the red and black at the same time—only will bet more on one to balance the bet. This is a fine way to

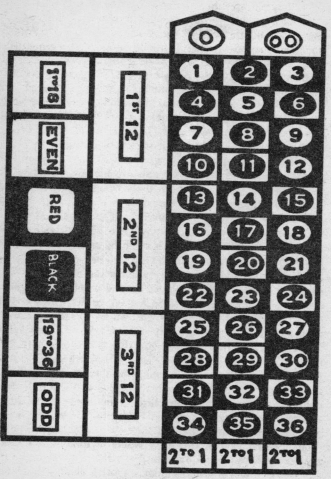

Nevada Layout—Roulette
(0-00 areas, green)

bet. They must lose one bet regardless of what happens, and if one of the green 0 or 00 shows they lose both bets. How anybody can play like that amazes me. I wonder how much they paid for the system.

Many a person will ask what all the colored chips stand for on a roulette wheel. There are six different colored chips and they are to distinguish to whom they belong to. When a player buys chips they are given a color and when six players are playing there are six different colors on the wheel layout, because if a number is hit and all the chips were the same color we wouldn't know who to pay. To avoid any arguments each chip has a different color and we know to whom they belong.

The chips have no value at all. They are used to play with. If after playing and you want to quit these chips must be cashed out at the wheel you are playing at. Many a player will take the chips with them when leaving and will try to cash them at some other club or at some other game in the same club they are playing and find the hard way, that they aren't worth anything. The player determines how much the chips are worth when he starts to play. On the strip in Vegas the smallest chip you can play is for ten cents a chip and you must buy a minimum of 20 chips—so that is $2 a stack. If the player wanted to play for higher stakes he could play 25¢ or $5 a stack or 50¢ chips at 10 dollars a stack and so on. Downtown in Vegas and other parts of the state you can buy chips for 5¢ or $1 a stack. There are 20 chips in a stack and that is how the bets are paid off in stacks of twenties. The roulette wheel is beautiful to look at. The colors are red, white, green and black as most of the wheel players are women. I think it is the colors that attract them and lure them to the game. Just imagine what would happen to a color-blind dealer—with all those colors and colored chips.

In looking at a picture of a wheel layout you will see that every number is squared off in a box, including the 0 and 00. In a wheel game, unlike any other game, the white lines that seperate the numbers all mean a different price payoff. If you bet a number straight up, which means you must put your chip directly on the number, it will pay 35 chips to 1. If you like to bet 2 numbers next to each other, you place a chip on the white line between the numbers, like 17 and 20 are next to each other, or 8 and 11 are next to each other. The odds are a little less. You receive 17 to 1. The more numbers you cover with one chip the less chips you win. If you want to bet 3 numbers with one chip, like 4-5-6 or 22-23-24, you place a chip on the white line where the 4 or 22 begins. If any of the 3 numbers hits you receive 11 to 1. If you wanted to bet on 4 numbers with one chip like 7-8-10-11, you place the chip directly in the middle of where the 4 numbers meet each other and if anyone of these numbers show you receive 8 to 1. If you wanted to bet on six numbers with one chip like 10-11-12-13-14-15, you place your chip between the 10 and 13 on the outside or end line and if any one of these numbers show you receive 5 to 1 for every chip you bet. Underneath the numbers 34-35-36 are 3 empty square boxes. They are called columns, and if you place a chip in one of these, that means you are betting on any one of the 12 numbers above where you have placed your chip to show and that pays 2 to 1 for every chip you bet.

There is one last bet made on the layout where you receive 6 to 1 for every chip you place, and that is the 0-00-1-2-3.

You place your chip on the outside or end line between the single 0 and 1. So you see you have to be careful where you place your chips and in what lines to put them on. On the outside of the layout you will see the numbers. 1st 12—2nd 12 and 3rd 12 and there is a white line that goes directly across the layout between each 12 numbers. That means if you think anyone of the 1st 12 like 1 to 12 will show you place your chip in the box, or the numbers 13 to 24 will show or 25 to 36 will show, you place your chip in the box and are paid two to 1. We call that betting the "dozens."

On the extreme outside of the layout are what are called the "even money bets." The odd or even number to show, red or black to show, 1 to 18, or 19 to 36 to show. Take your choice. They are even money. If you bet one chip on any one of these and you win, you will receive one chip in return.

Any time a player makes a bet on the wheel layout and wins, he is paid off, but the dealer leaves the original bet stay. The player must remove the bet if he doesn't think it will hit again. Many a player will bet silver and win and the dealer will pay them in silver or chips that are redeemable for cash, and the player will walk off leaving their original bet behind.

Before I go on, I must tell you wheel players that any bet you make on the wheel arrives at the same percentage for the club. It doesn't make any difference where or how you bet. The percentage will always be a 5-5/19 percent against you. Sounds funny but it is true.

Every wheel player has their own style of playing and their own numbers to bet on. Most good wheel players will bet what is called a section of numbers, five in a row or next to each other in the wheel head that spins around like 0-2-14-35-23 or 17-32-20-7-11 so that if the ball should drop around one of these numbers and bounce out it might bounce into a number next to it in the same section. Some players will just bet on a couple of numbers, others will bet all over the layout, as we say. Just keep on betting any place until the ball starts to drop and they must stop. Had a woman player who would bet 20 to 25 numbers every roll and if a number showed she didn't bet on, she would say, "I knew it, I should have had that number." After awhile I told her to bet on every number and she would have them all. She did. I told her that she would lose 2 chips on every bet she made as she was betting 38 chips and only getting a total of 36 chips back. She said, "I don't care. I am at least getting a winner."

There are winners at a wheel. It is just like any other game. Somebody must win sometime. In a club on the strip in Vegas two fellows were playing the wheel and were winning about $40,000. The bosses made them quit as they thought they were doing something to the wheel or had done something to the wheel earlier as some wheels aren't covered when not in use. So the bosses took the wheel head off and examined it from top to bottom. They also had the wheel leveled to see if it was off balance. They couldn't find anything wrong but are still convinced that something was done to them. The same thing happened in a downtown club. A player won $58,000 and the club did the same thing. Examined the wheel from top to bottom and couldn't find anything wrong. These players were just running lucky and taking advantage of their luck. They were betting 10 numbers a roll and hitting them. Many a gambler will say that if the wheel is off or not balanced right, it will favor certain numbers.

Where they got that idea from, I don't know. Even if a wheel is off what difference does it make. When the ball is spun, it is going in one direction and the wheel is spinning in the opposite direction. When the ball drops nobody is going to say where or what number the ball is going to drop into. Many a time on boats that had wheel games, the wheel would be at a 45 degree angle and the ball wouldn't drop in the low side. As long as the ball and the wheel are spinning in the opposite direction and it is a square wheel, your guess is as good as anybody's where the ball will drop.

We had a player come in and he started to bet on Number 5. He started off with a $5 a roll, lost $100 then bet $10 a roll, lost another $100. Now he bet $25 on each roll and lost $5,200. The five hadn't shown in 230 rolls. He walked out and we kept track to see when the 5 would show. It did—20 rolls later. This player had no chance to "get out" once he was hooked, because if the 5 did hit, he would only receive $875 and he would have to get many a hit to get even. The only chance those type of players have is when they hit the numbers in a few rolls—then they run. But they will stay until they are broke just to show the club that they can't be bullied.

In Cuba, in one club, they have let a player bet $500 on a number straight-up 35 to 1. Only 17,500 if the number is hit. But the catch was that he was over $100,000 loser and they could beat him for much more. He would need a few hits to get out, and it isn't easy to get them. Most all clubs have different limits on their wheel games. Some have $5 some $10, some $25 limit. That is on any one number. The limits vary, so if you have intentions of playing a high game, it is best to ask what the limit is before you sit down and play.

We have wheel players that are "tough" players, believe it or not. Like in any other game, there are the desperado players. They will come to the wheel and buy 20 silver dollars, play 5 numbers, betting $4 on each number straight up, and if one hits will spread all the money on the same 5 numbers, and if another one of these numbers hits—now the club is in trouble. He bets $25 on the same five numbers, and does the same thing if he keeps on hitting, when he loses he walks out. All he will lose is $20 and will win the "club" if his numbers show. That is a tough player, and the clubs could do without them—too dangerous.

Players have tried all different methods and systems to try and beat the wheel. I laugh out loud when somebody tells me that they have bought a book or system on a way to beat the wheel. Most all clubs will oblige any player with pencil and paper to play. Even give them free cigarettes and drinks, as long as they make a bet someplace in the layout. One of the simplest ways to beat a wheel is to try and cheat, if you can get away with it. As I have said, for every gambling game there is a way to beat it.

One of the most popular ways to beat a wheel is being done quite a bit in Nevada today. It is very strong if a dealer is caught sleeping or is busy. By sleeping I mean not paying attention to the game, and if it is a busy game the dealer is too busy picking up or "mucking" the chips as we call it. Many a time he will only pick his head up when the ball drops. That is what a cheater waits for.

One will stand at the head of the wheel, with a few $5 and $25 chips he bought at the cashier's window like he is going to play. The other will stand at the other end of the wheel where the high numbers are. As soon as the ball drops, the dealer must turn his head to look at the number, and if it should drop into one of the high numbers—that's all. Katy, bar the door! The cheater near the high numbers will in a flash move a $5 or $25 chip underneath a wheel chip on the number. This is done so fast, and these cheaters are trained to see that ball drop and move at the same time. Now the cheater that placed the chip will leave as soon as he does this. When the dealer is ready to pay off on the number, he finds a $5 or $25 chip on the bottom and the cheater standing at the head of the wheel politely says, "That is mine." Who is going to dispute him? Very neat, isn't it?

In the first place, anyone with sense would know that a player standing at the head of the wheel couldn't place a bet at the other end without knocking somebody over, or would need a long pole to reach a number in the last dozen, but when somebody is caught asleep, they must pay the penalty. Today most clubs will have the dealer put the $5 and $25 on the top of the other chips, unless they know the customer. If one is found underneath when a number is hit and they don't know the player, he wouldn't get paid. Another way is for a cheater to bet $100 or $200 in the last dozen which pays 2 to 1 and when the ball drops and doesn't fall in the last dozen, they will grab their money and run.

They don't have too far to go as the wheels are right in front in most casinos. If the ball drops in the last dozen, they stand there like gentlemen and wait to get paid 2 to 1. We counteract this move in our club by waiting until the ball has spun a few times, then the dealer will pick up the money and put some wheel chips in place of the money. Say the cheater bet $100 in the last dozen. The dealer will pick it up and put a wheel chip in place of it and say the chip is a $100 chip. That is the end of the "play." The wheel chip is worthless and if the cheater ran out with it he can't cash it out. He would have a $100 souvenier that cost 6 cents to make.

30

WHEEL SYSTEMS

It seems like all systems are tried on the wheel. Why? Because there isn't any thinking to playing the wheel. It is a simple game for simpletons to try a way to beat a game. The dealer just spins the ball and the system player bets and prays and if they are good church members their prayers might be answered, sometimes. Where these players concoct ways of beating the wheel is beyond me. I have seen the weirdest plays made and didn't think it was possible for a person to dream up so many different types of bets. If they would only realize that they all come out the same way, as most of the systems are progression bets. I don't care how they are started—that's how they finish. It all boils down to the fact that all systems are practically the same idea, only sometimes the betting is a little different. As I have said before, all a system does for the player is make their money last a little longer, but I have seen many a time where a system player has lost his money at the start of the system because nobody knows when the system is going to win.

There is only one way to play the wheel where you, the player, might have a chance. That is to bet the numbers, but not spread your chips around and all over the wheel layout. As the more numbers you bet, the less chance you have. The very good wheel players will bet about 5 numbers straight up. It doesn't matter what five you bet. It can be birthdays of your children, mother, fathers, dogs, cats—anybody's birthday or sections that are 5 numbers in a row. Talking about animals, a matronly woman playing the wheel was throwing her money around like it was going out of style, and drinking pretty good. I said to her, "Easy come, easy go. It's only paper." She said, "you are right. I own an animal farm. I have two big dog houses and one small cat house." That was the end of that conversation. Getting back to the wheel. In betting 5 numbers you are giving yourself a chance to win. If one of your numbers should show, you must add 3 or 4 more chips to the 5 numbers and if one should hit again do the same thing—just add a few more on each number. If your numbers don't show, just stay at your minimum bet all the time. Don't chase the numbers thinking they must show. If you do you are "gone". You must raise your bet only after you hit a number, not before. That way you are playing the wheel the way it should be played. You are in no hurry so don't get disgusted if your numbers don't show. We have a player that comes into the club about 4 times a year. He owns an electrical contracting company and only plays the wheel. He buys 10 cent chips, $20.00 at a time (10 stacks). His favorite number is 23 and he would what we call "star" it—that is he would bet 20 chips straight up on 23, 10 chips on the line between 20 and 23, 10 chips on the line between 22 and 23, 10 chips on the line between 23 and 26, and 10 chips between 23 and 24 (these are called splits) and 10 chips on single 0 and 10 chips on double 00. That was his style of betting. An investment of 80 chips or 8 dollars in cash. He would play this way all the time. He had a $500 credit, and if he would lose $100 he would quit for a while or if it was late go to bed. He would come in Friday and leave Sunday night. Many a time he would leave minus the $500, but he knew and we knew that he was a "tough" player. Because if any of these numbers hit, he would "press" up all the numbers and if the 23 hit he would receive $138—then he would bet $10 on all the numbers and if one hits would bet $25 on all the numbers, but if he missed a number in between he would start all over again—80 ten cent chips. He won $4,700 one trip and $2,300 another trip and many a time he would leave a little winner. He was and is a "tough" player. As far as we are concerned he could take his business to another club. Instead of us "grinding" him out, he is "grinding" us out and making us like it. That is the only way to play the wheel where you are giving yourself a chance, if you lose you are going down fighting. You may lose, but if you continue to play this way, we know that if your numbers should start to show you are in command and we are just standing by to cash out your chips when you quit. There is nothing else we can do but say to ourselves "tough player."

One of the toughest wheel players I have ever seen plays only one way and has been playing this way for 40 years!

He plays a dollar on 10-11-12-13-14-15 and 33 straight up. If you look at a wheel head, you will notice that the 7 numbers are almost evenly divided around the wheel. They are called "action numbers!"

When the ball starts to bounce, it must bounce around one of your numbers and with a little luck and a prayer, it might fall into one of your numbers. Whereas in playing the sections, the ball may be on one side of the wheel and your section on the other side. No chance for the ball to drop into your section. That is why these seven numbers are called action numbers." One of these is always in action.

This is the way this man progresses. One dollar on each number. If one of them hits, he bets three dollars on each number. If one hits again, he bets $10.00 on each number. If one hits again, he bets $25.00 on each number and stays there until he loses a bet, then back to one dollar again.

Boy is he tough!

He bets a little fast, but he gives himself every opportunity without hurting his bankroll. He has won thousands of dollars many, many a time, playing this way.

You don't have to play as high as he does. You can play with $.10 chips or $.25 chips, and progress the same way he does.

There is a local man that comes in for lunch now and then. He would bet 3 dollars each on the numbers 14, 17, and 20. He has lost many a time and he would invest $27—three bets on each number, but if one of these numbers would hit he would bet $25 on each number trying to get a repeater, which means a number showing twice in a row. He has done this a few times and walked out over $900 winner. All we could do is wait until he comes in the next time and try to grind him out at $27 at a time, because he will only lose $27—another tough customer. There is many a "tough" player at a wheel game, but the "soft" players outnumber them 1,000 to 1. So if you are or intend to be a wheel player, at least try to cut the odds down to where you will have a slight chance of winning. Don't try to abuse "lady luck" by playing all over the layout. Just play a few numbers and if they should hit, take advantage of it. Don't play any systems on the wheel—it is what we call a slow death and you can't win anything with a system. All you will receive is an ulcer, as it can become very aggravating when you have to bet a lot of money to try and win your original bet, because it looks so easy when playing red or black or odd and even. When any game looks easy in a gambling club, be careful read the fine print.

I have seen players stand at a wheel for hours, just keeping track of the numbers or colors—not make a bet and go home and try to figure out a way to beat the wheel. Then they come back to Vegas with a sure fire system, but it always seems to work out different when playing for money. It just seems that a player can't understand that what happened when they were keeping track or count in the past has nothing to do with the present. It is gone. When the ball on a roulette wheel is spinning it is for that roll only and nobody is going to say where it will drop. We had a player sitting at a wheel, not making a bet—just keeping track of the colors on paper. After 50 rolls he said in a loud clear voice, "The next roll will be red," and bet $100. Up came red. His chest swelled and he looked around to make sure everybody had heard him. He waited 20 more rolls then said, "the next roll is red." Up came black. He said it can't be and bet $500 on red. Up came black again. He sneaked out of the club. Another victim of the system.

Boredom

You've got to know your own personality in the games of gambling. For example on the dice table, there's probably 20 seconds between each roll of the dice, or less. On roulette, a little more. Blackjack is even faster as the cards go around the table, but in horse racing, there's 20 minutes or so between races. If you are the impatient type, and need constant action, stay away from the races. Time and boredom hang heavy and make you do things you wouldn't ordinarily do. You bet because there's nothing to do and not because there's a good chance of winning.

There certainly are gamblers who need constant action. You hear them at the dice table saying, "Roll the dice, let's get going!" Even if one of the dice goes off the table, they're impatient, and since many women are slow rollers, it drives them up the wall.

The same thing goes for the wheel, which starts off fast and goes slowly and slowly and slowly. In the meantime, they're biting their nails. They'd be happy if they could bet once a second.

New Games

From time to time, ambitious gamblers go to casino owners with new games they have invented—not roulette.

dice, the wheel, baccarat, etc., but something new. In all the years that people have been playing, no new game has come into being. Who knows? Maybe someday when we have a more intellectual society, they'll play chess or backgammon for money. But as yet, the time isn't right. However, I venture to say if you could come up with a new game and could copyright or patent it in some way, riches beyond the dreams of mere man would be yours.

31

QUESTIONS & ANSWERS

Remember the old question and answer programs on radio? Well, my job in the pit reminds me of it. I am constantly barraged by questions, some bright, some silly, but all illustrative when the answers are given. Maybe these questions and answers, real and unabridged, with their answers, will help you.

Q. Does it require intensified concentration to gamble?

A. I'd say yes. Though I must tell you than an oil man, one of Las Vegas' biggest gamblers, was playing high poker and at the same time playing gin with another player and also getting a shoe shine. And he won!

QUESTIONS AND ANSWERS

Q. In 21 do you get double for a "blackjack" in spades?

A. Not in Las Vegas, but for example in Reno some tables give you a $5.00 bonus for such a hand.

Q. What are the odds against hitting a $2,500 jackpot that has 6 reels?

A. Over 60,000,000 to 1 against you. Not very good odds.

Q. Is there such a thing as an off-balance roulette wheel?

A. Could be, but it wouldn't do the player any good. The ball goes one way, the wheel the other, it doesn't make any difference if there is a slight slant.

Q. Are there lucky players?

A. No just smart players.

Q. Are women better gamblers than men?

A. No usually.

Q. Would heat or cold affect the dice or the cards?

A. No.

Q. Are chipped or scratched dice crooked? I mean is that a sign that certain numbers will repeat themselves?

A. No. Casinos like to play with new dice as baseball teams like to play with new baseballs. But there's really no practical reason.

Q. How long do dealers work--or pit men?

A. They work in one, two or three hour shifts, get a 45 minute rest and then work again.

Q. Is there a best time of the day for players to gamble?

A. Yes, when you're fresh, and alert, not tired.

Q. Is it considered dishonest for the dealer to let you win?

A. It's dishonest but its done occasionally. Though there'd be few reasons why this would happen.

Q. How can you possibly say dice is a fame of skill?

A. Knowing first what to play and then the money management takes great skill. You can't control the dice but you can have an intelligent move for every contingency on the dice.

Q. Is there a 21 room?

A. No, dear. There is a Room 21 where you may sleep.

Or there is a 21 table where you may play.

Q. Can I pick a chip up off the floor?

A. Certainly, and you can keep it too—unless someone else owns it and catches you.

Q. What is the best game for making money?

A. Craps. The house takes the smallest bite.

Q. Is there any system at all in any game that's any good?

A. No. I'd like to open a club just for system players. I'd give them free pencils, paper, liquor, and food and I'd still make a fortune.

Q. Will dealers answer any questions?

A. No. Some dealers get so sick of foolish questions, they pretend to be deaf in one ear.

Q. Is the limit the same in most clubs?

A. No. In Puerto Rico, for example, its $50 limit on 21. If you go bad, you never can get out because you can't bet high enough to make up for your losses.

Q. Aren't most games just guess work?

A. No. You must have a style of play and stick to it. You shouldn't have to guess each move of the game.

Q. How about the crap-eleven that I hear many big gamblers say they bet?

A. It's a fast way to go broke. The house gets too much of a percentage on the crap and/or eleven.

Q. If you're losing, where do you stop?

A. In all the years I've seen people hocking everything they've had in order to make that last bet and get even, I've never seen anyone make it. Once on the toboggan there's no return. Down, down, down they go. My advice would be to stop playing as soon as you lose a few dollars. Go back when the table is hotter.

Q. Is there a "better" club to play in than others?

A. Some clubs give better odds. Actually you would divide the clubs into two categories—carpet clubs and sawdust clubs. Take your pick.

Q. Should I ever split 10's in 21?

A. No, never. Be happy you have 20. It's not easy to beat.

QUESTIONS AND ANSWERS

Q. Do dealers ever err?

A. Sometimes. There is no perfect dealer, everybody makes mistakes. Often dealers who shift from one city or from one casino to another, get mixed up in the rules and give you the rules of the wrong casino which often could give you a bad break.

Q. Who exactly are the big money players?

A. All I can tell you is that one night in the casino, a young fellow was betting $500 on every roll of the dice in the Field. Everyone was catering to this big bettor. Later we found out he was a bus boy getting $60 a week.

Q. When do you stop on a win streak?

A. You don't try to pick the spot. After a good streak stop after losing 2 or 3 bets. But don't be like a newspaperman friend of mine. He won about 10 hands in a row at 21 but said to me, "I think I'll quit—I'm winning on bad hands." Don't look a gift horse in the mouth.

Q. Are 21 dealers who lose money consistently fired?

A. Once in a while. Some clubs want dealers to find a winning average for the house. They expect it.

Q. What are cheaters called who hang around the dice table and claim bets that aren't theirs?

A. Claim agents.

Q. Really, how superstitious are big gamblers?

A. Very. At the Dunes one porter would hand certain players a towel and say, "Here's your lucky towel, Boss." He wouldn't take a tip either and would say, "If you win, you can slip me a little." Big winners have given him $100.

Q. If you are an expert in gambling, why aren't you rich?

A. I live comfortably and am a winning gambler. I pick my spots and don't gamble too often because I believe in control and self-discipline.

Q. What's a kicker?

A. I suppose you mean the extra card a poker player holds with a pair, usually it is an ace.

Q. If you ask for a wrong number by mistake at the mutuel windows can you turn it in for the right one?

A. A ticket seller will try to get rid of your wrong

number and if or when he does, he'll give you the right one.

Q. Will a casino sell me a pair of their dice?

A. No. They'll give you a used pair for the asking.

Q. Can a dealer fix the cards with a shuffle?

A. Some can if they want to. But why should they?

Q. What's the limit on a roulette wheel?

A. It's different all over. Usually $500 is top for an even bet and $25 on a number at 35-1.

Q. Do big casinos ever have losing days or weeks?

A. Yes. Even losing months. Sometimes experts are called in by worried bosses to find out why but they never find out anything unusual. Losses move in cycle.

Q. If I play every favorite to show every day, can I win?

A. Of course not. They won't pay enough money.

Q. What is the best method of play at roulette?

A. There is no best. But money management can make a difference here too.

Q. I hear there's a way of marking cards—like white on white that is very hard to catch. Would you comment on it?

A. Smart cheaters never mark cards. It can serve as evidence against them. They have better ways of cheating.

Q. Can you always split two pictures in 21?

A. Yes. If you split them you'd be an idiot, but its permissible.

Q. How do you know when a horse is going to try and win?

A. There's no sure way of knowing. Sometimes a look at the Form gives you a hint.

Q. Are jockey systems any good?

A. No better than any other systems.

Q. Are there any legitimate superstitions that have some bearing on the outcome?

A. If you believe you're going to lose because of walking under a ladder, it might influence your play so that you play to lose. Superstitions can only have bearing on the psychological, never the physical or mechanical—directly that is.

Q. Why in roulette does the wheel go one way and the ball the other?

QUESTIONS AND ANSWERS

A. So that there's less chance of any repetitions of blocks of numbers if something goes wrong with the wheel.

Q. Can bosses do anything more than worry if suddenly a dice table gets hot and stays hot?

A. One time about 20 people at a table were winning thousands of dollars. A floorman ran in to tell the big boss in his office. The floorman's question was, "What should we do?" "Are they our dice?" asked the boss. The floorman replied in the affirmative. "Then," said the boss, "we can do nothing".

Q. What happens if a man is caught cheating in a Las Vegas casino?

A. The State is very harsh with cheaters. He'd get a severe jail sentence.

Q. How many ways are there on the dice to hit a seven?

A. Six.

Q. Why are crap tables always green?

A. Because, as I understand it, green is easy on the eyes.

Q. Can a club close down a table if the dice are hitting big?

A. Yes they can. But, of course, they would create a lot of ill will.

Q. Can you ask the dealer to use a new deck of cards if you are unhappy?

A. Yes. And in most cases the dealer will oblige, though he doesn't have to.

Q. Is it true that some players with lots of chips at the dice table have some of them stolen.

A. Yes, by chip snatchers. The sad part of it is you never know it unless we catch them.

Q. Is it true men and women often leave their money on the table by mistake?

A. Yes, to the tune of hundreds of thousands of dollars.

Q. Isn't "Pass" and "Come" the same in dice?

A. Yes. But you bet on "Pass" on the first roll of the dice and on "Come " after that. They do mean you are betting with the shooter.

Q. Can you roll the dice if you are betting on other shooters but not yourself?

A. No. You must have a dollar on the line in order to roll.

Q. What happens as far as pay-off is concerned when two horses run a dead heat for first and you have a bet on one of them?

A. You win but you get less money than if the horse had won alone.

Q. How old does a person have to be to play in a legal casino? Are men's ages different than girls?

A. 21 years for both.

Q. Can you use foreign coins for the slots?

A. No. It's illegal. You can be arrested for it.

I leave you with a set of don't: Ten of them to abide by.

DON'T drink to excess when gambling.

DON'T be a wise guy when winning, you'll be losing soon enough.

DON'T be afraid to quit a loser. Take a walk. Don't ride a losing streak to the end.

DON'T be afraid to quit winner. A little winner is better than a big loser.

DON'T go overboard and borrow more money than you can afford to lose.

DON'T be afraid to ask questions. It's your money.

DON'T listen to everybody. Play the right way and stick to it.

DON'T play with strangers.

DON'T play a game you know nothing about. Learn first.

DON'T be superstitious. Knowledge will get you there.

IN CONCLUSION

If you know your way around Las Vegas, there are a lot of bargains and a lot of freebies. If you ask any dealer for cards or dice, they'll give you either free of charge. If you shop carefully, you can get a breakfast for 79 cents including ham and eggs. That's to draw you to the casinos. But you've got to know where to go.

It's foolish to drive your car up to the front of the hotel and have to pay parking charges. There are thousands of parking places all over the place. Hotels make sure of that. If you shoot dice, you can always ask the girl to bring you a drink, and it's free. You can tip her if you want to. That means any drink.

HOW TO WIN

In some of the hotels, the late night shows let you sit at a table where for one drink, a dollar or a dollar and a half, you can see one of the best shows on the Strip. If you are really a big roller, you can have anything. You can have girls, you can have food and drink and everything but money for gambling. If you're a high roller, there's no place in the world that treats you better than Las Vegas. You get the best suites, and the best service. Take advantage of them all, because the day may come when all you have left is six dollars to go to the races.

This is the cry of most people coming to a gambling center: "If you like gambling you must pay for it. We set aside a certain amount of money for shows, some for shopping, some for hotel and some for gambling. We are willing to pay for the fun we have on the dice tables."

That attitude will get you nowhere. Learn your game, practice on paper and then set your winning goal. When you reach it—quit.

Ninety percent of all players are stupid and ready to lose. The casinos have become fat and careless. They are ready to be taken if you are sharp and positive.

Study and then win.

EDITORS' SUPPLEMENT

[The following is a compilation of information
gathered by the editors of Holloway House.]

INTERNATIONAL GAMBLING

Gambling In England

In 1960, members of the English Parliament looked
around for a way to insure more income. Like many other
nations, states, principalities and municipalities they decided a gambling tax would be the least painful. For the

first time in a hundred years gambling was made legal in private clubs.

The law specifies (but doesn't always enforce) that games played must not favor the house. So the clubs, instead of getting a cut of winnings, charge "membership" fees that range from ten to fifteen dollars, depending on the exclusiveness of the club. There are taxes on games too. A single "shoe" at baccarat or chemin de fer, for instance, costs two dollars. In other words, you pay a fee but are even with the house on all odds. Some games of high stakes cost a considerable amount of money to play, but gamblers feel it is worth it because they play even with the house. There is no 5% take to the house, as in Las Vegas.

The clubs are big and swanky and depend a lot on tourists—most from America. They strive for elegance. The bookmakers are rich and respected.

There are a great many ways to lose your money in England. There are horses and dog tracks where you can bet with a bookmaker or parimutuel. Off the track you can patronize a cash-betting shop or telephone a credit bookie. There is bingo, roulette, slot machines, chemin de fer, poker, dice (popular with Americans) and blackjack. The Betting and Gaming act has had many consequences. Gambling in England has increased from under two billion to almost five billion. The horses still account for the most money bet.

Also, gambling is no longer a source of police corruption. Gamblers admit to constant bribery before legalized gambling. Food and drink are free and, at this point, the English government is realizing enough to pay for their defense budget.

Cash-betting shops have sprung up all over. Their sign "Licensed Betting Office" is limited by law to letters three inches high. But the shops get around this by using the term Turf Accountant. This lettering is often two feet high next to the small print. Most betting shops have cashier windows and counters for writing betting slips. There is a blackboard for prices and a "blower" describing races and track information. Betting shops keep hours like any other shop.

Old age pensioners use these shops almost as a club. Someone brings in bets from everyone else in the office. Some of these shops existed illegally before the gambling act and didn't do near the business. It is estimated that about 15,000 betting shops do business in Britain. No matter where you go there is some kind of shop. There are even betting shops on boats. There are also betting shops just for women, appropriately decorated, though surveys show women are generally interested in just bingo. Bingo is so popular (like all games, a membership fee is charged) that many movie houses and ballrooms have been turned into bingo parlors. Even the blind play with Braille boards.

One Parliament member says that when they legalized gambling it was thought there would only be a few clubs because there wouldn't be much profit in just membership fees. The ingenuity of the owners, however, triumphed by charging a fee per game.

While there are plush clubs however, the largest concentration of clubs is in the poorer neighborhoods. Since gambling has always been pigeon-holed as in sin, churchgoers explain that gambling is an extension of life and both are terribly uncertain.

Because of gambling, the National Union of Small Shopkeepers in Britain says its members have experienced a ten percent rise in bad debts since the act went into effect. The executives feel people are inclined to forego paying routine bills in favor of gambling.

But it isn't only the poor who are gambling. It is said the Queen has a footman bring her the race results every day. The wealthy who once streamed over the Channel to gamble in other countries now gamble at home.

A Royal Commission estimates that in any given day four of five families have something going in some gambling game when it was forbidden. But of course that is a fault of human nature.

The few who don't gamble are vociferous about gambling being born of either avarice or idleness. They in no way influence gamblers. For the in-betweens who, for moral reasons, can't see themselves betting on dice or roulette, they can place a pound or so on dominoes, crib-bage, darts or bar-billiards. Somehow they look on these games as less sinful, even though they are wagering.

The gambling act has in no way interfered with the lotteries. An Englishman can still bet a penny in a soccer pool and win a half-million.

While Americans take a beating in London clubs, there are exceptions. There is an unfounded story of a wealthy Texan making a big killing at the Pair of Shoes Club, which has since closed. He asked if he could make a single bet much over the house limit. The answer was, "You already own the first and second floor. You might as well own the third floor too." He crapped out though. The club owners of London say behind closed doors that the idea is to bleed the Americans as quickly as possible without spilling any of it on the floor.

The largest recorded win in English gambling history was a soccer pool win of $947,000. The winner was Percy Harrison, a motorman. What did he say when he accepted the check? "I'm sorry I got the money in the winter instead of the spring. I could have so much more fun in the spring and I feel better too."

The London clubs don't always win though. Much of their action is from sporting events. During a recent severe winter, for eleven weeks there were no sports and therefore no gambling. It was a tough time for the bosses.

England's most esteemed psychologists say competitive types of men favor man-against-man games such as black jack; intellectual types and women prefer more passive pursuits such as roulette; craps with its rattles, pitches and shouts of "Baby needs shoes!" attracts the assertive male. As for horseplayers, according to one sociologist, they like to bet long shots to assert their ability to make individual decisions in a depersonalized society.

Most clubs have had a problem over roulette. The Gaming Act says every game must be equally favorable to all players. Contrary to American roulette tables, the wheels in England have only one zero, and the house relies on seat money for additional profits. Some clubs in England allow he player to take the bank, but as you might guess, they seldom do, as a sizable bankroll would be required. So roulette has caused a problem. No one has yet to come up with any solution. However, roulette continues to be the most popular game in England and all of Europe.

Is British gambling 100% honest? No. There have been arrests for rigged wheels and loaded dice. But it is agreed that it is 99% honest, which is pretty good.

Gambling in Central Europe

Most of the casinos of Europe are respectable and middle-class. For example there is a sprawling mustard-colored casino at Bad Neuenahr on the Ahr River in Germany. Most of the people gambling there are middle-aged and not dressed in modern fashion. The most popular drink in the casino is mineral water. A few drink wine. Roulette is the most popular game. Betting pools and slot machines are common throughout West Germany.

There is a sign in Bad Neuenahr casino which is meant to salve the conscience of the religious. It reads: "The church has larger sins than gambling to worry about."

Casinos are illegal in Lower Saxony, North Rhine, Westphalia, Hamburg and Bremen, but there are thirteen licensed casinos in the rest of the country that net 75,000,000 a year. The average loss per person is $15, very small when compared to the average $50 loss per person in Las Vegas. The casino bosses boast that they haven't had any scandals or suicides in 20 years.

A fat, jolly German walked into a casino with a lovely but vacuous blonde. He seemed self-conscious and felt it necessary to announce, "I'm just trying to prove that gambling is not a substitute for sex."

In other parts of Europe all you need to get into the casinos is your passport and an entrance fee of about two dollars. In many cases, you have to sign a statement saying you'll follow house rules. You are not required to give tips, but the glares from the croupier will make you wish you had.

251

The Deauville Casino on the Normandy coast attracts the Riviera crowd in late summer. The requirements here are dinner jackets and evening gowns. Some of the Deauville casinos have fashion shows and it is strange to see a parade of the most beautiful girls in the world and men not even turning around from the tables to look at them. Closer to Paris is the casino at Enghien-les-Bains.

The top Italian casino is the Lido, off Venice and the Adriatic. That's for the summer. In winter the action moves to the Palazzo Vendranin on the Grand Canal. At a poker table in Lido a raise of the equivalent of $1,000 was made in an open poker game. The player hesitated as to whether to see the raise. An onlooker whispered, "If he's a German he'll throw his cards down and walk out. If he's French he'll see the raise. If he's Italian he'll raise no matter what he has." The man raised. Later the onlooker asked the man what nationality he was. He was Italian.

Then there's San Remo on the Ligurian Coast and Saint Vincent, north of Milan. Saint Vincent is also a health resort so if you ruin your health gambling at night you can build it up during the day at the baths.

There is gambling in Switzerland; however, it tends to be rather limited. The major casino is in Lucerne, but even that is small compared to those in other countries. The players chat with the croupier during the game and the evening is a social affair rather than a money-making event. Across Lake Lugano there are three popular small casinos: Campione d'Italia, Evian-les-Bains Di-vonne and Annecy.

Austria has many casinos. Some are large and beautiful some just an Alpine hut. The most formal are Vienna's Le Palais and Salzburg's Mirabell Castle. Bad-Gastein and Seebaden are more casual.

Two games are the mainstay of all these casinos—roulette and baccarat. The minimum bets are small.

Gambling In Eastern Europe

Marxist Eastern Europe is hot with gambling. It is one o the biggest businesses in the Communist bloc. The take i more than $1 billion a year.

It was originally held by the Red bosses that gambling was bad for Socialists—they should keep their noses to the grindstone and not to the wheel. But now gambling is legal and everyone approves. Racing in particular is popular and most bettors watch the morning line more than the party line.

In Yugoslavia the gambling fever is so high a newspaper editorial said the national flag should have two crossed croupier rakes on a green baize background. In parts of Yugoslavia many men on employment contracts put "gambler" as their occupation. It is not a stigma in this country.

Gambling in Yugoslavia is a state monopoly. The government take is high, sometimes as much as 50% (the maximum in Las Vegas is 22%). When there are complaints over this high take it is pointed out that the schools and libraries were all built with gambling profits. Czechoslovakia and Poland also have the gambling fever.

In Hungary, the biggest form of gambling entertainment is the lottery. The government does not give a lottery winner a chance to abscond with all his winnings. The governmental take is deducted before the winner gets his check.

Police in Hungary have printed lists of professional gamblers. These gamblers must wear a button to designate themselves as pros when they enter a casino.

Yugoslavia has twelve casinos at this writing. In some casinos, local people are not allowed. The government only wants to take tourists.

There have been some scandals in these Eastern European countries. For example, in a private casino in Budapest an extra prize at the roulette table was a nude airline hostess covered with chocolate. But all of this is excused by party leaders with "But look at the rewards for the state."

Gambling In Macao

Slowly, as Macao does add a touch of glamour, tourists come in to try their luck. When city fathers ordered the town glamorized, many of the citizens painted everything they had red. That was their idea of glamour. Casino owners say they are trying to imitate Las Vegas more than Monte Carlo, so the new Macao should be modern. Owners boast that not only do they have gambling but that it is served up amidst Portuguese charm and Chinese mystery.

The plan is to have a regular run of hydroplanes from Hong Kong to Macao. It takes forty minutes. Right now it is felt that it will take $5,000,000 to clean up the town.

In Macao there are natives, often doped on opium, who for a small fee will tell you what the next number on the roulette wheel will be. It doesn't come up right more than anyone else's guess but these "soothsayers" can still make a living from the superstitious.

The rich who have returned from some of the gambling in Macao shake their heads in wonderment saying, "This is one place where money is everything." The poor will offer to entertain winners by cutting off toes or fingers. Occasionally they find a sadist who goes for the horror.

Some of the religious sects in Macao do not allow their constituents to gamble. To enforce it, you will occasionally see priests standing near casinos to see that none of their congregation enters.

Gambling In The Caribbean

Most of the big islands of the Caribbean have race tracks, lotteries, cock fights and roulette wheels. A few have dice. Much of the Caribbean gambling grew up because Castro banned casinos in Cuba. Employees of Havana's gambling houses hastened to other islands. Under Batista, gambling casinos had flourished in Cuba, but under Castro, our sources of information indicate they are no longer open.

So gambling flourishes in Puerto Rico.

Gambling here is strictly supervised. Before granting licenses the government screens operators carefully. They must attend croupier's school and never gamble on the island. Inspectors open every pack of cards, okay every pair of dice and see that the limit of betting is strictly enforced.

There is the same strict surveillance in the Dominican Republic. Only here Americans run the exclusive casinos.

In Panama the government has a monopoly and the big casino is on the roof of the Panama Hilton.

Though this kind of gambling is on a level with Las Vegas with all the flourish and facade of class, superstition still runs in the undercurrent. For example, in the croupier schools a close eye is kept on each student. They try to have students emulate the know-how and friendliness of Las Vegas dealers, as it obviously means a greater turnover of dollars for the house.

It is said on the Island that while officially cheating gets a prison term of a year or so, it really means death. Somehow cheaters are usually found dead or badly beaten in prison.

In Panama one of the most sought after jobs is that of inspector of gambling. No one is respected more than an inspector of gambling.

When Batista ran the gambling in Havana, Americans flocked to the island from Miami. It was part of the tour. It was said that of every dollar gambled, Batista and his henchmen got five cents. Yet it was not unusual for a winner to put money on a past line for himself and then put down a bet for Batista.

Though Castro obliterated the beautiful casinos of Havana, it is said that Castro was an iron-nerved gambler himself who was once a consistent winner at cards.

The one underlying superstition that all island natives abide by is that it is terribly unlucky to bet winnings from cock fights on the horses. However, it is all right to reverse the procedure.

Old Las Vegas pros run the casinos in the Netherlands Antilles. Business is booming in Haiti and a new casino is being built in Aruba.

It is said that the world's biggest plungers gamble at the Bahamas' tables—even bigger gamblers than in London and Las Vegas.

Dice, roulette, chemin de fer and blackjack operate around the clock. Freeport, in the tiny Grand Bahama, the site of the biggest plunging, is not even marked on many maps.

Gambling in Monte Carlo

Monte Carlo (Monaco) is probably the most publicized gambling center in the world outside Las Vegas. This is unusual in that it only covers an area of 368 acres in the South of France.

Monte Carlo was originally a health resort (note how health and gambling resorts are so often intertwined). It actually started as a gambling center after several abortive starts when Prince Charles of Monaco learned that a Parisian named Francois Blanc was running a remarkably successful gambling casino in Hamburg. Charles got Blanc to come in and make a try with Monte Carlo.

Blanc immediately realized a whole town had to be built—hotels, restaurants, shops and also better traveling facilities. He had capital and experience. He first built a new casino and then a large hotel. He even built roads and modernized the harbor.

As the tourists started to arrive he took a daring step. Blanc reduced the zeros on the roulette wheel from two to one. It got much word of mouth and lessened the bank's advantage but it was a brilliant move.

Rival casinos were hurt and embarrassed by Blanc's strategy and a lot of publicity (phony) was distributed, telling about all the suicides that were happening at Monte Carlo. These tales are still repeated today yet they were not true.

But the casino prospered. When Blanc died in 1877 he left a large fortune. His son took over. Camille, his son, continued to improve the property and built a huge, new west wing. A new room was built in which only the very wealthy could afford to play. Then the casino was kept open all night. The games were roulette, trente-et-quarante, chemin de fer and baccarat. Since then, dice has been added.

The casino today is extravagantly decorated and identities of guests checked. One part of the casino is for those tourists who don't have a lot to gamble with. They are allowed in with slacks and the area is called "the kitchen." But most of the gambling goes on in the Salles Princes where you must be dressed and the entrance fee is $1. The stakes here are large and bets run as high as $5,000. And that is not unusual.

Bets are placed with rectangular colored chips called plaques. Before chips, gamblers often used gold coins.

When gambling stories are told they are usually told about Monte Carlo—the fabulous losses, the man who bet his wife on the spin of a wheel, the man who bet his gold button on a number, the fights, the losses, the suicides—but whether they are true, who's to say? President Teddy Roosevelt is supposed to have borrowed $10 for one play on the wheel and ran it into $25,000. Two movie moguls, Darryl Zanuck and Jack Warner, are supposed to have dropped $100,000 each in a night.

Twice men who claimed they were experts in extrasensory perception were challenged on the wheels to see the number about to come up. They failed. Criswell, the psychic, called three numbers correctly in a row on the wheel for a $3,000 win but then failed.

Prince Rainier once got the famed Albert Einstein to look at a book of roulette systems sold outside the casino to see if any had a chance of beating the wheel. The Einstein verdict was, "No, not if there is a limit on the game or a limit to the amount of the player's capital."

The casino does better on clear days than on rainy days. You'd think it would be the opposite because there'd be fewer outdoor activities on rainy days leaving the tourists with nothing to do but gamble. But the theory is that on clear days people feel more optimistic as to their chances and, as a consequence, gamble.

Because of the ambition of so many to break the bank at Monte Carlo, the axiom is, "Never play the chalk." That means never play the small odds bets. Take a chance. Go for broke.

Today with Prince Rainier III and Princess Grace Kelley

the reigning monarchs of Monaco, they attract many of the world's celebrities. These celebrities attract the tourists and the casino continues to thrive even though there have been periods of financial stress.

The casino is beautifully and efficiently run. Croupiers are trained and disciplined and equipment checked daily. Despite all the fiction and movies about robbing the bank of Monte Carlo, it's never been done and security is excellent. For years a detective named Monsieur le Broq ruled over the casino. He said he could tell dishonesty by gait. He was seldom wrong.

There was just one successful robbery of two cash boxes when thieves smuggled smoke bombs into the casino in brief cases, causing a panic. Now guests must check hats and brief cases before coming in.

Has the bank of Monte Carlo ever been broken? No. It has been hit for large losses, but never broken.

Bits And Pieces About Gambling Around The World

In the 16th Century, Sir Miles Partridge played King Henry VIII for the bells of St. Paul's cathedral and won.

One of the oldest gambling games is played by the natives in Africa and is called inpao (like chess). The players often bet their goats or their wives in the game.

Famous writer Feodor Dostoevski was a compulsive gambler spending every dollar he got from Russian publishers on roulette. He wrote of his experiences.

Gamblers Anonymous now has offices all over the world. They claim to cure (or arrest) about 100 gamblers a week of their curse.

Women more than men have practiced sadism through gambling. Among the items of proof is Parysatrs, Queen of Persia, who played craps with a slave for his life or freedom. She won and had him tortured to death.

A favorite story in Monte Carlo is of a man named Blanchard who, about to walk into the casino, had a pigeon soil his hat. He then won $15,000. Every time thereafter he walked in circles outside the casino hoping for another pigeon to soil his hat but none ever did.

The Greeks first gambled with a shell which was black on one side and white on the other. The betting was on which would come up, the black or the white.

The Department of Archaeology in the University of Rome has on exhibition signs from ancient taverns promising customers food and gaming tables.

In the Netherlands, the first gambling game on record was a simple stick on an axis (like spin the bottle) which was spun after each man put an equal amount of money down. The man the stick pointed to after the spin took the money. The church tried unsuccessfully to stamp out the game which became very popular.

King Henry III was such a devotee of gambling of any kind he instructed the clergy to stick to spiritual matters and not decry gambling. Dice was the game then.

The English Gaming Act of 1845 made it impossible to recover gambling debts by legal action. This act, pretty much enacted in most countries, is a tough one for illegal gamblers.

Three card monte (find the Queen) is a popular game on trains and boats throughout Europe and South America.

The most popular gambling game of the Eskimos is roulette.

In Australia the most popular game is two-up which is more or less just a coin tossing game. It is illegal to gamble on it.

In much of the Orient, and Korea, particularly, fan-tan is the popular game. The Koreans believe winners at fan-tan will have good luck come to them outside the game.

Some gambling games just die out. As an example you never see the put-and-take top anymore or the famous, and very contrived, shell game.

Egypt was the originator of the match game in which you try to guess how many matches someone has in his hand.

In China, mah-jong is still the most popular gambling game, as it has been for hundreds of years.

It is estimated twenty billion dollars is bet on football

and baseball games each year all over the world. In Japan they bet a lot of money on wrestling.

In Spain more money is bet on cock fighting and bull fighting than anything else. Most of it is done with book makers. In parts of the Philippines some $50,000 is bet during one cock fight.

The game of bridge is played in most English-speaking countries and a good deal of money is bet on it in card rooms and championship games. The same goes for gin rummy and pinochle.

Backgammon is very popular in the Middle East. In France it is called tric-trac, in Italy, favola reale and in Germany, puffspeil. The Chinese call it coan ke but it has different rules.

Dice are responsible for the movement in backgammon. Similar movement in similar gambling games are played in the Orient. In Japan it's sigoroku. In China it's Shing Kun. Dice weren't always six sided. Sometimes they were four sided.

The Innuit Eskimos gambled mostly with dominoes called ma zu a lot.

In the Bantu Armed Forces today, poker dice is the big sport for gambling.

The highest betting game in Russia for years was chase-the-ace. It's a take-off on three card monte.

The big Persian rummy game was as-nes. It is said Columbus and his men played this game on the ship on the way to America.

The English still gamble one-ruff, honors and whist. The older people like these games.

Basette, the banking game that became faro, was played in Italy and Spain in the 1600's. The rich were so affected by the game that the inventor, Cellini, was banished to Corsica.

France is given credit for introducing big time horse racing. Louis XIV inaugurated a meeting at St. Germain and offered to buy the winning horse for its weight in gold. That's how it became the Sport of Kings.

Harness racing is most popular in Europe. North America

ca and Russia. Roosevelt Raceway on Long Island handles the most betting money during a harness meet.

The French bet most of their money when betting the horses on Tierce. In this game you have to pick the first three horses in a race.

Britain was the original home of greyhound racing but the sport has died there and sprung up in America.

The lottery has helped raise money for foreign governments in past years. The Irish Sweepstakes is a financial must for Ireland.

Nick the Greek won his first fortune in Canada when he figured the odds properly and outsmarted the track bookies. There were no mutuel machines then.

Both Nero and Claudius were obessed with dice. They'd bet $50,000 on a throw. The madman Caligula gambled constantly, too.

Gambling with cards has been said to have changed the direction of America's Wild West.

Things have really changed, haven't they? There was a time when the police put their energy into chasing kids who were pitching pennies to the wall or to the line. Today, gambling has grown up into a multi-billion dollar profession. The question always has been: does legalized gambling bring criminals into the area? Perhaps. The question will never be answered. Obviously, if gambling is legal in every city and state in the country and in the world, it's a question, a good question, as to whether the gambling syndicates will control it or not. That remains to be seen.

In many European places, especially Monte Carlo, you can deposit a certain amount of money in the bank of the casino when you arrive and draw against it—$5,000 for free meals and free whatever you need.

In Las Vegas they recognize the big gamblers and give them these privileges so it turns out the same but there is a little more security in Europe. *It is not established that there will be casino gambling in Mexico which will be legal,* according to the Governor. The problem which will be licked eventually is security.

Mexico is known for its lax control of crime and Americans will be leery of taking big money out of the casinos and walking through those dark streets at night. The Governor is working on that now.

It is true that the 5-10 at Caliente is one of the most popular gambling games in the world, that of picking number winners between the 5th and 10th races, and the world pool is often well over $100,000, which gamblers have won with $32 worth of cross betting. It is done in the daylight so Americans can get back without problems. Also, if they wish they can have a check instead of cash. And that helps too. Caliente is now big and beautiful since the original burned down.

The big advantage of winning large amounts in foreign countries is that they do not do what is done in America now, where if you make a big hit they immediately take 20 percent out of the amount and it goes to the IRS. There has been much grumbling in racing circles from big betters about this and the lobbying is strong in Washington to eliminate the immediate tax.

The time might come very soon when this law will be stricken from the books. Actually it hurts the IRS rather than helps, because gamblers are reluctant to bet the kind of money that will make a big killing and then have to give 20 percent immediately to the IRS.

Luck or Skill

Over and over I'm asked, how big a part does luck and skill play in a game?

Well, obviously in roulette, the skill is in managing your money. There's no other skill because you are tied to the whims of the wheel. Unless you find a wheel that isn't exactly true, and one group of numbers comes up more than another, but you'll look a long time before you'll find one like that. However, it has happened.

Dice, I think, skill represents some twenty or 25 percent. There are players who play it safe and just play the pass and come lines, backing up their bets. But if you play sevens or elevens or hardways when the dice is running that way, or you hop on a long roll that some lucky player has, it's more than just luck. It's a bit of skill—but mind you, I said twenty or twenty-five percent.

Obviously, blackjack is more skill. I'd say blackjack is almost fifty percent skill. Know when to split, draw, take insurance, throw your cards in, to do some counting even with a shoe, to watch the dealers eyes, other players cards and eyes. Here you have some skill.

Horse racing? I have known players who have won steadily over the long years. My guess is that horseracing is seventy percent skill. Sure, you need luck, but those players who study the Form have information, know the blood lines, and remember the kinds of races horses have run, know how jockeys behave on certain horses, and they win. It's not an easy game to beat, even with the knowledge. But I think of all gambling games, horse racing requires a great skill.

When it comes to sports betting—football, I'd give it 25 percent skill and the rest luck. Conditions of the team players, the weather, the coach, where they're playing, the opponent of each team, enters into it.

The wheel and the casino and baccarat, I'd give the nod to money management.

When it comes to poker, I'd say it's 75 percent skill and 25 percent luck. Over a period of time, the good poker player playing with poor poker players will win over and over again.

I think that covers gambling games.

Of course nothing is more important than Lady Luck—for a while, anyway—for one night, perhaps. She's a marvelous lady to woo and have sitting on your lap for any game.

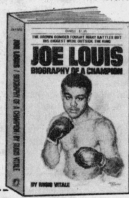

Black Lady Luck

BOREN & GUILD

BIOGRAPHY/ My name is Joan Boren. I'm not as young as I used to be, but I'm still beautiful, still Black, and can still manage any man alive. I know what to do with him in and out of bed. They called me "Lucky Joan" in Las Vegas because I was able to beat them at their own games, beat those "unbeatable" odds they stack up against you, even at roulette. I was incredibly lucky. It seemed every bet I made was a winner, everything I touched turned to riches. I was a queen in the world of big spenders and hard lovers. I even broke the bank at Monte Carlo. I was doing pretty good for a Black girl, living the dream of dreams. But hovering over my shoulder was that horrible specter that haunts all gamblers. When would Lady Lucky leave me and my winning streak run out? This is my story, the good and the bad. How each roll of the dice brought me closer and closer to paradise until I rolled them once too often and came up with snake eyes.

BH667 $1.95

OFFICIAL BAR & PARTY GUIDE

Makes entertaining fun!

The only book you'll ever need. Tells who and how many to invite, how to set up bar and food, what to buy and serve. Tips, ideas, recipes ... everything to make you the perfect host or hostess.

- Who—and How Many—to Invite
- How Long the Bash Should Last
- What Makes a Perfect Bartender
- Thrifty Ways to Shop for Liquor
- The Crucial Facts about Wines
- Is It Whiskey—or Whisky?
- Myths about Gin and Vodka

BH486
$1.50

... and more, more, more—including hundreds of recipes for cocktails, highballs, special drinks, and easy-to-prepare food. Plus tips that will save you time, money, and headaches ... and make you the perfect host or hostess!

THE BLACK EXPERIENCE FROM HOLLOWAY HOUSE

★ ROBERT BECK (under the pseudonym, "Iceberg Slim")

AIRTIGHT WILLIE & ME (BH636)	$1.95
NAKED SOUL OF ICEBERG SLIM (BH645)	1.95
PIMP THE STORY OF MY LIFE (BH628)	1.95
LONG WHITE CON (BH612)	1.95
DEATH WISH (BH609)	1.95
TRICK BABY (BH670)	1.95
MAMA BLACK WIDOW (BH657)	1.95

★ DONALD GOINES

BLACK GIRL LOST (BH656)	$1.95
DADDY COOL (BH649)	1.95
ELDORADO RED (BH647)	1.95
STREET PLAYERS (BH644)	1.95
INNER CITY HOODLUM (BH639)	1.95
BLACK GANGSTER (BH629)	1.95
CRIME PARTNERS (BH625)	1.95
SWAMP MAN (BH624)	1.95
NEVER DIE ALONE (BH623)	1.95
WHITE MAN'S JUSTICE BLACK MAN'S GRIEF (BH622)	1.95
KENYATTA'S LAST HIT (BH669)	1.95
KENYATTA'S ESCAPE (BH661)	1.95
CRY REVENGE (BH660)	1.95
DEATH WISH (BH626)	1.95
WHORESON (BH642)	1.95
DOPEFIEND (BH659)	1.95
DONALD WRITES NO MORE (BH511)	1.75
(A Biography of Donald Goines by Eddie Stone)	

AVAILABLE AT ALL BOOKSTORES OR ORDER FROM:
HOLLOWAY HOUSE, P.O. BOX 69804, LOS ANGELES, CA 90069
(NOTE: ENCLOSE 50c PER BOOK TO COVER HANDLING AND
POSTAGE: CALIFORNIA RESIDENTS ADD 6% SALES TAX.)

BOOK ORDER FORM

Dear Reader:

You'll find many other books of interest listed on previous pages. If they are not now available at your book dealer, we will be delighted to rush your order by direct mail. Fill in form below and mail with your remittance.

- -

SPECIAL ORDER BOOK DEPT.
8060 MELROSE AVE. • LOS ANGELES, CALIF. 90046

Please send me the following books I have listed by

Number . . . .

. . . .

. . . .

. . . .

I enclose 50¢ additional per order to cover hand-ling and postage on all orders under $5.00 (California residents please add 6% sales tax).

Enclosed is $ . . . . ( ) cash, ( ) check, ( ) money order payment in full for all books ordered above (sorry no C.O.D.'s). ( ) I am over 21.

Name . . . .

Address . . . .

City . . . . State . . . . . . Zip Code . . . . . .

- -